# Russia and the world economy

Economic failure, including an unprecedented collapse of production in a major economy in peacetime, played a significant part in the collapse of the communist system in Russia, and the break up of the Soviet Union itself. Despite its status as a major world power, the trade structure of the Soviet Union resembled that of a relatively backward Third World country dependent upon fuels, raw materials, precious metals, wood and lumber for 95 per cent of its exports to the industrial West. Its major industrial exports to non-socialist countries consisted of armaments, frequently delivered on credit to Third World countries.

This book analyses the economic, historical and political problems that will have to be overcome if a Russian government, however constituted, is to succeed in integrating the Russian economy into the world economy. It questions whether the assistance the West is proposing will be sufficient, and examines the consequences of failure for regional and international stability. Presenting largely unconsidered material from Soviet sources on the economic importance of the Soviet arms trade, and on Soviet exports of diamonds and precious metals, the author puts the case that the West has consistently overestimated Soviet hard currency earnings, and consequently underestimated the scale of the Russian government's problems.

**Alan Smith** is a Senior Lecturer in East European Economics at the School of Slavonic and East European Studies, University of London. He has been lecturing in Soviet and East European economic affairs for over twenty years, and acts as a consultant to companies involved in East–West trade. He writes from an economic perspective, but avoids technical terms in this book, ensuring that the analysis is accessible to all students of Russian affairs, and of international economic relations.

Also available from Routledge

**Why Perestroika Failed**
Peter J. Boettke

**Can Russia Change?**
Walter C. Clemens

**Restructuring the Soviet Economy**
David A. Dyker

**The Socialist Economies and the Transition to the Market**
Ian Jeffries

**Soviet Society Under Perestroika**
David Lane

**The Soviet Economic System**
Alec Nove

**Russian Politics and Society**
Richard Sakwa

**Resistance to Change in the Soviet Economic System**
Jan Winiecki

**The Disintegration of the Soviet Economic System**
Edited by Michael Ellman and Vladimir Kontorovich

# Russia and the world economy

## Problems of integration

Alan Smith

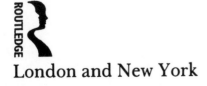

London and New York

First published 1993
by Routledge
11 New Fetter Lane, London EC4P 4EE

Simultaneously published in the USA and Canada
by Routledge
29 West 35th Street, New York, NY 10001

Typeset in Baskerville by
NWL Editorial Services, Langport, Somerset

Printed and bound in Great Britain by
Mackays of Chatham PLC, Chatham, Kent

*British Library Cataloguing in Publication Data*
A catalogue record for this book is available from the Bitish
Library

*Library of Congress Cataloging in Publication Data*
*has been applied for*


ISBN  0–415–08924–7
ISBN  0–415–08925–5 (pbk)

This book is dedicated to Ruth and Steven
and to the memory of my mother and father

# Contents

List of tables                                                          ix
Preface                                                                 xi

1  From the Soviet Union to Russia                                       1

2  Russian and Soviet economic development and
   foreign trade                                                        15

3  The organisation of Soviet foreign economic relations               36

4  The Soviet economic system and the
   demand for imports                                                   52

5  Soviet hard currency earnings                                        72

6  Soviet economic reforms and reform debates
   under Gorbachev                                                      99

7  The reform of foreign economic relations
   under Gorbachev                                                     121

8  Problems in exporting under Gorbachev                               138

9  Soviet balance of payments pressures 1985-91
   and their impact on the economy                                     156

10 The transition to a market economy in Russia                       177

11 Russian external trade and economic relations                      199

12 Russia and the world economy: problems of
   integration and the role of the West                               218

Bibliography                                                          239
Index                                                                247

# List of tables

2.1 Growth of Soviet production and foreign trade in
    real terms 1950–90      30

4.1 Soviet imports from non-socialist countries by
    broad commodity groups      56

4.2 Soviet imports of machinery and equipment from
    the industrial West      57

4.3 Soviet production, trade and domestic utilisation
    of grain 1961–90      69

5.1 Commodity composition of Soviet exports to the
    industrialised West and developing countries from
    country data 1972–84      74

5.2 Soviet exports to non-socialist countries by broad
    commodity groups      75

5.3 Soviet exports of diamonds and precious and
    other metals      77

5.4 Soviet energy exports to the industrial West 1972–89      81

5.5 Soviet exports of arms and defence equipment to
    non-socialist countries      91

5.6 Estimated Soviet arms sales for hard currency 1975-81      94

8.1 Soviet trade with non-socialist countries 1984–89      140

8.2 Soviet oil production and trade 1985–90      141

8.3 Soviet natural gas: trade and production 1985–91      141

8.4 Soviet exports to non-socialist countries 1984–89      142

8.5 Soviet hard currency exports 1984–90      143

8.6 Soviet trade surpluses and outstanding claims
    against Third World countries      149

8.7 Commodity structure of Soviet exports to non-
    socialist countries in comparable (1985) prices      152

8.8  USSR Ministry of Finance estimates of Soviet gold
     stocks and sales                                          154
9.1  Official estimates of Soviet balance of payments
     in convertible currencies on a transactions
     basis 1985–91                                             157
9.2  Soviet hard currency balance of payments and
     indebtedness 1985–90                                      159
9.3  Real volume growth of trade 1985-90                       165
9.4  Commodity structure of Soviet imports from
     non-socialist countries                                   167
9.5  Commodity structure of Soviet imports in
     comparable (1985) prices                                  168
9.6  Soviet energy exports to Eastern Europe
     (excluding GDR) in 1989 and 1990                          175
11.1 External trade of the RSFSR in domestic prices in 1988   201
11.2 Trade of the RSFSR outside the Soviet Union in
     domestic prices in 1988                                   202
11.3 Estimated exports of oil and gas from RSFSR in 1988      207
11.4 Russian balance of trade and payments in 1990
     and 1991                                                  209

# Preface

The purpose of this book is to examine the historic, economic and political obstacles that will have to be overcome if Russia is to become fully integrated into the world economy and the implications of this process for the advanced industrial economies. Although the book is the product of many years research into the foreign trade relations of the Soviet Union it was largely written during a period of study leave from the School of Slavonic and East European Studies at the University of London which also allowed me time to research into the relations of the emerging Russian Republic in the post-communist era. I would like to express my gratitude to my colleagues at the School who covered my teaching and administrative duties and offered their advice and without whose help the book would not have been completed. I have also benefited from advice from, and discussions with, a number of colleagues in other universities and colleges on the subject matter of this book over the years, including David Dyker of the University of Sussex (to whom I am indebted for comments on an earlier draft of the book), Philip Hanson of the University of Birmingham and Peter Wiles of the London School of Economics. Naturally I remain solely responsible for any errors of fact or judgement.

I also wish to express my appreciation to my wife, Ruth, and son, Steven, for their patience and help.

Alan Smith

# Chapter 1

# From the Soviet Union to Russia

## THE DISSOLUTION OF THE SOVIET UNION AND THE EMERGENCE OF THE RUSSIAN FEDERATION

The final embodiment of the Russian Empire in its communist form, the Union of Soviet Socialist Republics was formally dissolved on 26 December 1991. Following the failed coup against President Gorbachev in August 1991 and the failure of Gorbachev's subsequent attempts to establish a confederation of states (which was to be known as the Union of Sovereign States) to replace the Soviet Union, the heads of state of eleven of the fifteen republics which constituted the USSR signed a declaration at Alma Ata on 21 December 1991 agreeing to establish a far looser Commonwealth of Independent States (CIS). The commonwealth would not be 'a state or a super state structure' in itself with a central government and legislature, but would consist of independent states which would 'respect each others' territorial integrity' who would attempt to preserve 'allied command over military-strategic forces and over nuclear weapons' and who confirmed their 'allegiance and cooperation in the formation and development of a common economic space'. The Baltic Republics (Estonia, Lithuania and Latvia), who had been recognised by the outside world and the Soviet authorities as independent states in September 1991, and Georgia, which had claimed its independence in April 1991, did not sign the agreement.

The Alma Ata declaration was an extension of the agreement reached by the heads of three Slavic republics of Byelorussia, Russia and the Ukraine in Minsk on 8 December 1991 to establish a Commonwealth of Independent States to include Moldova, Armenia, Azerbaidzhan and the five central Asian republics

(Kazakhstan, Kyrgyzstan, Tadzhikistan, Turkmenistan and Uzbekistan). The declaration confirmed that with the formation of the Commonwealth of Independent States 'the USSR ceases to exist'. On the 25 December 1991 Gorbachev, the last president of the USSR, announced his resignation and the following day the Supreme Soviet of the USSR was dissolved as the Russian government began to take over the Kremlin buildings.

## THE ORIGINS OF THE RUSSIAN FEDERATION AND THE CIS

It is tempting to see the creation of the CIS as a means of preserving Russian control over its former empire, particularly as the Russian government was attempting to turn former Soviet (all-Union) economic and political institutions on Russian territory into Russian institutions under the control of the Russian government. It would probably be more accurate to view the establishment of the CIS as a defensive move by Russian politicians to replace central (Soviet) government structures, which were the principal means of economic and political administration in the Russian republic itself whose authority had collapsed. At the same time the establishment of the CIS provided the newly-formed Russian Government with the means to divest itself of some of the costs of empire which were placing an intolerable burden on the Russian economy and to accelerate economic reforms which did not command the whole-hearted support of the leadership of other republics, many of which contained former leading communists who had only adopted a more nationalist posture when the collapse of communism appeared inevitable.

Unlike the empires of other major European powers, which had largely involved the subjugation of distant lands that were territorially separate from the colonial power, the Russian Empire had expanded on a single land mass through the conquest and acquisition of neighbouring territories which were then incorporated into a unitary Russian state. This structure was only nominally altered by the formation of the Union of Soviet Socialist Republics on 30 December 1922, composed of the Russian Soviet Federal Socialist Republic (RSFSR), the Ukrainian Soviet Socialist Republic (SSR), the Byelorussian SSR, the Transcaucasian SFSR (which was divided into the Georgian, Armenian and

Azerbaidzhan SSRs in 1936 when the Kirghiz and the Kazakh SSRs were also created) each with the nominal right to secede from the Union, which provided the new republics with the semblance, if not the substance, of autonomy and established the nominal existence of a separate Russian Republic with its own territorial borders. The individual Soviet Socialist republics (which were extended to include the Central Asian Republics of Turkmenistan and Uzbekistan which were established in October 1924 and Tadzhikistan which separated from Uzbekistan in 1929 and which were incorporated into the Soviet Union at the time of their creation, the Baltic republics which were incorporated into the Soviet Union after the Second World War and the Moldavian SSR which was established in its present form in 1944) formally created their own separate national political, economic and cultural institutions, replicating but essentially subservient to the central all-Union institutions. The only exception was the RSFSR which was subject to a far greater degree of direct control and administration by Soviet (all-Union) institutions based in Moscow. As Russians largely controlled the central institutions of power the need for specifically Russian institutions to defend Russian interests was seen as superfluous. As a result, until 1990, Russia did not have its own national cultural institutions including a radio and television station, an Academy of Sciences and Trade Union bodies, or even a republican branch of the KGB and (except for a brief period from 1956–66) its own branch of the Communist Party. Although Russian branches of economic institutions and industrial ministries existed, Russian industry was subject to a far greater degree of all-Union control than that of other Republics, with 69 per cent of industrial output subordinated to central all-Union administration in 1989 compared with an (unweighted) average of 40 per cent for the other Republics (estimated from Narkhoz 1989: 331).

The emergence of genuine democratic movements in the Soviet Union in 1989 and 1990, encouraged by Gorbachev, led to the election of more independent and nationalist-minded parliaments in the individual republics who expressed their growing dissatisfaction with Soviet economic performance and Soviet dominance. This initially took the form of demands for greater republican autonomy but was subsequently extended to demands for outright independence from the Soviet Union. This created critical problems for Russian politicians, as the very nature of the development of the Russian Empire was such that for many Russians the concept of nation and empire were synonymous and had become associated with the existence and territory of the Soviet Union itself. For the first time in their history, the Russian people were being forced to examine exactly what Russia and being Russian actually meant (see Morrison 1991: chapters 11–12). Did being Russian just refer in a very narrow territorial sense to citizens of the RSFSR or was it an ethnic concept which embraced all people of Russian descent, no matter where they lived, did it include all those who chose Russian as their first language, or did Russia even embrace the citizens and territories of the whole of the Russian or Soviet Empire? The latter idea was being supported by many Russian communists, including Gorbachev, until the collapse of the Soviet Union itself. Others of a Russian nationalist persuasion (like Vladimir Zhirinovsky, who was born of Russian parents in Alma Ata, the capital of Kazakhstan, and who won seven million votes in the election for the Russian presidency in 1991) although fiercely anti-Soviet, also associated Russia with the Russian Empire and disdained separatist and non-Russian nationalist movements and urged a return to the Russian borders of pre-revolution 1917 (Steele 1992a).

There was also considerable popular and intellectual support within Russia for the Slavophile concept of a greater Slavic nation which was united by a common culture, a common orthodox Christian religion and a common Slavonic language base. For most Slavophiles this comprised (inside the Soviet Union) Russia, the Ukraine and Byelorussia but was extended to include Northern Kazakhstan (which had been extensively settled by Russians and which contains valuable mineral deposits) by Solzhenitsin in 1990. This idea was not supported by non-Russian Slavs, who were placing greater priority on complete independence from the Soviet Union. The Slavophile concept also implied a rejection of western economic and political concepts in favour of a return to a peculiarly pre-Soviet Russian economic system based on collective and spiritual principles. Slavophiles reject the increased use of markets, the spread of private property, the opening up of the economy to foreign investment and the export of Russian mineral wealth (Sutela 1991: 155).

At the other extreme a more pragmatic, western-oriented group of politicians proposed a thorough modernisation of political and economic institutions based on western principles of democracy and a market economy. The westernising school (who could be considered to working in a line of descent from Peter the Great through the nineteenth century anti-feudal westernising tradition) could be roughly divided into social democrats who, in the main, favoured a gradual transition to a market economy and greater measures to protect living standards in the short term (including foreign assistance and short-term imports of consumer goods) and more radical liberal market economists who supported a more rapid transition to a market economy. Many of the former however were, or had been associated with Gorbachev and the Soviet government, and had been marginalised as the impossibility of preserving Soviet power became apparent, while radical-liberal economists, who were accused by the Slavophiles of selling Russian interests to western businesses and the IMF, became associated with Boris Yeltsin and the Russian government. This group appreciated that if the Soviet Union could not survive it was essential to create national institutions for the Russian Republic as a matter of urgency.

From the end of 1989 onwards the preservation of the Soviet Union became the critical issue in both Soviet and Russian politics. The growth of demands for national independence and autonomy in the non-Russian republics and the potential secession of the wealthiest republics which supported the establishment of a market economy would have left the reform-oriented members of the Russian leadership with little support for market reforms from other Soviet republics in a reduced Union, and would have left the Russian republic to bear the entire burden of measures to redistribute income within the Union to support the living standards of the less wealthy republics. If non-Russian republics were free to secede from the Union, what advantages were there for the Russian Republic to stay in what remained of the Union, or should the Russian Republic itself secede? At the very least it was necessary to have a voice to articulate specifically Russian economic and political interests in the event of a breakup of the Union.

The first part in the process was the formation of Russian institutions of government and economic administration. Yeltsin was elected as Chairman of the newly established Russian Supreme Soviet on 29 May 1990 despite the opposition of Gorbachev, who was motivated in part by personal distrust for Yeltsin, and by the realisation that the emergence of a strong, popular Russian government articulating specifically Russian policies would come into direct conflict with the policies and power of the Soviet government. Yeltsin recognised that the Union could not hold in its current form and supported the secession of the Baltic republics, while simultaneously strengthening Russian power against the Soviet centre (see Morrison 1991: 136–52). In June 1990 the Russian parliament declared the primacy of Russian laws over Soviet laws and Russian control and sovereignty over Russian minerals and natural resources. Yeltsin also supported the Shatalin plan (see Chapter 6) for the rapid transition to a market economy, which left few powers to central authorities and continued to espouse radical market reforms (involving opening the Russian economy to foreign investment and competition) after Gorbachev had pledged his support for (inconsistent and unworkable) compromise proposals. Finally in June 1991, Yeltsin was elected to the new post of President of the Russian Federation by popular vote.

In the first half of 1991, Gorbachev was increasingly caught between conservatives in the Soviet leadership, who wished to preserve the Union by making as few concessions to the republics as possible, and the growing demands for autonomy. This struggle was reflected in the attempt to secure a new Union Treaty which would redefine the rights of the individual republics in relation to the centre, maintaining Union control over defence, law, foreign policy and the central budget, but leaving many other issues for joint decision between all-union and republican authorities. The Baltic republics together with Georgia, Armenia and Moldova continued to press for outright independence from the Union and refused to participate in a public referendum in June 1991 which resulted in majority support for the Treaty (see White 1992: 387–393).

The draft Union treaty, which would have substantially weakened Soviet authority, given substantial powers to the Republics and allowed the six non-participating Republics to exercise their right to secede from the Soviet Union, was scheduled to be signed by the leaders of the nine participating Republics on 20 August 1991. The day before the proposed signature a group representing conservatives in the Army, the KGB, the central state apparatus and the Communist Party staged an abortive coup which was designed to prevent the signature of the Treaty. This last attempt by conservatives to reassert Soviet central control over a disintegrating economic and political system accelerated the disbandment of the central institutions of the Soviet Communist Party and Soviet control and the Soviet Union itself. The highly visible role played by the popularly-elected Russian President Yeltsin in opposing the coup was critical in bringing about its failure and greatly strengthened Yeltsin's powers in subsequent dealings concerning the future of the Russian republic with the unelected Soviet President Gorbachev. Gorbachev's attempts to preserve a 'common economic space' and to establish a Union of Sovereign Republics which would retain the trappings of state authority were undermined by Yeltsin's opposition and by the widespread support for Ukrainian independence in referendum on 1 December, culminating in the Alma Ata declaration (see Roxburgh 1992: 384–7).

## THE ECONOMIC IMPORTANCE OF THE RUSSIAN FEDERATION

The RSFSR (which adopted the title of the Russian Federation on 25 December 1991) was by far the largest of the Soviet Republics to sign the Alma Ata Declaration. Its territory in 1991 encompassed 17,075,400 square kilometres, equivalent to 76.2 per cent of the land area of the Soviet Union or 12 per cent of the earth's land surface. According to the 1989 census the population of the RSFSR was 147.3 million, equivalent to 51.3 per cent of the population of the USSR, of which 81.5 per cent (120 million) described themselves as ethnic Russians and 27 million as non-Russians of whom Tatars (5.6 million) and Ukrainians (4.4 million) were the largest ethnic minorities. The majority of non-Russians were natives of the sixteen autonomous republics located within the RSFSR. Ethnic Russians living in Soviet Republics outside the RSFSR numbered 23 million in 1989, of which more than half were located in territories immediately bordering the RSFSR in eastern Ukraine and northern Kazakhstan (11 million Russians live in the Ukraine as a whole and a further 8 million in Kazakhstan with the remainder diffused throughout the Union). The RSFSR was the fourth richest of the Soviet Republics (behind the three Baltic Republics) with income per head 10 per cent above the Soviet average and roughly double that of the poorest republic, Tadzhikistan. More important, the RSFSR was the major source of Soviet industrial output and mineral wealth. In 1988 net output (value added in all sectors of the economy) per head in the RSFSR was 19 per cent above the Soviet average and the highest in the Union, while net industrial output per head was 24 per cent higher than the Union average (IMF *et al.* 1991, vol. 1: 214). In 1989 (before the figures were distorted by the collapse of Soviet production in 1990 and 1991) the RSFSR accounted for 61.1 per cent of Soviet net material product and 63.7 per cent of value added in industry (but only 50.3 per cent of value added in agriculture), 62.5 per cent of electric power, 57.9 per cent of steel production and 90.9 per cent of Soviet crude oil output, 77.3 per cent of natural gas production and 55.4 per cent of coal production (Narkhoz 1989: 338–41). Data on Soviet reserves and production of gold, diamonds and other precious metals are unreliable, but it appears that approximately 66–75 per cent of Soviet gold production was located in the RSFSR.

The most important sources of Russian mineral wealth are located in Siberia, whereas the major population centres are located west of the Urals in European Russia. In 1989 Siberia accounted for 74 per cent of Russian oil production and 88 per cent of natural gas production. During the 1980s approximately 70 per cent of Russian coal output came from Siberia, while Siberia accounted for the vast majority of Russian production of gold and diamonds. The sheer scale of Siberia and the Russian Far East creates major logistical, environmental and human problems for the exploitation of its mineral wealth and the transportation of this to areas of consumption. The area east of the Urals stretches across 130 degrees to Russia's easternmost point on the Bering Strait. The distance east from the Urals to the Bering Sea is nearly as far as that west from the Urals to Newfoundland. The Russian Federation also reaches northwards into the Arctic circle. This results in major climatic differences and substantial differences in the costs involved in developing different regions of Siberia and transporting resources to areas of consumption, which will continue to have major implications for Russia's external trade relations as well as for its relations with autonomous republics and other national groups inside Russia itself. Construction costs associated with oil and gas production in the westernmost regions of Siberia, closest to the Urals, are only 20–80 per cent greater than those typically prevailing in European Russia. As the more accessible deposits in western Siberia approached full utilisation, development was forced into the more distant northern and eastern regions of Siberia where the costs of exploration, extraction and transportation can be as much as 7–8 times greater than in European Russia. The average distance of transportation of Soviet oil and gas rose from 80 kilometres in 1970 to 1,910 km in 1980 and had reached 2,350 km by 1988 (Bradshaw 1992: 431). The problems of moving development north into the Arctic Circle are even more critical and have been analysed by Gustafson (1989: 160–4) who demonstrates that the 200 mile (320 km) distance north from the Urengoi deposits to the Yamburg peninsula (both of which are in the Tiumen' oil and gas fields which accounted for 65 per cent of Soviet oil production in 1988 and 72 per cent of proven gas reserves in 1980) involves crossing 'an invisible climatic and geological divide', north of which each additional 35 billion cubic metres of annual capacity would cost an additional 1.5 billion roubles (in 1980 internal prices) of capital costs in comparison with Urengoi alone. As a result energy development in Siberia entails rapidly rising marginal costs of production (not just to increase output but to maintain existing production levels as the most accessible fields are exhausted).

There are doubts about the political stability of the Russian Federation itself which is ethnically and culturally heterogeneous and contained sixteen Autonomous Republics (which have all declared the status of full republics for themselves) with a total population of 21.4 million within its borders at the end of 1991. A further four regions with a population of 1.6 million were awarded republican status in 1992. This raises the possibility that the Russian Federation will fragment into independent republics in much the same way as the Soviet Union did. Such doubts have been heightened by ethnic violence between the majority Chechens and the minority Ingush in the Chechen–Ingush Republic. Tatarstan with a population of 3.6 million (the second most populous republic after Bashkiria with a population of 3.9 million) voted in March 1992 for a form of sovereignty involving 'equal status' with Russia but stopping short of outright secession from the Federation at that time. All of the remaining nineteen republics (except Chechen–Ingush) signed a treaty maintaining their membership of the Federation, but on a basis which allowed them greater, but ill-defined, control over natural resources and greater powers of local taxation. Critically, many of the autonomous republic are rich in natural resources, especially

Yakutia which is the main source of Russian gold and diamond production. In addition, other energy deposits are located in regions and areas with an indigenous non-Russian population who are demanding greater control over natural resources. However, the native ethnic (titular) population form more than 50 per cent of the total population in only three of the Republics (Chechens in Chechen–Ingush, Ossetians in North Ossetia and Chuvash in Chuvashia), while in four republics (Dagestan, Tatarstan, Kalmykia, Kabardino-Balkaria) the titular ethnic group, although comprising less than 50 per cent of the population are the largest single ethnic group. In nine of the republics (Buryatia, Karelia, Komi, Mordovia, Udmurtia, Yakutia and the newly created Adygai, Gorno-Altai and Khakassia) people of Russian origin comprise more than 50 per cent of the total population, and in a further three republics where Russians comprise less than 50 per cent of the total population they still constitute the largest single ethnic group (Bashkiria, Mari and Karachai-Circassia). The predominance of Russians in the total population is seen as a major barrier to constitutional separation in those republics. Furthermore, the majority of the republics are bounded by the Russian Federation and do not have separate borders and will remain dependent on Russian co-operation for all trade flows and supplies.

## THE STABILITY OF THE CIS

Within months of its signature the loose agreement reached at Alma Ata was looking increasingly fragile, with Russia, the Ukraine, Azerbaidzhan, Bielarus and Moldova indicating their intention to establish their own separate armies and increasingly bitter disputes occurring between the Russian Federation and the Ukraine over the control over the Black Sea fleet (which comprised 380 ships and 70,000 men in Spring 1992) and nuclear weapons and over the territory of the Ukraine itself. Other economic disputes between the two republics have centred on the speed of price liberalisation in the Russian republic, which the Ukrainians argue has forced them to increase prices to prevent Russians buying up cheaper Ukrainian goods, and over Russian control over printing money. In the final analysis the resolution of the dispute between the Ukraine and the Russian federation is of the greatest importance for Russian trade relations as existing oil and gas pipelines delivering Russian exports of oil and gas to the remainder of Europe transit the Ukraine, and the Ukraine will remain an important transit route for Russian exports and imports to and from Europe.

Jonathan Steele (1992b) argues that a major irony of the disputes over the role of the CIS is that the republics that appear to have the most to gain in pure economic terms from the continuation of the CIS are those who are the least enthusiastic in support for it, while the Russian Federation, which would benefit most in economic terms from its peaceful fragmentation, initially appeared most intent on preserving it. Part of the answer on both sides is pure nationalism and national pride. Many leaders of the non-Russian republics still need to demonstrate their independence from Moscow to maintain popular support, while many Russians feel traumatised by the loss of empire and the sense of rejection, together with the realisation that the economic hardships they endured over decades to create a military super-power were in vain and now count for nothing. There are, however, other practical considerations, as Steele indicates. The Ukraine and Moldova consider themselves to be European states, like the East European countries (with whom they share borders that were redrawn after the Second World War) and the Baltic States, and see their trading future with western Europe and the EC. In the longer term, membership of the CIS may be seen as a barrier to recognition by the EC. Similarly, although the Central Asian Republics have a far stronger interest in maintaining trade links with Russia in the short term, the prospects of improved trade links with oil-rich states and with other Muslim states are beguiling. These republics are major cotton producers with potentially low labour costs whose long-term comparative advantage lies in the development of textiles and clothing but who would experience great difficulties in diverting exports of textiles and clothing to the satiated and highly protected markets of the industrialised West. The prospects for improved economic co-operation in the Black Sea area as a counterweight to the EC are also an incentive for the Transcaucasian republics.

## RUSSIA AND THE WORLD ECONOMY

This leaves the Russian government with a major problem. Despite its natural resources, a market of 148 million (relatively poor) consumers will not be large enough to sustain a modern, large-scale industry in the twenty-first century. Even if Russian terms of trade with other republics in the CIS have been unfavourable to Russia in the past, and if inter-republican trade cannot be sustained in the future, Russia would need to divert this trade to other parts of the world to avoid a continued, precipitous collapse in production. The collapse of Soviet trade links with Eastern Europe and of inter-republican trade was a major factor contributing to the fall in Soviet and Russian production in 1990–91. A continued collapse in industrial production would result in large-scale (and highly localised) unemployment with major problems for social stability. Russia has few practical alternatives to expanding its trade links with the world economy, if only to replace former links with eastern Europe and former Soviet republics who are seeking other trade partners, if it is to survive without major internal unrest which could have serious repercussions for world peace and stability.

The conclusion that Russia must strengthen its economic ties with the West forms a key part of the economic programme of the first Russian government which incorporates a rapid transition to a market economy. This is not an easy task and the full integration of the Russian economy into the world economy may take several decades to achieve. Foreign trade, foreign economic relations and the creation of an open economy in which producers and consumers can choose between domestic or external suppliers and markets will play a critical role in the transition process. External economic assistance could reduce the domestic costs (and the risk of generating hyperinflationary pressures) involved in the process of macroeconomic stabilisation by increasing the volume of consumer goods available to the economy and help to win popular support for the transition by providing labour incentives in the period before domestic production recovers. In the longer term an inflow of financial and physical capital in the form of foreign investment will be required to provide the resources for investment in industrial restructuring to stimulate economic recovery.

There are still major disagreements between Russian economists and politicians within the 'westernising' tradition who agree on the necessity for the introduction of a market economy but who disagree over the sequencing of the measures and the pace at which they should be introduced and their likely impact on the economy and society. At one extreme, radical free marketeers argue that the transition to a market should be achieved as swiftly as possible and should be introduced as a single package of measures in order to minimise the period during which mutually incompatible indicators and contradictory and irrational prices signals co-exist in a single economic system (e.g. energy subsidies combined with attempts to reduce energy consumption and decentralise decision-making to the market). At the other extreme it is argued that the institutions for a market economy are not in place and that individuals and enterprises who have little experience of a market economy will be slow to respond (or may even overreact) to market and price signals which will create large-scale economic disruption and hardship (e.g. peasants may refuse to sow above personal requirements if seed prices rise too quickly). It is also argued that the social costs of the transition (including hyperinflationary pressures combined with large-scale and highly localised unemployment as industrial restructuring commences) will threaten social stability and should be phased in gradually. Opponents of this view argue that arbitrary government decisions to maintain employment in one area, while exposing other areas to the full impact of market forces, will actually increase social unrest in the affected areas.

More worrying, however, is that pure market forces are incapable of distinguishing between basic necessities such as food, shelter and medicine and less essential consumer goods. The removal of subsidies on the former and the introduction of relative prices that correspond to price ratios in the industrialised market economies means that the price of basic necessities will rise faster than those of consumer durables, creating greater in-equality and at worst genuine poverty. Again western assistance may be required in helping to create a properly functioning welfare system to overcome these problems.

Strong opposition to the introduction of a market economy and to the integration of the Russian economy with the world economy remains among former communists and Russian nationalists who regret the passing of the Soviet Union and the end of the Russian empire. Slavophiles also oppose western investment in Russia and the sale to outside interestsof Russian energy and raw materials (which they feel should be preserved for future generations), while the native (non-Russian) population in regions producing raw materials also propose a greater degree of control over local resources.

## THE STRUCTURE OF THE BOOK

The purpose of this book is to analyse the prospects for Russian integration into the world economy and the problems that will be encountered in this process. The second chapter of the book examines the longer-term historical contribution of trade to Russian and Soviet economic development since the middle of the nineteenth century and examines how developed the Soviet economy really was at the time of the collapse of Soviet power. Chapter 3 analyses Soviet attitudes to foreign trade and how the institutions created by Lenin and extended by Stalin isolated the domestic economy from the international economy, and examines Soviet and western attitudes to East–West trade in the cold-war era. Chapter 4 examines the structure of Soviet imports from the West and technology in particular and their contribution to economic development. Chapter 5 analyses the structure of Soviet hard currency exports and the preponderance of exports of energy raw materials and arms, and asks whether the Soviet economy was systemically biased against the export of manufactured goods and what problems this will pose for the integration of the Russian economy into the world economy. Chapters 6 to 9 are concerned with the attempts to reform the economy, and Soviet economic relations with non-socialist economies under Gorbachev and their implications for reform in the new Russian Federation. Chapter 10 analyses the initial economic policies of the Russian government in the first stage of the transition to a market economy. Chapter 11 discusses Russian economic relations with the other republics of the former Soviet Union and argues that a common rouble zone is unsustainable. Finally, Chapter 12 examines the attempts of the Russian government to integrate the Russian economy with the world economy and the potential contribution of western assistance and investment to Russian economic development in the future.

# Chapter 2

# Russian and Soviet economic development and foreign trade

## THE LEVEL OF ECONOMIC DEVELOPMENT IN RUSSIA IN 1913

By most conventional indicators Russia was a relatively backward and predominantly agrarian economy on the eve of the First World War. Munting (1982: 26) estimates that income per head in the Russian Empire was about one-third of the level of Germany and one-sixth of that of the USA. He attributes the relatively low level of per capita income to the large proportion of the population employed in agriculture whose productivity was low in comparison with that of industrial labour in Russia and agricultural labour in the USA and Western Europe. Rapid population growth (from 74 million in 1860 to 116 million in 1890 and to 175 million in 1913), which was only exceeded in the developed economies by Australia, Canada and the USA as a result of immigration (Kennedy 1989: 255; Maddison 1970: 157) was concentrated in rural areas with poor soil fertility and a low level of capitalisation. This reduced the growth of agricultural output per worker and further deflated the growth of per capita income to only one per cent per annum in the twenty-five years before the war (Kennedy 1989: 302–3). Just over 82 per cent of the population (based on 1987 Soviet territory) lived in rural areas in 1913 (Narkhoz 1917–87: 374). This figure overstates the degree of dependence of the population on agricultural employment, as much of the rural population supplemented agricultural work with outwork and occasional employment in factories, mining and construction or were employed entirely outside agriculture. Of the population, 66 per cent depended on agriculture in 1914 but this created only 45 per cent of national income while only 5 per cent of the labour force was employed in industry and mining but that this accounted for 20 per cent of national income (Crisp 1976).

The first half of the nineteenth century was a period of sharp relative decline, although there was some expansion of the iron and steel and textile industries. Income per capita grew by only 5 per cent during the entire period from 1830 to 1860 and Russia was overtaken by Britain as the largest economy in Europe (Kennedy 1989: 218–20). However, the process of industrialisation was clearly under way by the second half of the nineteenth century and accelerated in the last quarter of the century. Industrial growth slowed down at the turn of the century but accelerated from 1907–14 after the introduction of the Stolypin reforms, which broke up the peasant communes and stimulated the movement of labour from agriculture to industry and helped to create an embryonic capitalist form of agriculture in the village. As a result Russia was the fourth largest industrial producer in the world in 1913 (behind Britain, the USA and Germany), the fourth largest producer of steel and fifth largest consumer of energy in the world (and the second largest producer of crude oil) and was responsible for 8.2 per cent of the world's output of manufactured goods (Kennedy 1989: 254–60). On a per capita basis, however, Russia dropped to seventh place among the industrialised nations (behind France, Italy and the Austro-Hungarian Empire) in 1913. Industrial employment was equally divided between very large-scale factories situated in the major Russian cities, which employed thousands of workers in highly labour-intensive processes including multi-shift working, and very small-scale workshops and handicrafts, with each sector employing roughly 3 million workers in 1913 (Munting 1982: 36–7).

## FOREIGN TRADE AND INVESTMENT BEFORE THE REVOLUTION

The exclusion of western capital and ideas was a major cause of Russia's relative economic and technological decline in the first half of the nineteenth century. Nove (1969) argues that the shock of defeat in the Crimean War, which was caused by economic backwardness including poor communications and obsolete weaponry, stimulated a radical reappraisal of the need for technical modernisation as well as improved systems of administration and training which opened the economy to western influence and capital. Poor transport and communications were also a major cause of Russia's economic backwardness. The population was concentrated in the poor soil regions around Moscow while difficulties in transportation hindered the development of the richer Black Earth soils in the South, both as a source of food for the North and as a surplus for export. Similarly the richest sources of minerals and raw materials were concentrated in the Eastern sector of European Russia, with the population centres in the west, while the major rivers flowed in a North–South direction and were of little use as a means of transportation. Consequently the construction of a railway network became an urgent priority for both strategic and economic reasons.

Railway construction raised a number of critical problems. Firstly, it entailed a long period between the outlay of investment and payback in income to investors. Secondly, the major benefits of the investment (e.g. reducing the costs of industrial production and agricultural exports and stimulating downstream production) would be external to the owners of the railroads themselves. This raised the question of whether private investors would be able to recoup an adequate return. Finally, Russia did not possess the technology or industrial capacity to create a railway network entirely from domestic resources. Government policy therefore became increasingly concerned with attracting foreign capital and loans to undertake and finance the construction of a state-owned railway. This involved currency stabilisation and restoring currency convertibility (which had been suspended in 1858) which in turn required a balanced budget and high levels of domestic taxation, as well as attempts to maintain a high level of exports to preserve foreign confidence in the currency. Despite these measures the value of the rouble continued to decline until 1896, when Sergei Witte (who was Minister of Finance from 1892–1903) placed the rouble on the gold standard, which by stabilising the value of the rouble made Russia more attractive to foreign investors.

Witte's policies succeeded in attracting a significant inflow of foreign capital both in the form of direct investment in industry and mining and in the form of financial capital in government bonds to finance railway construction. Maddison (1969: 91) shows that, by 1900, 70 per cent of the mining industry and 42 per cent of the metal industry were foreign-owned. Foreign investment also expanded in the second boom period in the decade before the First World War, and accounted for approximately 25 per cent of capital formation. Munting (1982: 34) shows that in 1914 foreign ownership extended to 90 per cent of mining, virtually all oil extraction, half of the chemical industry, 40 per cent of the metallurgical industry and 28 per cent of the textile industry (which had been almost entirely Russian-owned in 1900) while 46 per cent of government debt was held overseas by 1904, a proportion which had risen to 48 per cent by 1913.

Servicing international debt and maintaining a continued flow of imports of machinery and equipment placed a great strain on export earnings and living standards. After a period of relatively free trade from 1862–78 during which foreign trade moved from surplus into deficit, the state took a more interventionist role and tried to stimulate exports and discourage imports largely by price measures. The desire to push grain exports to the limit to help finance imports reached its apogee during the period when Vyshnegradsky was Minister of Finance (1887–92). The policy of 'export though we die' resulted in continued grain exports in 1891 despite a poor harvest and widespread famine. Other methods used by Vyshnegradsky to stimulate exports included charging low railroad freight rates to the ports and levying taxes on peasants immediately following the harvest period in order to force them to sell produce to exporters to raise revenue. Russian exports grew slowly when compared with the major expansion of trade in manufactured goods that was taking place in Europe during the last quarter of the century. Also, as the Russian government was increasingly forced to run trade surplus from 1880 onwards to service debt and to cover profit remittances and other invisible imports including freight, and insurance, balance of payments equilibrium could only be achieved by cutting imports.

In the 1880s imports were only approximately two-thirds of the level of the previous decade (Baykov 1946: 1). The newly emerging Russian industries were increasingly protected by tariffs from 1877 onwards, although these were removed entirely in 1898 for imports of agricultural equipment which did not compete with Russian-made goods, in order to stimulate agricultural exports. High tariffs were also levied on consumer goods and raw materials, in part to raise revenue, and in part to discourage consumption (Munting 1982: 34). A rapid expansion of trade took place after 1896 after the rouble was linked to the gold standard and Witte's expansionary policies, which significantly increased the demand for industrial machinery and raw materials as well as for imports directly associated with railroad construction. The development of the railways also stimulated exports of timber, minerals and agricultural products (Baykov 1946: 3). In the three years before the outbreak of war in 1914 the value of Russian imports and exports was four times higher than the level reached in 1891–95. Exports were still highly concentrated on agricultural products together with raw materials and goods with a low level of processing. Machinery and equipment and iron and steel products constituted less than 1 per cent of Russian exports from 1909–13. Food comprised 60.9 per cent of total exports over the same period (grain 40.1 per cent), timber 9.7 per cent, flax 5.7 per cent and oil 2.4 per cent (estimated from Baykov 1946). Producers goods made up 70 per cent of imports in 1913, of which imports of machinery and equipment constituted 16.6 per cent. Identifiable industrial raw materials constituted a further 46 per cent (energy 7.1 per cent, ores and minerals 6.9 per cent, chemicals and rubber 7.9 per cent and raw materials for the textile industries and semifabricates 21.2 per cent). Consumer goods made up 30 per cent of total imports in 1913 with foodstuffs (including luxury items such as tea, coffee and alcohol) approximately 20 per cent and industrial consumer goods 10 per cent (Vneshtorg 1918–66).

In summary, the economic structure of the Russian Empire in 1913 combined a relatively fast-growing industrial sector with a backward peasant agriculture. Although the pace of industrial growth matched that of the European industrial economies from the 1880s until the outbreak of war (with the exception of the period from 1899–1906), the impact on per capita incomes and the breakdown of employment between industry and agriculture was largely nullified by the explosive growth of the rural population, which in turn created a growing land hunger and social unrest and increased domestic food needs. However, Russia remained heavily dependent on exports of food (notably grain) and goods involving a low degree of processing in order to finance imports of machinery and equipment, industrial components and materials (and also luxury consumer goods) and to service the growing foreign debt. Russian industry was highly dependent on foreign investment, foreign technology and even foreign engineers as education and training failed to keep pace with the demands of industry.

## SOVIET FOREIGN ECONOMIC RELATIONS BEFORE CENTRAL PLANNING

### Economic strategy

Marx had anticipated that the first revolution would occur in an industrially advanced capitalist economy which would be followed by revolutions in other capitalist states. Economic relations between the newly established socialist states would be based on co-operation. The failure of revolutions to materialise in other industrialised countries presented the Bolshevik leadership with critical problems concerning the nature of the domestic economic system, the nature of economic relations between agriculture and industry and the role and conduct of foreign economic relations. The structural economic problems inherited from the Russian Empire were aggravated by the demands placed on the economy by the war, including the diversion of industrial production to military needs, the collapse of exports (to 9 per cent of their 1913 level in constant prices in 1917) which had led to the virtual doubling of foreign debt during the war and now presented problems in sustaining the desired level of imports; and the widespread seizure of land by peasants in the course of 1917, which threatened supplies of food to the towns and exports as former landless peasants moved towards production for self-sufficiency, rather than the market.

Lenin's initial concepts of planning and industrial organisation were influenced by the experience of German planning in the First World War and by socialist analyses of the role of financial capital and the large banks in the process of industrial development. Lenin outlined a system that could be described as State Capitalism (in the sense of state-directed capitalism). Nationalised banks would control the flow of capital to large-scale, highly-monopolised industry, which would remain in private hands but would be subject to instructions from the centre and to checks by workers' committees. The reluctance of private owners to cooperate with the government and the fear that large sections of industrial capital would end up under German ownership accelerated moves towards the wholesale nationalisation of the major branches of industry in June 1918. The use of the printing press to finance the Civil War (1918–21) and the resulting hyperinflation led to the collapse of the monetary system and the development of a form of moneyless economy known as 'War Communism' in which workers were paid in kind, or in goods that could be consumed or bartered and in which transfers of goods between nationalised enterprises were moneyless and were conducted on the basis of centralised instructions. Most critically the collapse of the monetary system deprived the peasant of the principal incentive to produce for the market and led to the collapse of economic relations between the town and the country. Armed forces were sent into the countryside to requisition grain to feed the towns as early as January 1918, a practice that was greatly extended during War Communism. At the lowest point of the Civil War, industrial output had fallen to 14.5 per cent of its pre-war level and the urban population had fallen by approximately 30 per cent as workers were driven from the towns to the villages in search of food.

Many Bolsheviks eulogised War Communism as a move, albeit premature, to a moneyless, communist society. Others, including Lenin, argued that with the end of the Civil War it was necessary to reintroduce a stable currency to provide the peasant with an incentive to produce food and agricultural raw materials for the towns as well as a surplus for export. This in turn necessitated the development of market relations between agriculture and industry and the provision of industrial consumer goods to the rural population to provide the peasant with an incentive to produce for the market. The resulting economic system, known as the New Economic Policy (NEP), involved the coexistence of a state sector comprised of nationalised, but commercially autonomous, large-scale industrial trusts which enjoyed a considerable degree of monopoly, with a private sector which consisted of small-scale industry and a predominantly private agricultural sector, all operating in a market environment.

NEP presented the Bolshevik leadership with a new set of dilemmas that formed the basis of the industrialisation debates of the 1920s, which can be examined (at the risk of over-simplification) in terms of the dispute between the left opposition whose major theorists were Trotsky and Preobrazhensky and the advocates of a policy of balanced growth, whose major theorist was

Bukharin (who initially had the support of Stalin). Firstly, would the increased role for private markets and private capital imply a return to capitalism and make the government dependent on the more prosperous farmers (kulaks), who produced the major share of the agricultural marketed surplus, and on private traders (nepmen), who controlled large sections of retail trade and who were predominantly opposed to the regime? Secondly, would it be possible to pursue a policy of industrialisation if output was to be determined largely by market forces which involved a continued supply of consumer goods for rural producers and, finally, what were the implications of this for foreign trade?

Bukharin argued that Russia's traditional comparative advantage lay in agriculture and that the development of a flourishing agrarian sector would have to precede industrial- isation. This implied that the size and structure of industrial output would be heavily influenced by peasant demand and that a significant proportion of industrial investment would have to be directed towards the production of consumer goods. It also implied that the private sector would continue to grow faster than the socialist sector. Bukharin argued that this policy would also generate a rapid pace of economic development, although many critics of his policies have argued that by slowing down the rate of industrialisation the opposite would be true.

The left opposition school argued that Bukharin's programme underestimated the danger to the regime that would result from continued dependence on the kulak and the nepman which would lead to the restoration of capitalism and that concentrating investment in consumer goods would leave the Soviet Union vulnerable to outside attack. They argued that socialism could only be guaranteed by a policy of rapid industrialisation concentrated in heavy industry and the production of investment goods, which would both increase the numbers of the industrial proletariat and strengthen defence potential. Preobrazhensky proposed that the strategy should be implemented by a policy of 'primitive socialist accumulation' which involved extracting a surplus from the population by price policy and taxation to pay for investment in heavy industry. As the peasantry were the most numerous section of the population this inevitably meant that they would have to bear a major part of the burden of financing investment either through direct taxation or through state administered prices which would depress the relative prices of agricultural goods. The major problem this strategy presented was whether the peasant would continue to produce for the legal state-administered market or would lapse back into self-sufficiency or production for the unregulated illegal market, either of which would require coercion of the peasantry to ensure a continued marketed surplus.

## Foreign economic relations under War Communism and NEP

The Bolshevik government had not envisaged a policy of complete autarky or economic isolation following the revolution, but had hoped that economic relations would be established with the new socialist states which had been expected to emerge as a result of the spread of revolution. It had initially been expected that economic relations with these states would be based on a joint plan, similar to the basis on which it was anticipated internal trade would be conducted (Bukharin and Preobrazhensky 1970: 326). It was now recognised that trade relations would have to be restored with capitalist nations, but it was intended that this trade should not determined by market forces, but should be directed and controlled by the state. A decree 'On the Nationalisation of Foreign Trade' was passed on 22 April 1918, which placed all foreign trade activity under the direct control of the Soviet state. The creation of a State Monopoly of Foreign Trade did not command unanimous support. The decree was largely motivated by Lenin's fear that Russian financial and industrial institutions would fall into foreign ownership and that this concentration of foreign capital would obstruct his plans to pursue a strategy of socialist economic development. Lenin also feared that foreign capitalists would exploit cheap Russian labour and engage in the wholesale extraction of Russian mineral resources for short-term profit, and that a liberal import policy would result in an influx of imported consumer goods at the expense of items that were considered essential for the policy of socialist construction. Lenin considered it necessary to restrict imports to commodities that were thought to be essential for long-term economic development and to prevent the export of essential raw materials and foodstuffs. Although these objectives could have been achieved by the imposition of tariffs, export duties, import and export quotas and restrictions on capital movements, Lenin favoured the construction of a legal fence around the economy, which illegalised all foreign trade transactions other than those which had been expressly permitted by the state (Quigley 1974: chap. 1 passim).

The establishment of NEP led to renewed demands for the abolition of the state monopoly of foreign trade. Bukharin argued that the central bodies responsible for conducting foreign trade were too isolated from domestic producers and actually prevented them from generating the required volume of exports needed to pay for imports, which hindered industrialisation. The left opposition countered that the abolition of the state monopoly would result in private traders seeking more profitable export markets and would encourage exports of grain and foodstuffs despite domestic shortages (as in 1891), which could result in famine in the towns and the exodus of urban labour to the countryside in search of food. Lenin's views prevailed (with the support of Trotsky and later Stalin) and the State Monopoly of Foreign Trade was retained throughout NEP despite the liberalisation of domestic trade.

The nature of Russian foreign economic relations was largely determined by Lenin's repudiation of all foreign debts incurred before the revolution and by the subsequent nationalisation of foreign property without compensation. Although this freed the economy of the enormous burden of debt service it had a major impact on foreign governments and potential investors. Russia was accused of breaking the foundations on which civilised trade and credit were based and isolating itself from the rest of the world (Hough 1991: 13). The antagonism of Russia's former allies towards developing economic relations with the new regime intensified following the signature of the peace treaty with Germany, which ceded large parts of Ukrainian territory to German control and also involved significant territorial losses from the old Russian Empire with the emergence of independent states in Poland, Finland and the Baltic Republics. Territorial losses resulted in a loss of population of 36 million but involved a more than proportionate loss of industrial potential and of the more developed dairy lands and timber regions that made a significant contribution to export earnings. The allied blockade of Russian ports and land frontiers and the imposition of an embargo on Soviet exports and a gold blockade by foreign banks and companies, who either refused to accept payment in gold by the Soviet government or only accepted it at a large discount

(Baykov 1946: 7), resulted in the collapse of foreign trade to virtually zero in 1919.

The blockade was partially eased in 1920 following the conclusion of peace treaties with the Baltic States and in 1921 trade agreements were concluded with Britain, Germany, Norway, Czechoslovakia, Austria and Italy and with states that had gained independence from the Russian Empire (Finland, Estonia, Latvia, and Poland). The treaty of Rapallo in 1922 opened the way to a more significant expansion of trade with Germany, who had been Russia's most significant trade partner in Tsarist times, accounting for 30 per cent of Russian exports and 48 per cent of Russian imports and 65 per cent of Russian imports of machinery and equipment in 1913 (Vneshtorg 1918–66). Despite the partial easing of international relations, Soviet trade levels remained depressed. A contemporary Soviet estimate, which took account of both price changes and boundary changes, calculated that Soviet trade turnover in 1930 was only 60.9 per cent of its comparable level in 1913, reaching 69.5 per cent in the peak year of 1931 (Baykov 1946: 43).

The basic problems were caused by the failure of the growth of exports and the inability to attract foreign credits and investment to cover the desired level of imports. Grain exports, which had averaged 10.6 million tonnes between 1909 and 1913 (on Soviet territories), grew slowly to 2.6 million tonnes in 1923–24, falling back to 569 thousand tonnes in 1924–25 and only averaged just over 2 million tonnes a year in 1925–26 and 1926–27. Similarly exports of timber only averaged just over 2 million tonnes per annum from 1923–26 compared with an annual average of over 7 million tonnes from 1909–13. The major success was exports of crude oil and products, which had reached 2 million tonnes by 1926 and peaked at 6.2 million tonnes in 1932 compared with average annual production of 859 thousand tonnes from 1909–13. Although exports of industrial and processed goods grew faster than agricultural exports the former (with oil, timber and furs comprising 41 per cent of total exports in 1927–28) overtook agricultural products as the main source of export earnings from 1927–28 onwards, they failed to reach pre-war levels despite the fact that pre-war levels of industrial production had been reached by 1926. The growth of domestic consumption particularly for food (partly affected by population growth) had again outstripped the growth of domestic production, slowing down the potential growth of exports.

This had a major impact on the Soviet Union's ability to import, which was exacerbated by the lack of access to long-term credits. Imports initially recovered faster than exports with items for consumption accounting for just over half of total imports in 1921–22. The government was forced to finance imports by sales of gold and foreign currency. From 1923 onwards producers goods predominated and industrial raw materials (notably cotton and ferrous metals) predominated in imports and from 1926 until the outbreak of war accounted for approximately 90 per cent of total imports. Imports of machinery and equipment for industrial modernisation, however, remained relatively depressed and were below the average level recorded in 1909–13 until the late 1920s (Baykov 1946: 41–63).

## THE STALINIST GROWTH MODEL AND IMPORTED TECHNOLOGY

### Extensive growth and non-indigenous technology

The essence of the Stalinist growth model was that it attempted to achieve a rapid growth of industrial output by the mobilisation of inputs of capital, labour and raw materials into the industrial sector. The strategy, which was described as 'extensive growth' by Soviet economists, depended on generating a rapid growth of inputs into productive industry to realise the growth of industrial output, rather than on improving the efficiency with which resources were used by the development of new processes and production techniques. The growth of the industrial capital stock was generated by concentrating a high proportion of GNP into investment and especially into investment in heavy industry and the production of raw materials. The growth of the industrial labour force was achieved by the forced transfer of labour from agriculture into industry and by a significant increase in female participation rates in the industrial labour force. During the first five-year plan, the proportion of GNP devoted to investment rose from 15 per cent in 1928 to 44 cent in 1932 (Ellman 1975) while the industrial labour force more than doubled from 4.3 million to 9.4 million over the same period (Narkhoz: various years).

The model also depended on the rapid diffusion of existing world (i.e. non-indigenous) technology to generate an improvement in labour productivity. Bergson (1989: 106) makes the analytical distinction between 'technological progress proper', which involves generating a growth in economic efficiency (more output for a given unit of input) through the development of new production methods and processes, and 'technological progress extended', an inclusive term which embraces all forms of generating a growth of output with a given supply of inputs, including the acquisition and diffusion of existing non-indigenous technology which taken in its widest sense includes benefiting from the experience of more advanced economies, including copying systems of management, incentive schemes, etc. The Stalinist model depended more on 'technological progress extended' than on 'technological progress proper' to achieve rapid industrialisation.

The acquisition, application and diffusion of technology that originated outside the domestic economy is a common source of growth for medium-developed economies. A study of the relationship between the absolute level of, and the rate of growth of labour productivity (output per worker) in 55 countries ranging from the USA to Burma, conducted by Gomulka (1971) discovered that economies with an intermediate absolute level of output per worker were capable of growing faster than economies with either a very high, or a very low, absolute level of output per worker. This suggests that countries with a very high level of output per worker have a greater proportion of workers who are already utilising the most advanced technology in the world and who therefore depend on new technological innovations (technological progress proper) to generate further growth in labour productivity. It is also probable that economies (and firms) that possess a relatively advanced technological production structure will also have a relatively high research and development capability and will depend to a greater degree on domestic innovation to generate productivity growth than less technologically advanced economies. The most plausible explanation for the observed link between very low absolute levels of labour productivity and a low growth of labour productivity is that the very poorest countries do not have either the physical infrastructure (roads, power networks and communications) or an educated and trained labour force in sufficient quantities to be able to benefit from the transfer of non-indigenous technology to their economies.

The acquisition of non-indigenous technology during the first five-year plan was reflected in the growing proportion of imports of machinery, electrical equipment and spare parts, which according to Soviet official data grew from 6.9 per cent of total Soviet imports in 1923–24 to 19.6 per cent in 1929, reaching 48.4 per cent in 1932 (Baykov 1946: Appendix, table VI) while imports of iron and steel products rose from 4.8 per cent of the total in 1923–24 to a peak of 20.6 per cent in 1931. Figures provided by Baykov (1946: Appendix, Table II) indicate that imports of producers goods ranged between 88 and 93 per cent of total Soviet imports during the first five-year plan, compared with 70–72 per cent from 1909–1913. During this period the Soviet Union became the world's largest importer of machinery and equipment, receiving between 33 and 50 per cent of world exports of machinery and equipment in 1931–32 and thereby helping to maintain the relative world price of manufactures in relation to agricultural products and raw materials which led to a major deterioration in Soviet terms of trade and created acute balance of payments pressures (Koves 1985: 36). Soviet imports were drastically curtailed after 1931, with the effect that the volume of imports of machinery and equipment fell to just over 40 per cent of the 1930 level in constant prices in 1933, falling further to only 32 per cent of the 1930 level by 1938 (Vneshtorg 1918–66). Machinery and equipment, however, still constituted 34.7 per cent of the value of Soviet imports. At the same time imports of consumer goods and cotton and foodstuffs, including tea, rice and fish, were drastically curtailed while exports of grain were expanded in 1930 and 1931.

## Soviet perceptions of the need for technology imports

The prevailing view among western analysts of the Soviet economy was that the Soviet Union displayed a strong preference for autarky during the Stalinist era, indicated by the low level of trade in the 1930s. Holzman (1974: 54–60) contends that the Soviet government pursued a deliberate policy of limiting their trade dependence on what was seen as a hostile capitalist world after 1931 when import possibilities were not fully utilised. This policy was facilitated by the initial spurt of imports of machinery and equipment from 1928–31, which had built up domestic production capacity, thus limiting subsequent dependence on imported products. Koves (1985: 37–40) argues that import cuts were forced on the Soviet Union by balance of payments pressures resulting from the recession and the collapse of world market prices for Soviet staple exports of grain, timber and oil, which limited the ability of the Soviet Union to import and were not the result of a deliberate policy to limit dependence, although Soviet trade specialists then rationalised this as deliberate policy.

Methods other than importing technology embodied in machinery and equipment were used to acquire foreign technology on a wide scale in the 1930s. These included searches of technical and scientific literature, purchasing single items of equipment for dismantling and copying (reverse engineering) and hiring foreign engineers in order to acquire their expertise and technical know-how (Sutton: 1968). The impact of this policy on economic growth is controversial as estimates of Soviet growth rates during this period vary substantially. Soviet official statistics claim that the gross output of large-scale industry grew just over fourfold (an annual average rate of 20 per cent per annum from 1929–36), followed by a slowdown from 1937 until the outbreak of war. Western re-estimates by Kaplan and Moorsteen (1960) based on Soviet data, indicate a slower, but still impressive rate of industrial growth of just over 10 per cent per annum from 1927–37 (this is contested below), followed by a fall to an annual rate of 1.9 per cent from 1937–40.

The import pattern of the 1930s was repeated in the immediate post-war period, when imports of machinery and equipment rose to 40 per cent of total imports in 1946 before falling in relative and absolute terms to less than 9 per cent in 1948. These figures underestimate the scale of acquisition of foreign machinery and equipment which was supplemented by substantial requisitioning of German equipment from Germany itself and its former allies in Eastern Europe in the form of reparation payments and virtual confiscation of German property found elsewhere in Eastern Europe.

In 1951 Stalin formulated the idea that Marx's 'universal world market' had been irrevocably divided into two separate and independent world markets, socialist and capitalist (the latter included developing countries), and that economic relations between the two would be severely restricted. This was facilitated by the development of trade links with the new Socialist Republics in Eastern Europe and China, which partially substituted bloc autarky for purely Soviet autarky (Holzman 1974: 60–5). The

*Table 2.1*   Growth of Soviet production and foreign trade in real terms 1950–90 (annual average rate of growth per five-year plan period)

|  | 1951–55 | 1956–60 | 1961–65 | 1966–70 | 1971–75 | 1976–80 | 1981–85 | 1986–90 |
|---|---|---|---|---|---|---|---|---|
| Industrial output | 13.1 | 10.7 | 8.6 | 8.5 | 7.4 | 4.7 | 3.6 | 3.2 |
| Net material product | 11.3 | 9.1 | 6.4 | 7.7 | 5.6 | 4.3 | 3.2 | 1.4 |
| Exports: Total | 12.1 | 11.2 | 8.8 | 9.9 | 4.9 | 4.8 | 1.9 | 0.3 |
| CMEA | 10.5 | 13.0 | 9.6 | 9.9 | 5.3 | 4.7 | 0.3 | −1.3 |
| Industrialised West | 15.5 | 14.6 | 8.7 | 7.8 | 4.8 | 2.8 | 2.8 | 2.3 |
| Developing countries | 33.5 | 20.5 | 28.8 | 11.7 | 3.8 | 7.8 | 3.3 | −2.6 |
| Imports: Total | 13.2 | 13.8 | 5.8 | 6.4 | 10.4 | 5.8 | 6.0 | 1.0 |
| CMEA | 11.0 | 12.5 | 9.7 | 6.0 | 7.0 | 5.7 | 6.4 | −0.2 |
| Industrialised West | 10.8 | 21.0 | 8.6 | 11.2 | 17.1 | 6.4 | 3.8 | 0.3 |
| Developing countries | 11.1 | 21.2 | 11.6 | 7.4 | 9.8 | 2.9 | 7.4 | 7.1 |

*Sources:* Growth rates of industrial output and net material product from Narkhoz various years. Export and Imports from Vneshtorgs 1922–81 and 1990. (see note on statistical sources at end of Bibliography).

Soviet Union has pursued a more open trade policy with non-socialist countries since the death of Stalin in 1953. Soviet official trade statistics which show that imports from the industrialised capitalist economies measured in 'comparable prices' (the methodologically suspect Soviet version of 'constant' prices) grew faster than net material product (NMP) produced in each five-year plan period from 1955 to 1985 indicating a greater degree of openness to trade with the West (see Table 2.1).

The first significant expansion of imports from the West started with Khrushchev's chemicalisation programme in the late 1950s. Khrushchev's speeches at this time also included favourable assessments of the managerial methods employed by western multinationals to boost efficiency and stimulate economic integration in the EC (Khrushchev 1962). At the same time Soviet economists in Gosplan were 'rediscovering' the theory of comparative costs and developing new methods to assess the effectiveness of foreign trade, which compared the domestic production cost of import substitutes with the domestic cost of producing exports that were required to pay for imports and which specifically mentioned the expansion of trade links with advanced capitalist states (Smirnov, Zotov and Shagalov 1964).

The opening of the Soviet economy to imports from non-socialist countries was not limited to machinery and equipment as Khrushchev initiated purchases of grain from Australia, Canada and the USA, following the poor harvest of 1963. Although Khrushchev retained the concept of 'two world markets' he revised the approach towards developing countries, arguing that non-aligned countries could be won over to the socialist camp (Valkenier 1983), and developed a series of bilateral economic relations with Asian and Middle Eastern non-aligned states, notably India, Egypt and Indonesia which became major sources of imported cotton and rubber. In the period from 1959–64, however, trade links were expanded with emerging 'revolutionary democracies' which eventually proved to be a major drain on Soviet resources (Smith 1985a).

Many western studies of Soviet trade policy since the war have concentrated on the contribution of imported machinery and equipment to Soviet economic growth and on Soviet perceptions of the importance of technology imports (see Hanson 1981, Parrott 1983, Sokoloff 1987). This partly reflected western political concerns during the cold war period that the Soviet Union, through the acquisition of western technology and know-how that it could not generate domestically (and which could make a multiplied contribution to Soviet growth rate, over and above the contribution of the imported equipment itself) gained considerably more from West–East technology transfer than did the West.

Parrott (1983: 181–229) argues that, following the fall of Khrushchev in 1964, Kosygin initiated a reappraisal of Soviet economic capabilities, which led to a rejection of the assumption of Soviet technological supremacy over the West and a recognition of the barriers to innovation and diffusion of technology under the traditional Soviet economic system, with the possibility of a widening technology gap emerging between the Soviet economy and the advanced capitalist states. This more realistic assessment of the relative technological capabilities of the Soviet Union and the industrialised capitalist economies resulted in a major political disagreement in the post-Khrushchev Politburo concerning trade and defence policy. Conservatives argued that the recognition of greater western capability increased the threat from the West and necessitated increased expenditure on domestic research and development and on defence. Less orthodox members of the leadership argued that this analysis pointed to the need for greater economic contacts with the West, which would in turn require a reduction in East–West tensions and domestic economic reforms to improve Soviet performance in western markets. Parrott concludes that Brezhnev initially supported conservative arguments but eventually moved to a more centralist position in which he saw imports of western technology as a substitute for deeper economic reform.

## Technology transfer and economic growth in the post-war period

Soviet statistics and western estimates indicate a major acceleration of growth of industrial output in the immediate post-war period. Official statistics show an annual industrial growth rate of more than 20 per cent from 1947–50 as the USSR rebuilt its war-damaged economy and benefited from improvements in international technology that had taken place since the first industrialisation drive. Official statistics indicate that, although the rate of growth of industrial output and net material product (NMP) declined after the initial period of reconstruction had been completed in the late 1950s, the rate of growth of industrial output was still impressive by international standards (averaging 13 per cent per annum in the 1950s). Extrapolations based on the differences between the official Soviet and US growth rates stimulated Khrushchev's claim in 1961 that the Soviet Union would overtake the USA in the per capita production of major industrial items and win the war between capitalism and communism by means of peaceful competition by the early 1980s.

Official statistics of Soviet growth from 1960 onwards indicate the emptiness of Khrushchev's boast, while there is growing evidence to suggest that the official figures also overstated the real rate of growth. Official statistics indicate that there has been a secular decline in the growth rate of industrial output, with the growth of industrial output declining in each five-year plan period since the war (except 1966–70). Furthermore, although there was a decline in the growth rate of the industrial labour force and the industrial capital stock over the same period, these continued to grow faster than the growth of output, indicating either a decline in efficiency of capital and/or major diseconomies of scale, possibly associated with the need to utilise less accessible sources of energy and raw materials. The rate of decline of the growth rate since the mid-1970s is greater than would be expected from the overall secular downward trend in growth rates and the growth rate itself actually started to lag behind that of the USA, with the result that even Soviet official figures show that Soviet national income fell from 67 per cent of US national income in 1980 to 64 per cent in 1986 (Narkhoz 1987: 623). Gomulka's work indicates that the Soviet Union, as a medium developed country should have been capable of benefiting from the international transfer of technology and therefore growing faster than, and narrowing the gap with, more developed economies. Finally, in 1990, official statistics recorded that both Soviet national income produced (minus 4.0 per cent) and industrial output (minus 1.2 per cent) fell for the first time in peace time, a decline which accelerated in 1991 to minus 15 per cent and minus 7.8 per cent respectively (Ekonomika i Zhizn 1991, no. 5 and 1992, no. 6).

Western analysts of Soviet economic performance have treated Soviet official growth rates with scepticism. The principal causes for concern (among many) have been that Soviet statistics attach artificially high values to the fastest growing products and thus bias growth statistics upwards, that Soviet statistics underestimate deterioration in the quality of production and overestimate quality improvements, and that Soviet statistics significantly underestimate actual price increases (hidden inflation) and consequently overestimate the real rate of growth. These criticisms refer as much to the poor methodology of Soviet statistics, as to deliberate falsification by the central authorities (although it is widely accepted that enterprises and other organisations routinely falsify the information they provide to higher authorities to secure bonuses). Most western estimates of Soviet growth (including those of the CIA) are based on recalculations of Soviet official data and indicate a far more serious set of problems, with lower growth rates and a far wider gap between US and Soviet output and consumption levels. More alarmingly there is evidence to suggest that the degree of hidden inflation has increased over time and that official statistics considerably underestimate the deterioration in Soviet economic performance from the late 1970s. A study by Ellman (1982) was among the first to suggest that growth had not merely slowed down but had actually stopped altogether in 1978 and that per capita incomes did not increase between 1979 and 1981, while certain social indicators (death rates, queues and shortages) actually deteriorated. Similar conclusions were reached independently by Wiles (1982) who arrived at slightly higher growth rates than Ellman, but more gloomy social indicators. Similarly Bergson (1987), in a series of articles originally published in the 1970s and 1980s, predicted an eventual decline in Soviet output, if systemic changes were not enacted.

A devastating critique of Soviet growth statistics and economic performance over the period from the second half of the 1920s up to the current day was published in the literary journal *Novy Mir* (under the title 'Cunning Figures') by two Soviet economists, Seliunin and Khanin, in 1987. Their most significant claim is that national income grew by only 6–7 times between 1928 and 1985 (p. 192) compared with official claims of an 86-fold increase over the same period and 137-fold increase from 1913–1985 (Narkhoz: various years). Aslund estimates this is equivalent to an annual rate of growth of between 3.2 and 3.5 per cent per annum (Aslund 1990: 46). While Seliunin and Khanin accept that this is an acceptable rate of growth, particularly given the level of war damage, it is roughly comparable with US growth over the same period and implies little or no narrowing of the gap between the two.

Seliunin and Khanin contend that national income only grew by one and a half times between 1929 and 1941, implying an annual average rate of growth of national income of only just over 3 per cent. They agree that there were deep structural changes in the economy during the 1930s, but that this progress was limited to the development of heavy industry, construction and transport, while agricultural output fell substantially and 1928 levels of grain and livestock production were not reached until the 1950s (Seliunin and Khanin 1987: 193). As a result it seems more accurate to use the terms 'extensive industrialisation' or even 'extensive change' instead of 'extensive growth' to describe of the process of Soviet industrialisation during the 1930s.

Seliunin and Khanin argue that the 1950s were the most successful period of Soviet economic development when an (unspecified) high rate of growth was achieved by greater efficiency in the use of resources (intensive growth) as well as by the rapid growth of the industrial labour force resulting from demobilisation. They attribute this largely to a balanced growth policy which placed as much emphasis on the production of consumer goods, agriculture and housing as on heavy industry, combined with a stable monetary policy which equated the supply and demand for consumption at an inflation-free level. This policy was not sustained in the 1960s and 1970s. Seliunin and Khanin's analysis of growth rates in this period again indicates a secular decline in growth, but at a substantially lower level than most conventional estimates with growth falling to 1 per cent per annum in 1976–80 and 0.6 per cent per annum in 1981–85 (including a fall of national income of 2 per cent per annum in 1981–82 (Khanin 1992: 10), despite the fact Soviet terms of trade moved sharply in their favour following the increase in world oil prices in 1974.

Khanin (1991: 33; 1992: 10) also argues that the officially recorded fall in production from 1990–91 is underestimated and that after correcting for hidden inflation the real fall in national income in the last quarter of 1990 compared with the last quarter of 1989 was of the order of 13.5 to 14.5 per cent. The continued fall in national income in 1991 (officially given as 15 per cent, which if the rate of hidden inflation was unchanged at 5 per cent implies a fall in output of 20 per cent) makes the collapse in national income produced over the two years greater than 30 per cent, which is more than that experienced during the American depression. Aslund (1990: 49) argues that Soviet GNP per capita in 1985–86 was less than a third that of the USA. On this basis the collapse in Soviet production in 1990–91 would have left the former Soviet Union with a per capita GNP less than 20 per cent of that of the USA, equivalent to approximately $3,500 per head.

# Chapter 3

# The organisation of Soviet foreign economic relations

## THE DOMESTIC PLANNING SYSTEM

The structure of Soviet foreign trade was determined by the policy of forced rapid industrialisation and the institutional structure that was created to implement the strategy which was designed to ensure that basic economic decisions concerning production and consumption reflected the preferences of the ruling elite within the Communist Party. This process entailed strengthening the planning instruments that had been developed during NEP into institutions which not only influenced the level and structure of investment in the economy, but exercised strong central control and direction over a myriad of economic decisions that would normally have been taken at the level of the enterprise or the corporation in a market economy. The basic features of the centrally planned economy had been established by the mid-1930s and, although subject to numerous attempts at refinement after the death of Stalin in 1953, remained relatively intact until the system virtually collapsed under the simultaneous pressure for change from above and below in the late 1980s.

The process of central planning can be divided into two basic elements: the problem of plan formulation (drawing up optimal or feasible plans) and plan implementation (providing a set of instructions to ensure that plans are implemented at the enterprise level). This involved the creation of a planning hierarchy in which information about production potential flowed up the hierarchy from production units (enterprises) through intermediate agencies to planners who processed the information into plan instructions, which were then sent back down the planning hierarchy to enterprises. The principal central agencies involved in the process of supply planning were the Politburo of the Communist Party of the Soviet Union (CPSU), which was responsible for establishing the main directions of economic policy and state agencies including the State Planning Committee (Gosplan) and the State Committee for Material Supply (Gossnab, which was created in 1965) and industrial ministries, which were responsible for the operation of exceedingly large industrial sectors (e.g. Ministry of Heavy and Transport Machine Building) and also for the detailed implementation of central plans. The central organisations of Soviet authority were replicated by 'national' organisations at the Republican level. The Politburo played little or no role in the minutiae of day-to-day decision-making in the economy, but determined the main features of the economic agenda by setting plan growth rates for national income and other major economic aggregates over the medium and long term and the distribution of national income between investment and consumption as a whole, the level of investment in light and heavy industry, defence and infrastructure on the basis of information provided by Gosplan (Hewett 1988: 106). The Politburo determined or approved a range of economic issues with social, political or ideological ramifications from quite basic economic questions such as as changes in prices in state stores, to more overt political questions concerning the nature and conduct of trade relations with specific countries regardless of profitability.

Gosplan was the principal agency responsible for the formulation of both long-term or perspective (15-year) plans, medium-term (five-year) plans and for the construction and supervision of operational (one-year or less) plans, in accordance with the Politburo's objectives. Gosplan attempted to maintain a balance between the supply and demand for approximately 1,500–2,000 broad commodity groups by means of a system of material balances which measured the availability or planned supply of goods in physical units (the planned level of domestic production plus stock reduction plus planned imports) against the planned demand (planned domestic consumption or usage plus stock building plus planned exports). These were supplemented by more detailed balances constructed by Gossnab, which covered approximately 20,000 products.

Perspective and medium-term plans were important for determining the broad direction of economic activity and in highlighting imbalances between domestic supply and demand over the long term, which allowed Gosplan to draw up investment programmes to overcome the most critical bottlenecks in the economy. While this had many advantages it had the substantial disadvantage that major volumes of investment that had already been determined by past decisions could not incorporate the most recent technological changes, making the economy slow to respond to changing parameters in world markets. The major function of Gosplan, however, was not forward planning but the formulation and supervision of operational plans. Production potential in the short term is determined by existing production facilities in the economy plus any new plant coming on stream minus any planned closures of plant and equipment. As Gosplan was under political pressure to meet the target growth level contained in the five-year plan, it initially based output targets for individual industries for the current period on plan targets and attempted to stimulate increased production from existing plants by setting plan targets that were 'a few percentage points' higher than the output level achieved in the previous planning period (Birman 1978). These targets were passed to the industrial ministries who passed them down the planning hierarchy in the form of plan directives. At each stage in the process, the appropriate planning authorities included a greater degree of detail to the plan target, normally by adding the required growth target to the data on plan fulfilment that they had received from subordinate authorities in the process of plan formulation.

Finally, the enterprise received its annual plan, which included detailed instructions specifying what the enterprise should produce (in physical quantities or value parameters); its allocation of inputs (energy, materials, components) and labour and labour productivity plan; a plan for the introduction of new products and processes; and a financial plan which specified planned costs (including wages) planned revenues and planned profit levels, which was a reflection of the value of the planned level of inputs and outputs. Enterprise managers and supervisory authorities were motivated to implement plan targets by the payment of money bonuses for the fulfilment or overfulfilment of the most important targets, which in most cases was gross output which tended to re-emerge in one form or another despite persistent attempts to reform the system of indicators to reflect other variables under Khrushchev and Brezhnev.

The system resulted in widespread 'socially irrational' or economically inefficient behaviour. Enterprises had an incentive to understate their production potential to planners in order to obtain plan targets that could be easily achieved. Similarly, the enterprise had an incentive to over-indent for inputs of energy, raw materials, components and labour to ensure it received an adequate supply. However, the principle of increasing enterprise targets from the level achieved in the preceding plan period, meant that once an enterprise had successfully obtained a 'slack' plan it had no incentive to overfulfil it by too much as this would affect subsequent output targets. In addition, if it succeeded in obtaining surplus inputs, it had no incentive to economise on their use, as this would affect the allocation for subsequent years. Enterprise managers actually had a perverse incentive to overconsume excess inputs of energy and raw materials that could not be stored or bartered to another organisation.

The distortions generated by material incentives on the quality and assortment of output were equally serious. Enterprises were not concerned about either the quality or range of their products provided they satisfied plan targets. Soviet economists and citizens frequently complained that the quality of basic consumer goods such as television sets, fridges and washing machines did not meet world market quality standards. If aggregated output targets were specified in terms of weight, enterprises had an incentive to concentrate production on the heavier items in their production profile. Similarly, if targets were specified in terms of volume, enterprises tended to concentrate on the production of items for which the highest volume could be achieved with a given level of inputs.

## SOVIET FINANCIAL AND MONETARY PLANNING

The distinguishing feature of the Soviet monetary system was that money was 'passive' in most spheres of operation, in the sense that the possession of money did not automatically give the holder the right to demand resources, particularly in the case of transfers of resources between enterprises. In a market economy an enterprise demands inputs from suppliers by paying it money which creates revenue for the supplying enterprise and which in turn enables the latter to purchase inputs from its suppliers. In the Soviet economy the distribution of inputs between enterprises was conducted by Gossnab according to instructions contained in the State plan. The enterprise maintained accounts with the State Bank which had the sole power to administer and supervise the financial affairs of the enterprise and which was not supposed to sanction payments for inter-enterprise transfers that had not been included in the enterprise plan. As a result flows of goods between enterprises did not involve cash payments; the enterprise accounts at the State Bank were either credited or debited with the book value of outputs supplied and inputs received, in accordance with directives contained in the state plan. In practice, the State Bank did not have the authority to bankrupt an enterprise that failed to meet cost targets and would underwrite above-plan consumption of inputs by granting credit. Consequently, Soviet enterprises had soft-budget constraints which meant that they knew that financial provision would be made for inputs that were required to meet plan targets, regardless of the demand for the end product or the efficiency with which the inputs were used. This also applied to labour inputs. Enterprises facing difficulties in attracting labour paid out wages in excess of wage ceilings established in plan targets which were then sanctioned by the State Bank.

Money played a more active role in the retail sector where holders of money could choose between the goods made available to them in state stores before making their purchases, although this remained a limited form of 'active money' as the level and structure of household demand had no direct effect on either the supply or price of consumer goods in the state sector, either in total or for individual products. Similarly, indications of unsatisfied consumer demand had no direct impact on the level or structure of investment in the consumer sector. Prices in state retail stores were highly inflexible and, in the case of the majority of basic staple goods, remained unchanged between the early 1950s and April 1991 with the difference between production cost and prices covered by subsidies from the state budget. This degree of price inflexibility created two major problems of disequilibrium in consumer markets. Firstly, low relative prices for subsidised goods increased the demand for those specific goods. As the authorities did not automatically respond by increasing the supply to meet available demand or by operating an effective rationing system, this simply resulted in queues, shortages and black markets for the goods in question.

Secondly, price inflexibility meant that retail prices were unable to rise in response to inflationary pressures caused by a more rapid rate of growth of money demand in relation to the supply of consumer goods, particularly when enterprises violated their wage plans. Retail demand was injected into the economy with the payment of money wages and transfer payments (pensions, welfare payments, etc.). The problem of macro-economic equilibrium in the state sector could be reduced to the problem of equating the flow of money incomes minus personal (direct) taxes minus savings to the value of the supply of consumer goods (including turnover taxes) and services over a given period. In a market economy excess demand in the consumer sector that cannot be met by an increase in the supply of domestically produced consumer goods will result in a combination of an increase in the level of retail prices as a whole (inflation) and an increase in imported consumer goods until the excess demand has been equilibrated by an increase in the nominal level (money value) of consumption. In the centrally planned economy, the combination of inflexible prices and the state monopoly of foreign trade (see below) prevented these automatic responses to an increase in the level of aggregate demand in the economy, which resulted in macroeconomic disequilibria reflected in repressed inflation and a 'repressed balance of payments deficit' in the sense that the central authorities used physical controls to prevent the demand for imports by individuals and enterprises at prevailing exchange rates creating an actual balance of payments deficit.

Repressed inflation was principally manifested in the form of 'involuntary savings', as consumers' desired spending plans were frustrated and they were forced to hold a higher level of savings balances in relation to income than they wanted. This in turn led to the phenomenon of 'inflationary overhang' caused by the accumulation of idle money balances over time, which added to the level of demand for consumer goods in any given period, increasing the disequilibrium between available supplies and monetary demand.

## THE OPERATION OF THE STATE MONOPOLY OF FOREIGN TRADE

Central planners could not have exercised detailed control over the flow of resources inside the economy, if they had been unable to control the flow of resources into and out of the economy. The centralised administration of foreign trade, vested in the State Monopoly of Foreign Trade which prevented individuals and enterprises from engaging in any import or export operations without a specific directive to that effect from the national planning authorities, was an essential feature of the traditional, unreformed Soviet economic planning system. Although the basic features and operating principles of the State Monopoly of Foreign Trade were established by Lenin during the NEP period in the 1920s, and co-existed with a mixed-market economy, they were considerably modified and strengthened by Stalin with the advent of central planning in the 1930s. Despite criticisms of the system in the 1970s, the basic system of administering foreign trade was largely unaltered until Gorbachev's first attempts at reform in 1987.

The principal executive bodies involved in the administration and conduct of foreign trade relations when Gorbachev came to power in 1985 were the Ministry of Foreign Trade, the State Committee for Foreign Economic Relations (GKES) and an agency of the State Bank which specialised in foreign trade matters known as the Foreign Trade Bank (Vneshtorgbank). These organisations worked closely with other state organisations involved in economic planning, including the State Planning Committee, the State Committee for Material and Technical Supply, the State Committee for Science and Technology, the Ministry for Finance and the State Bank.

The central apparatus of the Ministry of Foreign Trade was subdivided into six regional chief administrations which were specialised according to geographical and political trading regions (e.g. the Americas, European Socialist countries), eight main administrations which were specialised according to product groups and fifteen functional administrations (Gruzinov 1979: 23–4). The Ministry's operations were conducted by Foreign Trade Associations or Organisations (FTOs) which were specialised along product lines and were the only organisations empowered to enter trade negotiations with foreign suppliers and customers, and to conduct import and export activities on the basis of instructions received from the chief administrations. In 1985, 90 per cent of foreign trade was conducted by 50 FTOs which were directly responsible to the Ministry of Foreign Trade, while the remaining 10 per cent of trade operations were conducted by nine foreign trade organisations responsible to the GKES (Pozdnyakov and Sadikov 1985: 23). The GKES was largely concerned with export activities involving large-scale construction projects in third world and socialist countries, some of which were part of the Soviet aid programme (Pozdnyakov and Sadikov 1985: 42).

The formulation of foreign trade plans was the joint responsibility of the Ministry of Foreign Trade and the State Planning Committee and was largely determined by the system of planning by material balances. Gosplan drew up an initial production plan which highlighted the most important imbalances in the domestic economy and which served as the basis for constructing import and export plans. In theory, the import plan consisted of commodities that could not be produced domestically in sufficient quantities to satisfy the needs specified in the state plan, commodities that could not be produced domestically at all (as a result of either the lack of technical capability or lack of capacity) and commodities that were identified as excessively costly to produce domestically. The export plan was largely composed of items for which there was excess domestic capacity in relation to domestic demand. This could result from one of or a combination of the following factors: favourable endowment with exploitable natural resources over and above domestic consumption requirements (e.g. raw materials and energy); a deliberate investment policy to create an export-oriented sector and the existence of domestic production capacity that exceeded domestic demand as result of market saturation resulting from an earlier crash programme to overcome domestic shortage. Finally, the plan could also include items that could be identified as cheap to produce domestically in relation to world market prices.

The distinguishing feature of foreign trade planning was the essentially anti-mercantilist (or even anti-Keynesian) attitude towards exports. Exports were not seen as a positive extension to the domestic market, or a source of external wealth creation, but as a diversion of domestic resources away from domestic uses, which was solely justified by the need to meet import plans. The whole system was therefore driven by the need to overcome the most critical domestic supply constraints identified by Gosplan in the process of drawing up long-term perspective, medium-term and operational plans.

A critical (but probably heavily censored) analysis of the highly bureaucratic procedures used to plan and execute foreign trade decisions was published in the late 1970s following a management research project into the operations of the Ministry of Foreign Trade conducted by V.P. Gruzinov. Gruzinov (1979: 31–3) demonstrated that the decision to import a piece of machinery could involve as many as forty different stages in the planning process, which for purposes of simplicity could be narrowed down to seven major stages. Firstly, a decision to import the item was taken by the council of Ministers; secondly, the decision was passed to the appropriate FTO; thirdly, the FTO sought tenders from foreign suppliers; fourthly, the tenders were passed on to the Soviet customer; fifthly, the Soviet customer approved the tenders; sixthly, the FTO signed the contract with the foreign supplier and, finally, the machinery was delivered and installed under the supervision of the FTO which was responsible for ensuring that the terms of the contract were fulfilled. At each stage in this process the FTO had to receive approval from its superiors in the Ministry as well as to liaise with the receiving enterprise.

A similar process (although effectively reversed from stage three onwards) was conducted in the case of exports. The FTO sought potential foreign customers for Soviet products and made them an offer which included provisional specifications concerning price, quality, terms of delivery, etc.; if these were accepted by the customer, further detailed negotiations were held before a contract was drafted; the contract was then submitted for approval to the head of the FTO and to other departments of the Ministry that might be involved; the contract would then be sent to the foreign customer for signature after internal approval had been received; finally, the FTO was responsible for making arrangements with the appropriate enterprise (issuing mandatory orders) and delivering the goods according to the contract.

While this cumbersome procedure ensured that central planners could maintain detailed control over the size and composition of imports and exports, it also meant that production enterprises were isolated from potential foreign customers and suppliers and had little or no direct knowledge of changing demand conditions or product specifications in world markets. The centralised administration of foreign trade also reinforced the monopoly position of enterprises and ministries in the domestic economy and increased their protection from foreign innovations. Industrial ministries had no incentive to request imports that would be competitive with goods produced within their own ministry and, through membership of the Council of Ministers, could veto the import of goods that would affect their domestic monopoly.

## The role of prices and exchange rates and the contribution of foreign trade to the State Budget

Domestic wholesale and retail prices which were determined by the central authorities bore little relation to world market prices and changes in the latter had little or no effect on the level or structure of prices of goods produced domestically. The internal financial and price system was formally (but entirely notionally) linked to the international financial system by the official exchange rate for the rouble, which was set in 1961 at 0.987412 grams of gold per rouble (equivalent to $1.11 per rouble) until the demonetisation of gold and the abandoning of fixed exchange rates in 1971. Subsequently the rouble has been linked to a basket of western currencies and has tracked international fluctuations in exchange rates. The convertibility of the rouble, however, was entirely notional. The rouble was basically commodity inconvertible in the domestic economy in that the holder of roubles could not automatically convert them into goods, other than the limited supply in the state retail market. The rouble was also financially inconvertible (that is, it could not be exchanged into other currencies) in two critical senses: firstly it was domestically inconvertible in the sense that Soviet citizens (or other residents or visitors to the Soviet Union) could only convert roubles into foreign currencies (or vice versa) to cover their immediate needs under very limited conditions (e.g. after obtaining permission to travel abroad); secondly, the rouble was externally inconvertible in the sense that roubles could not (legally) be taken out of the country and that the rouble was not traded on international currency markets. The rouble could not be used to finance normal trade transactions (current account convertibility) or investment or other capital transactions (capital account convertibility).

This enabled central authorities to maintain the fiction of an official exchange rate that was highly overvalued in relation to the rate at which the domestic rouble would have traded on the basis of either internal or full convertibility. As a result the economic significance of the official exchange rate was largely limited to operating as a tool for the conversion of foreign trade operations (which in the case of trade with the West were conducted in the currencies of the partner country) into roubles for statistical and accountancy purposes.

Soviet domestic prices and world market prices were equated for accountancy purposes by a system of taxes and subsidies that is normally referred to by the German term, the 'preisausgleich' (or price equalisation), as the practice was first highlighted by studies of the East German economy. The operation of the preisausgleich can be simply illustrated by the case of trade with western market economies. The Ministry of Foreign Trade purchased exports from Soviet suppliers and paid for these in roubles at domestic wholesale prices plus a markup to cover the additional costs involved in producing for western markets. These goods were then sold to the western customer for payment in hard currency at the prevailing world market price. This process was reversed in the case of Soviet imports from the West. The Ministry of Foreign Trade now purchased imports from western suppliers at world market prices and paid for these in convertible currency, and then sold them in the domestic market to Soviet consumers or enterprises, at the prevailing domestic wholesale price for the nearest Soviet analogue for the product. The difference between the rouble earnings acquired from the sales of imports in the domestic market and rouble expenditure for exports accumulated to the State Budget and has been a significant item of budget revenue for some years.

The basic features of the operation of the system (and some of its practical shortcomings) can be illustrated the following theoretical example which is derived from the analysis provided by Lavigne (1985 and 1991a: 32–6). In order to achieve an optimum level of trade the Ministry of Foreign Trade should import commodities that have a relatively high domestic cost of production (or social utility) in relation to hard currency expenditure and should export goods with a relatively low domestic cost of production in relation to hard currency earnings. If we take the (unrealistic) assumption that Soviet internal prices reflect the real opportunity costs of production (or marginal social costs) and that domestic retail prices reflect the marginal social utility of consumption, then an optimising, centralised Ministry of Foreign Trade would draw up import and export schedules whereby it would rank imports according to the domestic costs saved per unit of foreign exchange expended and would proceed to import first those goods with high domestic cost (price) in relation to a unit of foreign exchange. Similarly, the export schedule would be drawn up on the principle of exporting goods with the lowest domestic production cost in relation to a unit of foreign exchange earned.

The ministry would continue to import goods and export goods to pay for them until it reached the point where the domestic cost of production of the marginal unit of exports is exactly equated to the domestic cost of production of the imports acquired in exchange. Any trade beyond this level would result in economic losses in that the domestic cost of producing exports would exceed the domestic cost of producing the import obtained in exchange. Trade below this level would be suboptimal, in that the potential gains from trade would not be maximised, and a higher level of domestic consumption could be achieved by increasing the volume of exports and obtaining a higher level of domestic value in exchange. Assuming that the Ministry of Foreign Trade buys exports from domestic producers at prices that reflect production costs and sells imports in the domestic market at prices that reflect domestic production costs or utilities, the entire gains from trade (or rental earnings) would accumulate to the Ministry of Foreign Trade and could be passed on to the state budget. This could be also be considered to be a genuine socialist solution in that profits arising from international differences in costs of production and from resource endowments would accumulate to the state not to private owners of land and capital.

The optimum exchange rate in the above example would occur at the point where the domestic cost of earning a unit of foreign exchange was equated with the costs of production saved by the marginal import. An identical trade pattern could be achieved, in theory, if all enterprises were permitted to engage freely in foreign trade and operated on the principle that they would export any goods for which the ratio of domestic production costs was below the world market price converted at the optimum exchange rate and imported goods for which the domestic production cost exceeded the world market price converted at the optimum exchange rate. Under these circumstances, however, the profits arising from trade would accumulate to the enterprise, not to the state budget, although a proportion of the gains could be appropriated to the budget by a combination of tariffs, profits tax and export taxes (particularly on raw materials).

In practice the operation of the State monopoly of foreign trade differed substantially from the optimising model outlined above. Firstly, the Soviet domestic price system was fixed arbitrarily and did not reflect genuine domestic opportunity costs or social utility and did not function as an adequate guide to decision-making in foreign trade while the exchange rate was not set at an equilibrium or optimum level but was artificially overvalued. These factors complicated the operation of the preisausgleich and affected the efficiency with which foreign trade could be conducted. In theory the overvaluation of the exchange rate had a relatively small impact on the price of imports. For commodities for which a domestic analogue or close substitute existed, the price paid for the imported good by the end user was in principle equivalent to the domestic wholesale price of the Soviet substitute (Gardner 1982: 55). The preisausgleich operated by converting the world market price of imports into domestic roubles at the official exchange rate and then adding on a tax to arrive at the price at which the good was sold by the Ministry of Foreign Trade in the domestic market. Under these circumstances the overvaluation of the exchange rate simply increased the proportion of the price of the imported good that was accounted for by tax. Treml and Kostinsky (1982: 20–1) and Gardner (1982: 58) show that precise domestic equivalents could not be established for many imported goods and under those circumstances the domestic price of imports was derived directly from the world market price by means of variable coefficients.

As far as exports were concerned the principle of the preisausgleich meant that the world market price of the exported good was converted into domestic roubles at the official exchange rate and a tax was either deducted from this sum, or a subsidy added to it, to equate it with the domestic wholesale price. If the exchange rate had been set at the optimal or equilibrium level (and domestic prices had reflected domestic production costs) all desirable export activity would have been profitable, and all exports could have been subject to differential taxation to equate domestic costs with international prices. However, the use of an overvalued exchange rate meant that some profitable export activity (measured in terms of the domestic cost of production of the imports acquired in exchange) appeared unprofitable when world market prices were converted into domestic prices at the official exchange rate, and consequently the domestic costs of production had to be covered by a budget subsidy over the domestic price.

In the majority of cases manufactured items produced for export had to meet the quality specifications of the market in question, which differed substantially from the requirements of the undemanding domestic market. The FTOs played a major role in monitoring and evaluating the quality requirements of western markets, which serve as guidelines for the award of the State Certificate of Quality for domestic products. In practice many products that had been awarded the State Certificate did not meet the standards required for western markets and required substantial modification before they could be exported (Gruzinov 1979: 209). Consequently the FTOs had to relay very detailed instructions concerning quality specifications from foreign customers to enterprises and were responsible for monitoring quality control throughout the production process.

Starting in 1958 enterprises received a supplement over the wholesale price to compensate them for the additional costs involved in the production for export markets of a number of export items including machinery and equipment, chemicals, wood products and lumber, and refined oil products (Gardner 1982: 56). Although the supplements were varied according to such criteria as destination, quality specifications, and punctuality in meeting delivery schedules, etc., the starting point was always the domestic wholesale price (Gruzinov 1970: 206). Treml and Kostinsky (1982: 20) estimate that export supplements ranged between 30 and 40 per cent of the domestic wholesale price in the early 1980s compared with a wider range of between 5 and 95 per cent estimated by Gardner (1983: 56) for 1976, which had remained relatively constant since 1964.

Despite these attempts to motivate enterprises to boost exports it appears that the system provided inadequate incentives for enterprises to overcome their aversion to exports. Enterprise managers argued that the supplements paid for exports were too low and barely rewarded them for the extra costs involved in producing for export, and provided no additional incentives to produce for the export market. An additional complaint by enterprise managers was that the need to meet the detailed specifications required by export orders meant that these could not be fulfilled from series production, resulting in the need to retool for small production runs, which prevented enterprises from fulfilling gross output or sales targets which resulted in the loss of bonuses (Bash, Belous and Kretov 1986). Enterprises simply preferred to produce for the softer, low quality, domestic market.

## CONCLUSION

The Soviet economy operated in a very different way from the standard textbook model of a market economy which had a direct impact on the structure of foreign trade, the legacy of which has implications for economic reform and opening up the economy to greater trade links with the West. The essence of the planning system was to generate additional production from existing resources. The major problem confronting both planners and enterprises in the Soviet economy was to mobilise resources to meet targets imposed from above. The major problem confronting an entrepreneur or profit-oriented manager in a market economy (during peacetime) is to secure a market for the product which will generate revenues to pay for inputs. This process was reversed in the Soviet economy, where enterprise managers were provided with a guaranteed 'market' for their output in the form of government directives but faced difficulties in obtaining the supply of inputs needed to meet the output target contained in the plan, meaning that they were supply-constrained not demand-constrained. Imports were seen by planners and enterprises as a means of alleviating the most critical supply constraints.

In a demand-constrained market economy exports are seen as a potential and welcome extension to the market. In a supply-constrained economy, export orders are viewed by managers as an unwelcome addition to their output targets. The higher quality specifications demanded by foreign markets and specific alterations required to meet export orders made it harder for enterprises to meet gross output targets. Soviet enterprises preferred to concentrate production on a relatively narrow range of low-quality products that could be sold on the domestic market, which made their manufactured goods relatively uncompetitive in foreign markets.

Although the state monopoly of foreign trade helped central planners to exercise strict control over trade flows and prevented the emergence of open balance of payments pressures, the extreme protectionism it provided to domestic enterprises reinforced the monopoly position they enjoyed as single producers on the domestic market and removed one of the major incentives for the enterprise to introduce new products and cost-saving processes, which in turn reduced their ability to compete on export markets. Although the monopoly allowed planners to concentrate available hard currency on machinery and equipment in order to implement Politburo investment priorities, this aggravated disequilibria in the retail sector.

# Chapter 4

# The Soviet economic system and the demand for imports

## INTRODUCTION: SYSTEMIC FEATURES AND THE DEMAND FOR IMPORTS

It was argued in Chapter 3 that the demand for imports was initially determined by the creation of material balances which highlighted the major items in deficit supply in the economy, which planners attempted to fill with imports. In this section I shall argue that the deficits between domestic supply and demand resulted from a combination of the policy of extensive growth (which increased the demand for investment goods, labour and raw materials at a rate that did not automatically correspond to the potential growth of supply from domestic sources) and the planning system which provided producers and consumers with little or no incentive to either increase production or reduce consumption of items for which domestic demand was growing faster than supply.

The rigidity of wholesale and retail prices deprived enterprises and consumers of the incentive to economise on the consumption (or to increase the production) of scarce or deficit goods and planners of an automatic signal of sectors in which demand was growing faster than supply. Similarly, the principle of 'planning from the achieved level' meant that enterprises had no incentive to increase production of deficit goods (which would lead to higher plan targets in subsequent periods) or to economise on the consumption of scarce inputs (which would similarly lead to a reduced supply of inputs in subsequent periods) and had an incentive to conceal accurate information on production possibilities from planners. Central planners who were accustomed to dealing in physical units and mobilising resources to achieve output targets instead of adjusting output targets downwards to the available supply of inputs, attempted to impose output targets which incorporated a high rate of growth of physical output, under the assumption that additional supplies of inputs could be found from under-utilised domestic capacity or from hitherto unexploited sources of energy and raw materials. Consequently planners were frequently unaware of emerging bottlenecks and supply shortages until they had become critical.

Planners were then faced with the problem of either increasing domestic production of deficit items, which could involve new investment which in turn created further requirements for imported machinery and equipment and/or importing the deficit item to alleviate the bottleneck. If it proved impossible to expand domestic production (e.g. by a high priority investment programme) or to reduce domestic consumption of the bottle-neck item, this process would establish a permanent demand for imports of specific goods which would thereafter be included in import plans.

## Trade with the Council for Mutual Economic Assistance (CMEA)

Trade with CMEA partners, which was conducted on the basis of long-term agreements was of little value in filling short-term Soviet bottlenecks. The structure of Soviet trade with Eastern Europe was largely determined by the imposition of Stalin's priority on heavy industry in Eastern Europe, following the out-break of the Korean War in 1950. As a result, all the East European countries were forced to accelerate their already ambitious plans to develop metallurgy and heavy engineering industries in their first (1951–55) five-year plans. This policy effectively ignored both the long-term comparative advantage of the East European economies and (with the exception of Poland and Romania) their relatively unfavourable endowment with raw materials and energy. As a result, the Soviet Union was required to meet East European demand for energy and raw materials, which it supplied in exchange for imports of industrial goods (and machinery and equipment in particular) produced by the newly created industries.

The problem was further complicated by the replication of the Soviet planning system in each of the East European CMEA economies, as a result of which each of the East European economies developed their own national planning hierarchies, separate price systems and even state monopolies of foreign trade and consequently suffered from the systemic economic problems of irrational price systems, passive money, supply constraints and poor quality production outlined in Chapter 3. Therefore, each of the centrally planned economies regarded imports as a means for alleviating the most critical domestic supply constraints and exports as an unwelcome, but unavoidable, diversion of resources from the satisfaction of domestic needs. The absence of an incentive to export resulted in strict bilateral balancing of trade between CMEA countries (until the mid-1970s) as each country was unwilling to supply exports unless it was guaranteed the supply of an equivalent value of imports in exchange. Trade between the member countries was nominally based on world market prices 'cleansed of monopoly factors' which, after 1958, were established for each five-year plan period on the basis of the average world market price for the preceding five-year period.

The pattern of Soviet trade with Eastern Europe (known as the 'radial pattern' because it resembled the spokes of a wheel radiating out from Moscow) proved highly resistant to change following the death of Stalin in 1953, as the South-East European economies were reluctant to jettison their plans for industrialisation and the Central–East European economies were reluctant to rationalise or close down industries involving more simple labour-intensive technologies. The radial trade pattern, however, started to impose significant costs on the Soviet economy as the Soviet Union was increasingly required to develop the more costly sources of oil and gas in Siberia to meet both Soviet and East European energy demands.

This became a major concern for Soviet economists in the mid-1960s. It is even possible that the Soviet Union incurred absolute losses in its trade with Eastern Europe in the 1950s and 1960s in that the cost of supplying oil and gas to Eastern Europe actually exceeded the domestic (Soviet) production cost of the goods the Soviet Union imported from Eastern Europe. Most attention, however, has concentrated on the opportunity cost to the Soviet economy in terms of the benefits forgone by supplying oil and gas to Eastern Europe in exchange for low quality manufactured goods instead of exporting them to the West for hard currency, which could be used to purchase goods that could satisfy more pressing Soviet needs.

The opportunity cost of supplying energy to Eastern Europe was significantly increased by the two major increases in world oil prices in 1973/4 and 1979. Although the intra-CMEA price system was adjusted in 1975 and 1976 to introduce the principle of 'sliding world market prices' (whereby the price of energy was altered each year to reflect an average of the preceding five years' world market prices), intra-CMEA energy prices were still substantially below world market prices from 1975 to 1984. Furthermore, the Soviet Union started to run substantial surpluses in its trade with Eastern Europe over the next ten years as the East European economies were unable to increase their exports to the Soviet Union. In 1980 the Soviet Union supplied Eastern Europe with 85 million tonnes of crude oil and 5 million tonnes of refined oil products (worth approximately $20 billion on world oil markets) at a cost of 5.9 billion roubles (equivalent to $9.1 billion) and 30 billion cubic metres of natural gas (Stern 1982: 22; Smith 1985b: 116–18). A major study by Marrese and Vanous (1983) suggests that the opportunity cost to the Soviet Union of trade with Eastern Europe amounted to $90.4 billion between 1974 and 1982, reaching $18.6 billion in 1981 alone. Other western estimates (e.g. Poznanski 1988: 302) arrive at substantially lower estimates (approximately half the above) of the cost of trade with Eastern Europe to the Soviet economy (for a fuller discussion see Smith 1992).

## The structure of trade with non-socialist countries

The structure of Soviet imports from non-socialist countries by broad commodity groups during the Brezhnev era is illustrated in Table 4.1. Soviet imports from non-socialist countries largely consisted of machinery and equipment, other manufactures including specialist steels and metal pipes (for use in major energy projects) plus spare parts and components for industrial production, energy products from third world countries (which were normally re-exported) and foodstuffs (including tropical foods from third world countries that could not be produced domestically), chemicals and a relatively small proportion of industrial consumer goods. Since the 1970s imported foodstuffs included substantial quantities of grain and animal feedstocks, which are principally, but not entirely, imported from the American continent, Australia and New Zealand.

*Table 4.1*    Soviet imports from non-socialist countries by broad
             commodity groups (million roubles)

|                          | 1972  | 1975   | 1980   | 1982   | 1984   |
|--------------------------|-------|--------|--------|--------|--------|
| Total                    | 4,791 | 12,700 | 20,813 | 25,596 | 27,112 |
| Machinery and equipment  | 1,138 | 3,635  | 4,713  | 6,021  | 6,060  |
| Fuel and energy          | 195   | 648    | 931    | 2,010  | 3,107  |
| Ores and metals          | 537   | 2,131  | 3,359  | 3,711  | 3,398  |
| Chemicals, fertilisers   | 311   | 737    | 1,528  | 1,496  | 1,718  |
| Wood and paper and products | 188 | 503   | 747    | 693    | 631    |
| Textiles                 | 397   | 598    | 860    | 749    | 931    |
| Foodstuffs               | 1,322 | 3,173  | 6,361  | 7,576  | 8,052  |
| Industrial consumer goods | 439  | 757    | 1,194  | 1,648  | 1,680  |
| Unspecified              | 264   | 518    | 1,120  | 1,692  | 1,535  |

*Sources:* Estimated from Vneshtorg (various years). All figures estimated as
residuals from percentage commodity breakdowns of Soviet imports from all
regions minus imports from socialist countries.

## SOVIET IMPORTS OF MACHINERY AND EQUIPMENT

### The quantitative importance of imports of western machinery

An aggregated summary of the development of Soviet imports of
machinery and equipment from the industrialised West from
1950–88 is provided in Table 4.2. The periods in the table have
been selected to highlight significant changes in the proportion of
machinery and equipment in imports from the West and in the
proportion of imported equipment that originated from the West.
Three major surges in the proportion of Soviet imports of
machinery and equipment imported from the West can be seen in
the periods from 1959–64, from 1968–71 and from 1975–78 when
the proportion of imports of machinery and equipment in total
imports from the West exceeded 40 per cent of the total (Table
4.2, column 4). On each occasion the peak annual level was followed
by a fall in the absolute volume of imported machinery and
equipment from the West. Finally, a minor surge in imports of
machinery and equipment from the West in 1982–83 was followed
by cuts in the absolute level from 1984–87. This pattern repeats

Table 4.2  Soviet imports of machinery and equipment from the industrialised West

| | Annual average imports of machinery (million roubles) | | Imports of machinery and equipment from the West (as a percentage) | |
|---|---|---|---|---|
| | Total from all sources | From West | Machinery Imports | Imports from West |
| 1951–58 | 733 | 153 | 20.8 | 32.5 |
| 1959–64 | 1,821 | 457 | 25.1 | 40.6 |
| 1965–67 | 2,452 | 521 | 21.2 | 33.1 |
| 1968–71 | 3,546 | 938 | 26.4 | 40.0 |
| 1972–74 | 5,350 | 1,497 | 28.0 | 31.7 |
| 1975–78 | 11,659 | 4,580 | 39.2 | 41.3 |
| 1979–81 | 15,120 | 4,512 | 29.8 | 28.8 |
| 1982–85 | 22,961 | 6,013 | 26.2 | 31.4 |
| 1986–88 | 25,732 | 5,533 | 21.5 | 35.9 |

Sources: estimated from Vneshtorg (various years).
Notes: Data for 1975–78 include small amounts of imports of equipment for pipelines listed separately in Vneshtorgs for 1977 and 1978.

the experience of a surge in imported equipment followed by cutbacks observed during both the first five-year plan and the immediate post-war period.

The initial growth of imports of western machinery and equipment in the Khrushchev era reflected the impact of the chemicalisation programme, which included major imports of complete installations (turnkey) projects from the West which were intended to provide an immediate boost to chemical production, particularly for the provision of fertilisers for the lagging agricultural sector. The expansion of the chemical industry was also accompanied by a smaller increase in imported equipment for the food industry and in ships and port equipment. All of these imports reflected Khrushchev's preoccupation with investment to overcome the problem of food supplies.

Following Khrushchev's fall from power in 1964 the proportion of imported machinery and equipment which originated from the West fell from 25.1 per cent in 1959–64 to 21.2 per cent from 1965–67. An agreement was reached with Fiat during 1965–66 for the construction of the Tolyatti car plant which contributed to the growth of imports of machinery and equipment from the West from 1968–71. However, the major expansion of Soviet trade links with the West did not take place until after the Nixon–Brezhnev summit of 1972, which formally initiated the policy of detente and was a direct result of the quadrupling of world oil prices at the end of 1973, which contributed to a 150 per cent increase in the value of Soviet hard currency earnings derived from exports to the industrialised West between 1972 and 1974.

According to Soviet trade statistics the proportion of all Soviet imports of machinery and equipment (including the 'omitted' pipeline machinery) which came from the industrialised capitalist countries peaked at 43.4 per cent in 1976. This figure substantially underestimates the proportion of western equipment imported for investment in civilian industry for a number of reasons. Firstly, the prices and exchange rates used to evaluate machinery imports from the CMEA overestimate their value in relation to imports from the West. Sokoloff (1987: 96) estimates that after allowing for this the proportion of western equipment in machinery imports could rise by 8 per cent. In addition, CMEA exports to the Soviet Union include substantial (but difficult to estimate) quantities of military equipment and transport equipment including ships and lorries with military uses and agricultural equipment in the machinery category. When these factors are taken into account the proportion of western equipment in imported equipment for industrial capital formation could reach 60 per cent in 1976–77. Hanson (1981: 129), however, estimates that imported western machinery and equipment accounted for only 5.7–6.1 per cent of total Soviet investment in machinery and equipment in the mid-1970s. He obtained this result by taking western data on exports of machinery and equipment to the Soviet Union, adjusted them for price changes in world machinery markets and then converted them into domestic roubles at a realistic, but generalised rouble:dollar exchange rate.

Sokoloff's estimates (1987: 67 and 197–201) indicate a higher proportion of western imports in Soviet new productive investment in machinery. Sokoloff used Soviet data on imported machinery and equipment which he converted into domestic prices (using a conversion coefficient derived specifically for machinery and equipment by Treml and Kostinsky (1982)) and expressed this as a proportion of the sum of 'new productive investment in machinery and equipment'. He then apportioned imported machinery between 'western' and 'others' according to the proportions indicated by Soviet foreign trade statistics. He concluded that imported equipment accounted for 27.1 per cent of new investment in machinery and equipment in 1975 and that western supplies accounted for 39.9 per cent of total machinery imports, implying therefore that western equipment accounted for 10.8 per cent of total investment in machinery and equipment in 1975. If we take account of the relative overvaluation of imports of machinery and equipment from the CMEA, the proportion of equipment of western origin in investment in the industrial civilian industry would rise still further and could even have been as much as 15 per cent or higher in 1975.

This was the peak period of Soviet imports of western machinery (until 1989). The value of Soviet imports of western machinery and equipment fell from 5.1 billion roubles in 1977 to only 4.3 billion in 1981. After allowing for the inflation in imported machinery prices from 1978–81 of approximately 10 per cent per annum, this represented a fall in the real volume of equipment imported from the West in the order of 30–40 per cent from 1978–81. The proportion of total Soviet machinery imports originating from capitalist countries fell to below 29 per cent in the early 1980s, falling further in the early Gorbachev years and reaching a low of 19.2 per cent in 1987.

## The role of machinery and equipment imports in the traditional growth model

Imported machinery and equipment served two main purposes in the traditional Stalinist growth model. Firstly, they were a source of embodied technology transfer which contributed to the process of overcoming technological backwardness and which could then be diffused through the economy, leading to additional gains in productivity. Research by Gomulka (1971, 1986) indicates that a technologically backward economy can benefit from an initial 'catch up' period during which the 'stock' of international processes that can be relatively easily identified and absorbed into the economy are utilised. As the economy matures it will become increasingly dependent on more sophisticated international developments and on the flow of new innovations, generated either at home or abroad to stimulate further economic growth. Continued dependence on unsophisticated imported technology in this period indicates an inability to generate and diffuse domestic technical progress.

Secondly, imported machinery and equipment serves the more orthodox function of widening the capital stock and increasing production potential in specific branches of industry, which cannot be expanded either sufficiently quickly or cheaply from domestic sources. Imports that fulfil this function are consistent with the bottleneck theorem. Sokoloff (1987: chapters 8–10) argues that, although the technological content of imported equipment was important to the Soviet authorities, the principal purpose of machinery imports was not to acquire technology in the pure sense of 'know-how' embodied in the machinery (much of which could be obtained more cheaply by the purchase of licences), but was to generate an immediate and direct increase in domestic production capacity that could not be obtained from domestic sources. This view is supported by Hill (1983: 50), who argues in a detailed study of Soviet imports of machine tools that 'the greatest incentive to the USSR to import on this scale is likely to have been the securing of production capacity, followed by the subsequent experience gained in the day-to-day operation of the actual machines supplied'.

Although there is some disagreement among western specialists on precisely what constitutes high technology, an examination of Soviet import statistics confirms that the majority of Soviet imports of machinery and equipment from advanced capitalist countries could not be classified as high technology products according to most standard definitions, particularly as the Soviet Union was denied access to imports of high technology goods by western export controls administered by CoCom (the Coordinating Committee for Multilateral Export Controls, which was established in 1950 to coordinate western controls on the export of militarily useful technology to communist countries). In the peak year of 1977, imports of equipment for the chemical industry accounted for 31 per cent of Soviet imports from the West, equipment for the prospecting, extraction and transportation of energy accounted for 15 per cent, shipping and port equipment 8.5 per cent, equipment for car plants, cellulose, food and textile industries 11 per cent, and metallurgy and machine tools 8 per cent.

The periodic spurts in imports from the West also indicate that Soviet imports of machinery and equipment from the West have been determined more by short-term domestic economic priorities and the desire to overcome domestic shortages than by the pursuit of a consistent policy to overcome technological backwardness. Gustafson (1989: 196) for example, notes that Brezhnev's import policy was marked by the tendency to use 'imported equipment and know-how to give a fast start to the government's highest priority tasks, ranging from passenger automobiles to defense electronics'. It is possible that the centralisation of investment and import decisions actually reduced the average technological requirements for machinery imports by linking these to the low technology investment projects which the leadership was capable of understanding and approving. A leadership that did not fully understand the potential of modern technology and was unwilling to decentralise decision-making to those who did (as well as fearing the political impact of information technology) gave excessive emphasis to large-scale civil construction projects that utilised relatively simple processes that they could comprehend (Gaidar and Yarushenko 1988). This was reflected in an import structure in which preference was also given to imports of machinery and equipment and intermediate manufactures associated with large-scale civil engineering projects (gas pipelines, turnkey projects, hydroelectric dams) in place of imports of more sophisticated engineering products whose appraisal required more detailed and sophisticated knowledge of both the technical specifications of the product itself and of the technical requirements of the end user, which in turn required decentralisation of import decisions.

## Lessons from the chemical industry

The chemical industry, which accounted for a quarter of Soviet imports from the West from 1960–79, provides interesting evidence of the successes and failures of Soviet import programmes. In 1960–61 imports of equipment for the chemical industry accounted for 11 per cent of total Soviet equipment imports from all sources and for 30 per cent of total equipment imports from the West. In the first three years of the programme (1959–61) the West provided 72 per cent of imported chemical equipment. From 1976–79 imports of equipment for the chemical industry totalled more than $4 billion, equivalent to 27.5 per cent of all imported equipment from the West and 79 per cent of all imports of equipment for the chemical industry. In 1980 when Soviet imports from the West were cut by 40 per cent from the previous year, imported equipment still accounted for 68.1 per cent of supplies of machinery and equipment to the chemical industry while imports from capitalist countries accounted for 44.3 per cent of total supplies (Narkhoz 1989: 658).

The most successful part of the chemical programme involved the expansion of production of mineral fertilisers, with the result that by 1986 the Soviet Union was the world's largest producer of mineral fertilisers and Soviet production was 50 per cent higher than that of the USA (Gaidar and Yarushenko 1988: 76). This appears to be a classic case of a successful attempt to import and diffuse existing western technology in order to overcome a domestic bottleneck that had largely been created by the failure to invest in agriculture in the 1930s and early 1950s and the wholesale destruction of livestock during collectivisation. Hanson's case study of the Soviet mineral fertiliser industry (Hanson 1981: chapter 10) reveals that the Soviet authorities made extensive use of imported western technology (supplemented by smaller-scale imports from Czechoslovakia, the GDR and Hungary) to develop nitrogenous and compound fertilisers, while phosphate and potash fertiliser production was expanded, using Soviet and Polish equipment. Hanson estimates that by the mid-1970s a quarter of Soviet consumption of fertilisers was produced by western equipment and that this contributed to between 0.2 and 1.1 per cent of net agricultural output. Hanson argues that the returns to the Soviet economy from investment in imported equipment for the fertiliser industry were high and that equivalent benefits could not have been achieved by investment in domestic research and development to develop indigenous technology.

The picture for imports of chemical equipment as a whole is less encouraging. Gaidar and Yarushenko (1988: 76) note that Soviet production of synthetic fibres and plastics in 1986 was only 25 per cent of the original forecast and 18 per cent of the US level, despite major investment in this sector. The Soviet Union remained a substantial net importer of chemicals, fertilisers and rubber throughout the 1980s, with a deficit in trade with non-socialist countries which averaged more than $1 bn per year in the 1980s.

Hanson's study also reveals other weaknesses related to the

import of technology for the chemical industry. Lead times involved in buying and constructing plants based on western technology were significantly longer than occurred in trade between West European partners, and it was clear that there was no evidence of a reduction in lead times as experience was gained, and that subsequent domestic diffusion and modification of chemical technology was very limited (Hanson 1981: 201). This was not confined to the chemical industry. Hill (1983: 70–1) estimates that the time-lag between the receipt by a UK company of an order for machinery in general from the USSR and the final commissioning of the plant was, on average, between two and three times longer than for a comparable deal with another western company. Hill attributes some of the delay to lengthy negotiation procedures and suggests that this may have offered significant advantages to the Soviet purchaser in the form of increased information about technical and commercial conditions associated with the plant, but concludes that the major causes of the delays were 'bureaucratic inefficiencies and poor project management'.

Crash investment programmes have not resulted in long-term solutions to the problems concerned and have not led to the development of a flourishing export sector in areas in which imported equipment has been concentrated and in some cases have resulted in longer-term dependence on imports. Hanson demonstrates that industries which became 'addicted' to imported western technology were able to obtain additional imports of plant almost as a matter of routine, even if the industry concerned no longer had a high priority. This can in part be attributed to the need to import compatible equipment and components to repair and modernise existing plant. While imports of equipment for the chemical industry fell to under 5 per cent of total machinery imports and to 6–7 per cent of imports from the West in the mid-1980s, the chemical industry could not rid itself of its dependence on imported equipment. Despite Gorbachev's initial attempts to limit dependence on imported equipment, imported equipment for the chemical industry accounted for 61.4 per cent of all machinery supplied to the industry in 1989 (compared with 55.5 per cent in 1985) while imports from developed capitalist economies rose from 23.6 per cent to 40.6 per cent of all equipment used by the industry over the same period and accounted for 12 per cent of imports of machinery and equipment from the West (Vneshtorg and Narkhoz 1989).

## The importance of imports of technology to the Soviet economy

Much western research has been concentrated on the contribution that western capital goods and western technology made to Soviet economic growth. In a comprehensive survey of this work, Gomulka and Nove (1984: 25) conclude that technology embodied in imports of machinery and equipment made a relatively minor contribution to the process of technology transfer from the industrialised West to the Soviet Union, and that other forms of disembodied technology transfer (journal search, etc.) were of greater importance. The evidence that Soviet machinery imports were not highly concentrated in high-technology sectors provides some support for the notion that the acquisition of technology through imported equipment was not a major factor determining the Soviet leadership's priorities in this sector. Gomulka and Nove (1984: 39) also argue that the impact of imported western machinery on Soviet economic growth was 'either small or uncertain'.

## EXTENSIVE GROWTH AND THE DEMAND FOR INDUSTRIAL INPUTS

The strategy of extensive growth incorporating rapid industrialisation created a growing demand for industrial inputs including fuels, energy and raw materials and labour. The Soviet Union remained a net exporter of energy and raw materials and the effect of the growth of domestic demand on net availability of exports from these sectors is examined in Chapter 5. The growth of the industrial labour force also created a growing demand for food supplies and consumer goods to satisfy the demands of the urban population. During the first five-year plan an (over) rapid growth of the industrial labour force was created by the policy of agrarian collectivisation, whereby small and medium-scale private farms were forcibly amalgamated into larger units which permitted a greater degree of mechanisation and drove labour out of the agricultural sector into industry. This created an increased demand for agricultural equipment, which was initially met by imports of tractors and combine harvesters, in addition to demand for industrial equipment.

## The demand for labour

The policy of devoting a large proportion of GNP to investment in industry enabled the industrial capital stock to grow more rapidly than the industrial labour force during the 1930s. As the industrial sector as a whole was faced by a shortage of capital in relation to labour this policy enabled an increasing proportion of the industrial labour force to be equipped with machinery, sometimes by the simple expedient of transferring labour from manual tasks to more complex mechanised tasks within the same factory. This strategy both stimulated full employment and facilitated an increase in output per worker. However, as a growing proportion of the labour force was mechanised and optimal capital:labour proportions were reached, the growth of the industrial capital stock started to exceed the growth of the industrial labour force, creating labour shortages.

Some Soviet estimates (Malle 1987) claimed that the stock of under-utilised labour available for transfer to industrial employment had been virtually eliminated by the mid- to late-1960s. The growth of industrial employment in the USSR declined in the 1970s and 1980s to an annual rate of just over 2 per cent and the number of workers employed in industry peaked in 1986 and by 1989 was below the level recorded in 1980 (Narkhoz 1989: 52). These problems were complicated by demographic and geographic factors with the growth of the working-age population declining more rapidly in the European Republics than in the Central Asian and Transcaucasian republics, where family size remained substantially higher and the proportion of women employed in the labour force was lower. From an economic perspective the slowdown in the growth of the industrial labour force required planners to either concentrate labour intensive investment in the Central Asian republics or to encourage migration from the Asian republics to the European republics.

The slower growth and ultimate decline of the labour force had major implications for the optimal structure of investment and imports of machinery, shifting the demand for machinery away from simple labour-augmenting capital to labour-saving capital which reduced the demand for labour in a specific area and permitted labour to be released to other areas of production, and/or reduced the aggregate labour:capital ratios by requiring less labour to operate the plant than the existing average. This required a shift in emphasis from investment in turnkey projects to investment in the modernisation, replacement and re-equipment of existing plant. This in turn implied giving enterprises greater powers to make investment decisions, which logically implied dismantling many aspects of the foreign trade system including the separation of domestic and world market prices and artificial system of exchange rates in order to allow enterprises to estimate the return on imported equipment in terms of domestic cost savings. Such radical reforms were not seriously contemplated by the Brezhnev leadership. Soviet policy during the Brezhnev era concentrated on trying to increase the provision of labour supply by improving the use of labour time. Ironically, as Malle (1987) shows, the methods employed to achieve this provided enterprises with an incentive to increase the rate of investment in labour-scarce areas in order to fulfil indicators for the 'efficient' use of labour.

In an open market economy growing labour scarcity tends to increase the demand for imports of labour-intensive products from cheaper labour areas as well as for labour-saving machinery. Hanson (1981: 178) shows that the growth of production of chemical fertilisers resulting from western machinery imports permitted a substantial reduction in the demand for, and use of, agricultural labour. However, it also appears that in most areas the labour-saving gains arising from imported technology were not maximised owing to overmanning. Western firms involved in exporting and installing chemical equipment reported that Soviet enterprises in the chemical industry employed on average between 50 and 70 per cent more labour with imported equipment than would have been expected in a comparable western plant (Hanson 1981: 192). UK executives in the machine-tool industry interviewed by Hill (1983: 71) also indicated that overmanning on projects utilising imported technology was widespread and attributed this to lower skill and training levels of the Soviet workforce, poor motivation and poor supervision, together with the policy of full employment which made it difficult to make under-utilised labour redundant.

## The growth of wages and consumer demand

The growing demand for industrial labour and the priority accorded to investment also aggravated the problems of equilibrium in the consumer market. Enterprises that were concerned primarily to maximise gross output had an incentive to continue to employ labour provided it made some positive contribution to gross output (i.e. at any point above that where the marginal physical product was zero), even if the wage paid to the individual worker exceeded his/her marginal product. The rapid growth of demand for industrial labour during the 1930s was accompanied by a fivefold increase in state retail prices from 1928–37 as the central authorities lost control over the supply of money and inter-enterprise credit (Garvy 1977: 172–7). During the period of rapid expansion of the labour force in the 1940s and 1950s tighter controls on both prices and wages were implemented, which allowed turnover in the state retail sector to grow faster than total wages and incomes in the state and co-operative sector. At the same time the growing number of family members participating in the labour force enabled family income to rise faster than wage rates, with the result that consumption in the state retail network grew by 120 per cent between 1950 and 1960. In the last years of Khrushchev's leadership, the growth of total wage payments (and money incomes) substantially exceeded the growth of retail turnover (and consumption) as households built up savings. When the growth of the total labour force started to decline in the late-1960s and central controls over wage rates were relaxed, enterprises found themselves in an increasingly competitive labour market with a growing incentive and power to raise wages faster than both productivity and the planned rate of growth of consumption from domestic production. The average wage grew by 5 per cent per annum between 1965 and 1970 compared with an annual average of less than 3 per cent during the preceding 15 years.

In a market economy that is open to foreign trade with a fully convertible currency any excess of disposable income over the supply of domestic consumer goods and services will result (if immediate corrective government action in the form of increased taxation is not taken) in a combination of the inflationary pressure on retail prices and/or the diversion of production away from consumption to investment and/or an increase in the supply of imports which will put downward pressure on the exchange rate which in turn will result in a combination of an outflow of reserves, an increase in interest rates and/or devaluation. In a centrally planned economy with a state monopoly of foreign trade, in which domestic retail prices are determined by the central authorities, the government must either take deliberate action to increase the supply of consumer goods (either from domestic production or from imports) or must increase state retail prices (by increasing turnover taxes) or must allow suppressed inflation (manifested in the form of involuntary savings) and legal and illegal secondary market activity to develop.

The Soviet authorities traditionally maintained a high level of subsidies for basic staple goods sold in the state retail network, including foodstuffs whose prices remained fixed until 1990–91, despite rising demand. Under these circumstances imported consumer goods can help to alleviate both microeconomic imbalances caused by excess demand over domestic supply for specific goods and macroeconomic imbalances caused by excess demand in the aggregate over the supply of consumer goods and services in the aggregate. The problem of specific imbalances in the supply of consumer goods has been most serious in the case of foodstuffs and grain. As shown above, the first major expansion of imports of machinery and equipment from 1959–64 was associated with investment projects designed to improve the production and distribution of foodstuffs, which was in part stimulated by the bad harvest (102.6 million tonnes) of 1957. A disastrous harvest in 1963 resulted in a fall in reported grain output from 140.2 million tonnes in 1982 to only 107.5 million tonnes, with wheat production particularly badly affected. Although the Soviet Union had always imported a small amount of grain (reaching a maximum of 781,600 tonnes in 1957) it had been a net grain exporter each year since the 1917 Revolution and a substantial net exporter of grain since collectivisation. In 1964 grain imports came to 7.4 million tonnes as the Soviet Union became a net grain importer for the first time. Although the Soviet Union restored its position as a net grain exporter from 1967–1971, it again became a major net importer of grains from 1972 onwards and a substantial importer of grain from 1979 onwards. The estimates of Soviet grain imports in Table 4.3 (derived from the partial data provided in Soviet trade statistics and trade partners' data) show that Soviet imports continued to rise in the late-1970s, reaching 27.8 million tonnes in 1980 and more than 40 million tonnes in 1984–5. Soviet imports from non-socialist countries of foodstuffs other than grain also grew significantly in the late 1970s, rising from 1 billion roubles in 1976

Table 4.3    Soviet production, trade and domestic utilisation of grain
1961–90

| | Harvest | Annual average (million tonnes) | | | |
| | | Imports | Exports | Net imports | Domestic use |
|---|---|---|---|---|---|
| 1961–63 | 126.1 | 1.3 | 7.2 | –5.9 | 120.2 |
| 1964–66 | 148.1 | 7.1 | 3.8 | 3.3 | 151.4 |
| 1967–71 | 170.0 | 2.0 | 6.6 | –4.6 | 165.4 |
| 1972–75 | 181.6 | 15.6 | 5.0 | 10.6 | 192.2 |
| 1976–80 | 205.0 | 20.6 | 2.0 | 18.6 | 223.6 |
| 1981–85 | 189.1 | 37.6 | 2.8 | 34.8 | 223.9 |
| 1986–90 | 211.8 | 32.2 | 1.7 | 30.5 | 242.3 |

Sources: Exports, imports from Vneshtorg (various years). (Aggregated data for
1977–86 are not provided in Vneshtorg and have been estimated from data on
exports to individual countries, except 1980, 1985, 1986 from Narkhoz 1989.)
Harvest figures from Narkhoz, annual plan reports.
Note: Harvest figures for 1990 have been adjusted upwards for consistency with
earlier years.

to 5 billion in 1981. As a result, in 1981 Soviet imports of foodstuffs
from non-socialist countries cost 9.8 billion roubles (US $13.5
billion) and comprised 37.8 per cent of all non-socialist imports.
Similarly, Soviet imports of industrial consumer goods from
non-socialist countries were increased from 0.7 billion roubles
($1 bn) in 1979 to 1.8 billion roubles ($2.5 bn) in 1981.

The growth of imports of food and consumer goods from
1979–81 permitted a degree of stabilisation of the domestic retail
market at the expense of imports of machinery and equipment,
despite the doubling of world oil prices and increase in the world
market price of gold and silver. Aggregate consumption actually
grew faster than aggregate money incomes from the end of 1979
to the end of 1982, alleviating suppressed inflation and leading to
a temporary slowdown in the rate of growth of savings deposits.
The improvement in Soviet export prices enabled planners to
increase the volume of imports from non-socialist countries by
21.7 per cent between 1979 and 1981, while the volume of exports
only grew by 2.3 per cent. The impact of this on domestic consumption was nullified by a series of poor harvests which
continued throughout the early 1980s, as a result of which
increased grain imports were required purely to maintain
consumption levels (see Table 4.3).

The deterioration in Soviet terms of trade from 1982 onwards (which became acute after the fall in world energy prices in 1986) was associated with a major growth of disequilibrium in retail markets. From 1982 to 1989 disposable income grew by 50 per cent while consumption grew by only 36 per cent, with the result that virtually 28 per cent of additional income went unspent. The cumulative effect was that the stock of personal savings in the State Savings Bank and in cash virtually doubled over the period to 443 billion roubles at the end of 1989, equivalent to 90 per cent of aggregate annual consumption (including housing and utilities). This problem is examined in Chapter 9.

## CONCLUSION

Soviet imports from the West can be divided, somewhat arbitrarily, into two main categories: goods intended to increase the productive potential of the Soviet economy in the medium to long term (principally machinery and equipment, industrial components and materials), and goods for more immediate consumption (principally foodstuffs and animal feedstocks and industrial consumer goods). Treml (1983: 37) estimated that imported consumer goods (including those from CMEA countries) accounted for 14–15 per cent of the value of sales in the state retail network and that imports of food and agricultural raw materials (principally animal feedstocks) accounted directly and indirectly for 20 per cent of the Soviet calorie intake in the late 1970s and early 1980s.

If, as suggested above, the acquisition of technology that cannot be obtained through other channels is not the main or only explanation for Soviet imports of machinery and equipment, why did the Soviet Union import equipment from the West, why has the proportion of machinery and equipment in total imports from the West fluctuated in the manner it has and what are the implications for future trade flows and Russian economic prospects in general?

Some general conclusions can be reached. Firstly, throughout the Soviet period, the Soviet economy has not been either totally dependent on, or independent of, imports of western machinery and equipment, whose quantitative importance in Soviet investment has been neither large nor negligible, whichever measure is chosen. Secondly, imported machinery and equipment were not the major vehicle of either technology transfer or technology generation in the Soviet Union. The Soviet Union maintained a large R & D sector (by international standards) which, although relatively inefficient in generating new innovations (measured by the inability to generate international patents in relation to the resources devoted to this sector) and diffusing them through the civilian economy, together with other conventional and unconventional methods of acquiring information on foreign technology were the major sources of domestic innovation. A new Russian government will have to decide to what extent the poor economic contribution of the R & D sector was caused by the economic and political system and consequently what improvement will result from domestic reforms. The government will then need to decide whether the Russian economy possesses a long-term comparative advantage in some sectors relying on innovation (e.g. avionics) and, if so, how to improve the performance and efficiency of this sector, or whether to place greater emphasis in future on conventional market-oriented methods of acquiring non-indigenous technology.

# Chapter 5

# Soviet hard currency earnings

## THE SIGNIFICANCE OF THE CAUSES OF EXPORT DIFFICULTIES

It was argued in Chapter 4 that hard currency shortages in relation to the demand for imports, combined with the reluctance of the leadership to sustain anything other than a modest level of debt in relation to the country's apparent earning capacity, necessitated cuts in imports of western machinery and equipment on three separate occasions (in the mid-1960s, the late 1970s and the mid-1980s) in order to restore equilibrium to the current account balance of payments, following short periods in which deficits were incurred. This raises critical questions about the Soviet ability to generate exports which have major implications for the ability of the Russian economy to increase trade with the industrialised Western economies.

It is important to discern whether the initial pressures on the hard currency balance of payments were caused by macro-economic pressures (i.e. excess demand resulting from overtaut planning, which led to an increased volume of imports despite the state monopoly of foreign trade) or whether they were caused by more serious microeconomic factors (i.e. an inability to produce the goods demanded in hard currency markets) and, if so, what is or was the cause of this inability? If macroeconomic pressures were the major cause of balance of payments problems, then reducing the level of imports to the level of exports that could be sustained in the short-term, combined with measures to eliminate excess demand in the domestic economy, was the most appropriate response available to central planners. It also follows that if such an economy were to be marketised and opened up to foreign trade, conventional techniques of demand management and exchange rate policies should be successful in restoring equilibrium to the balance of payments in the medium to long term, although deficits may need to be covered by borrowing in the short term.

If, however, balance of payments pressures are/were caused by a structural inability to produce the commodities demanded in world markets, deep seated structural reforms (probably involving large-scale unemployment) will be required before there will be any significant increase in export earnings and consequently any increase in the volume of imports. This could, in turn, considerably extend the period over which large sectors of the population suffer from the costs of the reform process before experiencing any benefits. Furthermore, if the economy is incapable of sustaining the desired volume of hard currency exports, any structural modernisation of the capital stock which required foreign inputs would have to be accompanied or preceded by a major inflow of foreign capital, either in the form of equity finance, private loans or government loans and grants. Private capital is only likely to be forthcoming if investors are convinced about the long-term prospects for a successful transition, including the ability to sustain a flow of exports in the long term. The prospects for the latter will in turn be affected by the degree to which the structural inability to export itself is caused by economic-systemic factors (including the nature of the planning system and the foreign trade system) and could therefore be expected to be overcome by radical change to the system or whether they were determined by specifically 'Russian' factors, which are harder to define but include geographical, demographic and cultural factors.

## THE STRUCTURE OF SOVIET EXPORTS TO NON-SOCIALIST COUNTRIES

Two features of Soviet exports to non-socialist countries are immediately apparent from the data in Table 5.1. The first is the predominance of energy, raw materials and goods embodying a low degree of processing (and the correspondingly low proportion of manufactured goods) in Soviet exports to the industrialised West and the second is the predominance of arms and goods with potential military uses in exports to developing countries.

*Table 5.1*　Commodity composition of Soviet exports to the industrialised West and developing countries from country data 1972–84 (million roubles)

| | 1972 | 1975 | 1978 | 1981 | 1984 |
|---|---|---|---|---|---|
| **Total** | **4,449** | **9,450** | **14,427** | **25,940** | **32,277** |
| **Industrial West** | | | | | |
| **Total** | **2,441** | **6,140** | **8,701** | **17,247** | **21,349** |
| Energy | 792 | 3,398 | 5,545 | 13,343 | 17,036 |
| of which: oil | 647 | 2,870 | 4,503 | 10,130 | 13,357 |
| gas | 19 | 192 | 729 | 2,946 | 3,130 |
| Diamonds total | 205 | 302 | 619 | 511 | 745 |
| of which:　cut | 58 | 138 | 349 | 222 | 296 |
| uncut | 147 | 264 | 270 | 289 | 449 |
| Non-ferrous and precious metals | 319 | 251 | 337 | 469 | 700 |
| Other ores and metals | 133 | 230 | 122 | 148 | 222 |
| Minerals | 42 | 158 | 87 | 82 | 80 |
| Furs and textile materials | 201 | 263 | 329 | 414 | 159 |
| Timber and wood and paper products | 354 | 841 | 694 | 742 | 716 |
| Chemicals | 64 | 184 | 189 | 490 | 747 |
| Machinery | 90 | 261 | 285 | 352 | 315 |
| Identified non-engineering | 2,110 | 5,627 | 7,922 | 16,199 | 20,405 |
| | 86.4% | 91.6% | 91.0% | 93.9% | 95.6% |
| **Exports to developing countries** | | | | | |
| **Total** | **2,008** | **3,310** | **5,726** | **8,693** | **10,928** |
| Arms and defence goods | 1,240 | 2,026 | 4,316 | 5,753 | 7,503 |
| | 61.7% | 61.0% | 75.3% | 66.2% | 68.7% |
| Energy | 76 | 338 | 388 | 1,436 | 1,796 |
| of which: oil | 71 | 307 | 370 | 1,399 | 1,744 |

*Sources:* Estimated from data on Soviet trade with individual countries in Vneshtorg (various years).
*Notes:* Energy and energy products, chemicals, furs and textiles, wood and wood and paper products and machinery were all obtained by addition of entries in data with individual countries. All other entries estimated from residuals (see text for details). Arms and defence goods: see text and notes to Table 5.5.

*Table 5.2*    Soviet exports to non-socialist countries by broad commodity groups (million roubles)

|  | *1972* | *1975* | *1980* | *1982* | *1984* |
|---|---|---|---|---|---|
| **Total** | **4,449** | **9,450** | **22,732** | **29,029** | **32,277** |
| Machinery and equipment | 760 | 1,081 | 1,708 | 2,174 | 2,561 |
| Fuel and energy | 879 | 3,739 | 12,598 | 16,684 | 18,906 |
| Ores and metals | 547 | 578 | 844 | 817 | 976 |
| Chemicals, fertiliser etc | 97 | 302 | 669 | 695 | 1,045 |
| Wood and paper and products | 412 | 713 | 1,228 | 813 | 904 |
| Textiles | 161 | 245 | 297 | 352 | 93 |
| Foodstuffs | 196 | 337 | 297 | 294 | 442 |
| Industrial consumer goods | 138 | 264 | 541 | 415 | 413 |
| Unspecified | 1,259 | 2,191 | 4,550 | 6,785 | 6,937 |

*Sources:* Vneshtorg (various years).
*Note:* For methodology see text.

Trade in military goods is concealed in Soviet trade statistics and has to be estimated indirectly. Soviet trade statistics included a percentage breakdown of total trade and trade with socialist countries expressed by very broad commodity groups (until 1989 when the commodity breakdown for socialist countries was replaced by one for capitalist countries). From these figures it is possible to estimate a breakdown of trade with all non-socialist countries as a residual which is shown for selected years in Table 5.2. These figures combine data on trade that is conducted in hard currency with trade conducted on a bilateral or soft currency basis and cannot be taken as a guide to Soviet hard currency earnings. These estimates show that, of total Soviet exports to non-socialist countries of 32.3 billion roubles in 1984 (the year before Gorbachev came power), exports of fuel and energy amounted to 18.9 billion roubles (58.9 per cent of the total). The next largest specified category is machinery and equipment, which accounted for 2.6 billion roubles or 7.9 per cent, followed by chemicals, fertilisers and rubber, which came to 1 billion roubles or 3.2 per cent. Exports worth 6.9 billion roubles or 21.5 per cent of the total cannot be identified.

A more detailed breakdown of the commodity structure of Soviet exports can only be obtained by the lengthy process of aggregating the data on exports to individual countries and cross-referencing this with more detailed data of the commodity composition on total exports to all sources. Table 5.1 has been estimated on this basis. The data on exports to individual countries indicates that, in 1984, identified Soviet energy exports accounted for 79.8 per cent of total Soviet exports to the industrialised West of 21.3 billion roubles ($28.7 bn) and amounted to 17 billion roubles ($22.9 bn) composed principally of crude oil and refined oil products ($18.3 bn) and natural gas ($4.2 bn). No data on the volume of oil and gas exports were provided for that year. The commodity composition of exports to the value of a further 1.8 billion roubles to the industrialised West cannot be identified from the data relating to exports to the individual countries themselves. A major share of this can be identified by using a methodology first outlined by Kostinsky (1973) as comprising diamonds (745 million roubles) of which cut diamonds accounted for 296 million roubles and uncut diamonds for 449 million roubles. Cut diamonds have been identified as the difference between Soviet exports of industrial consumer goods to non-socialist countries (included in the aggregated data for exports) and items included in that category in the data on exports to individual countries. Uncut diamonds have been identified as the difference between total Soviet exports of non-metallic minerals, earths and clays (CTN 25; see Notes to Table 5.3) and those items that are included in this category in the data on exports to individual countries. Other unclassified non-ferrous and precious metals have similarly been identified as the difference between Soviet exports in the category of ores, concentrates and metals which cannot be identified from the data on exports to individual countries and which came to 700 million roubles in 1984. Small amounts of industrial diamonds (which cannot be identified) are also included in the category 'machinery and equipment'.

Estimates of exports of diamonds and precious metals obtained by this method (converted into dollars) for 1972–89 are provided in Table 5.3. Total exports of diamonds, non-ferrous and precious metals increased from $634 million in 1972 to $2.1 billion in 1980. The increase in the value of exports of precious metals in 1979 and 1980 coincides with a tenfold increase in silver prices in the

*Table 5.3*   Soviet exports of diamonds and precious and other metals ($ million)

| | Unidentified exports | | | Identified exports | | Total |
|---|---|---|---|---|---|---|
| | Diamonds | | Non-ferrous and precious metals | Ores and metals CTN 24 and 26–9 | Other minerals CTN 25 | |
| | cut | uncut | | | | |
| 1972 | 70 | 178 | 386 | 161 | 51 | 846 |
| 1975 | 191 | 366 | 348 | 319 | 219 | 1,443 |
| 1976 | 223 | 328 | 563 | 287 | 149 | 1,550 |
| 1977 | 298 | 405 | 477 | 243 | 158 | 1,581 |
| 1978 | 511 | 395 | 493 | 179 | 127 | 1,705 |
| 1979 | 334 | 603 | 691 | 250 | 119 | 1,997 |
| 1980 | 627 | 571 | 927 | 368 | 110 | 2,603 |
| 1981 | 308 | 401 | 651 | 205 | 114 | 1,679 |
| 1982 | 419 | 337 | 783 | 266 | 196 | 2,001 |
| 1983 | 377 | 378 | 1,006 | 189 | 151 | 2,101 |
| 1984 | 362 | 663 | 705 | 272 | 98 | 2,100 |
| 1985 | 474 | 510 | 736 | 361 | 122 | 2,203 |
| 1986 | 661 | 623 | 1,039 | 412 | 82 | 2,817 |
| 1987 | 723 | 665 | 1,607 | 376 | 114 | 3,485 |
| 1988 | 708 | 895 | 2,725 | 524 | 170 | 5,022 |
| 1989 | 624 | 1,156 | 3,486 | 822 | 200 | 6,288 |

*Sources:* All figures estimated from Vneshtorg (various years).
*Notes:* Unidentified exports
a) Diamonds. Difference between aggregate exports of industrial consumer goods to non-socialist countries and that identified from data on trade with individual trade partners.
b) Uncut diamonds. Difference between exports of CTN 25 (Minerals, earths and clays) and exports identified in this category from trade with individual countries(column 6) from Vneshtorg (various years).
c) Non-ferrous and precious metals. Difference between aggregate exports of ores and metals to non-socialist countries and that identified from trade with individual countries. Until 1976 exports of non-ferrous metals (copper, nickel, zinc, aluminium, bronze, cadmium, etc.) were identified in data on exports to individual countries. These have been included in data on non-ferrous metal exports for 1972–76 for consistency.
CTN = CMEA Trade Nomenclature (the system used for trade notation by CMEA countries).
Identified exports: CTN 24, 6–9. Ores and metals includes ferrous and non-ferrous ore and concentrates, ferro-alloys, metal scrap and waste, and some steel products (which are not predominant in exports to the industrial West). CTN 25: Other minerals; identified trade in this category includes asbestos, sulphur, apatite. These have not been identified individually since 1976. It is possible that some exports of uncut diamonds and non-monetary gold have been included in this column.

autumn and spring of those years. Despite this growth, the proportion of diamonds and precious metals in exports to the industrialised West fell from 16 per cent in 1972 to 6.8 per cent in 1984 as energy export grew in importance. There are few signs of a significant and successful attempt to increase exports of these items to overcome hard currency shortages under Brezhnev, although a major growth took place in the late 1980s (see Chapter 9).

Other major items of exports to the industrialised West in 1984 (which can be identified directly from Soviet data on exports to individual countries) also involved a low degree of industrial processing including timber, pulp and paper products (716 million roubles); ferrous metals (including scrap), ferrous and non-ferrous alloys and iron ores and concentrates (222 million roubles); furs and textile raw materials (159 million roubles); earths and clays other than uncut diamonds, including asbestos, sulphur and apatite (79 million roubles) and food products (164 million roubles). Chemicals (and predominantly unsophisticated chemicals including ammonia, acids and plastic mass) comprised a further 747 million roubles. Consequently exports totalling 20.6 billion roubles (96.3 per cent of total exports to the industrialised West) could be identified as having a high raw material content and embodying a low degree of industrial processing. Of the remaining exports that could be identified only 315 million roubles (1.5 per cent of total exports to the West) consisted of machinery and equipment of which the single largest item was a total of 110,526 passenger cars at a value of 118 million roubles (equivalent to a delivery price of $1400 each).

Soviet exports to 'developing countries' in 1984 were given as 10.9 billion roubles. Of these only 5.3 billion could be identified by country of destination, leaving 5.6 billion roubles (51.4 per cent) unidentified (which is referred to hereafter as the LDC residual). As the comparable figure for imports from developing countries that are unidentified by country of origin is 2 per cent, this cannot be attributed to the failure to include important trade partners in trade data. Most western specialists believe that the LDC residual is primarily associated with arms sales that have not been identified by country of destination for strategic reasons (see Lavigne 1991a: 305). However, this figure is not an inclusive figure for the total value of unspecified exports to the Third World and probably significantly underestimates the volume of Soviet arms exports (Smith 1985a). As noted above total 'unidentified' exports to non-socialist countries amounted to 6.9 billion roubles in 1984, of which an estimated 0.7 billion roubles could be attributed to exports of uncut diamonds and other unidentified precious metals to capitalist countries. The commodity structure of a further 656 million roubles of Soviet exports to developing countries in 1984 is not identified in the data on exports to individual countries (the intra-country commodity residual or ICC residual). The ICC residual is subject to considerable variation from year to year and in 1982 was as high as 1.6 billion roubles. The ICC residual is highly (but not exclusively) concentrated on Afghanistan, Algeria, India, Iraq, Jordan, Syria and South Yemen, all of whom were identified by SIPRI as recipients of Soviet defence equipment. If this is added to the LDC residual we obtain a figure of 6.2 billion roubles for 'unidentified military exports in 1984'.

A further residual can be discovered by examining the data on exports of machinery and equipment to individual countries. In 1984 exports of machinery and equipment to developing countries amounted to 2.2 billion roubles. Of this figure, 341 million roubles cannot be more closely identified from the data on exports to individual countries. Once again the residuals were highly (but not exclusively) concentrated on identified recipients of Soviet arms. Finally, a further 306 million roubles of exports to developing countries that are identified in the trade statistics fell into the category of heavy vehicles (which includes military vehicles and other vehicles with military uses) and 538 million roubles fell into the category of aircraft and aircraft equipment. The principal recipients of these items were Afghanistan, Angola, India, Libya, Iraq, Syria, Ethiopia, and Nicaragua. Consequently, it appears that more than half of Soviet exports of machinery and equipment to developing countries (equivalent to 1.2 billion roubles) in 1984 consisted of military or military-related equipment which would have been produced by military factories, not by civilian enterprises. If these figures are added to the unidentified items they indicate that total exports of armaments and military related equipment to developing countries came to 7.5 billion roubles in 1984, equivalent to 68.5 per cent of all exports to developing countries that are designated as non-socialist in Soviet trade statistics. An estimate of arms trade for other years will be given in Table 5.5 (see p. 91).

## SOVIET EXPORTS TO THE INDUSTRIALISED WEST DURING THE BREZHNEV ERA

### Energy exports

Tables 5.1 and 5.4 demonstrate the impact of the two major increases in world oil prices in 1973–74 and 1979 on the value of Soviet energy exports to the West. Before the first increase in world oil prices Soviet energy exports to the industrialised capitalist countries came to 795 million roubles equivalent to 32.5 per cent of Soviet exports to the West by value. By 1984 they had grown to 17 billion roubles, equivalent to 79.8 per cent of exports to the West. Soviet exports of crude oil and refined oil products in 1972 came to 107 million tonnes out of a total production of 400 million tonnes, of which 42 million were exported to OECD countries for $781 million according to Soviet statistics. Nissanke (Chadwick *et al.* 1987: 104–7) shows that although the Soviet Union was experiencing hard currency balance of payments problems during the 1972–73 period (which necessitated an increase in foreign borrowing) and Soviet oil availability (production plus imports) was growing by 25–30 million tonnes a year in the early 1970s, oil exports to the OECD virtually stagnated from 1970–73 and were actually reduced in 1974 as the pressures of domestic demand and meeting the demands of socialist partners grew. The net effect (according to estimates based on Soviet data) was that although annual oil output grew by 106 million tonnes from 1970–74, domestic consumption grew by 86 million tonnes and net exports by only 20 million tonnes, while exports to socialist countries grew by 21 million tonnes and exports to the OECD actually fell by just over 1 million tonnes. Exports to the OECD recovered their 1973 level of 46 million tonnes in 1975 as a result of a further growth in output of 32 million tonnes, while domestic consumption and exports to socialist countries grew by 26 million tonnes. The quadrupling of oil prices, however, meant that the value of Soviet oil exports to the industrialised West rose to $4.0 billion in 1975.

The Soviet authorities appear to have been content to benefit from the windfall gains arising from the change in world oil prices in 1973–74 which relieved some of the immediate pressures on the hard currency balance of payments, but were either unwilling or unable to revise the policy of extensive growth in the domestic

Table 5.4 Soviet energy exports to the industrialised West 1972–89

| | Crude oil and oil products | | | | | Natural Gas | | |
| | Prod | Exports | | | $ mn | Prod | | Exports |
| | | million tonnes | | | | bn cubic metres | | $ mn |
| | | crude | products | total | | | | |
|------|------|------|------|------|------|------|------|------|
| 1972 | 400 | 22.1 | 17.7 | 39.8 | 781 | 221 | 1 | 23 |
| 1975 | 491 | 19.2 | 23.4 | 42.6 | 3,977 | 289 | 8 | 184 |
| 1976 | 520 | 32.3 | 23.5 | 55.8 | 5,243 | 321 | 12 | 369 |
| 1977 | 546 | 35.0 | 22.0 | 57.0 | 6,235 | 346 | 16 | 533 |
| 1978 | 572 | 36.7 | 26.9 | 63.6 | 8,118 | 372 | 20 | 1,067 |
| 1979 | 589 | 36.9 | 22.0 | 58.9 | 11,156 | 407 | 25 | 1,302 |
| 1980 | 603 | 33.4 | 23.6 | 57.0 | 14,157 | 435 | 26 | 2,841 |
| 1981 | 609 | 29.4 | 24.1 | 53.5 | 14,066 | 465 | 29 | 4,090 |
| 1982 | 613 | 36.8 | 32.2 | 69.0 | 16,592 | 501 | 26 | 3,777 |
| 1983 | 616 | 44.6 | 33.3 | 77.9 | 17,522 | 536 | 24 | 3,281 |
| 1984 | 613 | 49.6 | 31.8 | 81.4 | 16,596 | 587 | 29 | 3,832 |
| 1985 | 595 | 37.7 | 29.7 | 67.5 | 12,692 | 643 | 30 | 3,898 |
| 1986 | 615 | 37.6 | 40.3 | 77.9 | 7,888 | 686 | 38 | 3,800 |
| 1987 | 624 | 43.4 | 40.4 | 83.8 | 11,214 | 727 | 40 | 2,839 |
| 1988 | 624 | 54.6 | 40.7 | 95.3 | 10,537 | 770 | 43 | 2,653 |
| 1989 | 607 | 38.0 | 40.4 | 78.4 | 10,613 | 796 | 49 | 2,806 |

Sources: Production figures from Narkhoz (various years). Export volumes: 1972–84 OECD data (from Nissanke 1987: 82–3, Stern 1987: 94–5); 1986–89 from Vneshtorg (various years).
Notes: Prod = production.
Export values estimated from Vneshtorg( various years) translated into dollars at average official exchange rate for the year. All export data include Finland.

economy or those of their socialist partners during the five-year plan period of 1976–80 in the light of the major increase in the opportunity cost of domestic and East European oil consumption resulting from the increase in world oil prices. The Soviet Union did not publish data on the volume of oil exports from 1976 to 1986 (although some data has subsequently been made available on a piecemeal basis) and for most years the volume of Soviet deliveries to the West can only be estimated from western statistical sources. Table 5.3 utilises OECD data for export volumes from 1972–85 which have been collated by Stern (1987: 92–3) and Nissanke (Chadwick *et al.* 1987: 82–3). The use of trade partners' data can be hazardous for estimating a country's total trade flows and consumption patterns, particularly in the case of the oil industry where a considerable volume of entrepôt and spot trade is involved, and where the statistical authorities of the importing country may have difficulty in recognising the proper country of origin. OECD returns on the volume of imports from the Soviet Union are in general lower than the comparable Soviet data for exports to the OECD, but by a variable amount from year to year, leading to problems of comparison and interpretation.

OECD data show a sharp increase in the volume of OECD crude oil imports from the Soviet Union at the beginning of the 1976–80 five-year plan, as a result of which OECD crude and product imports from the USSR rose from 42.6 million tonnes in 1975 to 55.8 million tonnes in 1976, reaching 63.6 million tonnes in 1978, after which they decline each year until 1981 (despite rising Soviet production) when they reached 53.5 million tonnes. The total increase in domestic production of 83 million tonnes from 1976–80 was divided between increased domestic consumption of refined oil products (64 million tonnes) as domestic refining capacity was expanded (Chadwick *et al.* 1987: 29) and increased exports of crude oil and products to Eastern Europe, which reached 81 million tonnes in 1980, while from 1978–81 Soviet domestic consumption actually rose faster than output.

These figures indicate that the central authorities were either unable or unwilling to expand oil exports to the West after the five-year plan had started, even though they were faced with the need to cut imports of machinery and equipment from the West in the late 1970s to restore equilibrium in the hard currency balance of payments as grain purchases were increased.

Once again, the Soviet leadership was initially content to benefit from the windfall gains resulting from the world price increase of 1979, which took the value of Soviet oil exports of 57 million tonnes to the OECD in 1980 to $14.1 billion, but not to drastically revise or reappraise industrial output targets or improve the efficiency with which energy was used, which could have resulted in reduced consumption and either greater availability for export or could have led to a reduction in the use of short-term secondary recovery measures, including water injection, which were jeopardising production in the longer term (Goldman 1980: 173; Gustafson 1989: 114–16).

Articles by Soviet economists in the early 1980s showed a greater awareness of the opportunity cost of domestic oil consumption and of the cost of providing oil exports to Eastern Europe, including a downward revision of East European energy needs in published Soviet estimates (Smith 1985b: 116–21). The Brezhnev leadership's belated response to the benefits of reduced domestic and East European energy consumption was partly motivated by economic factors (including the need to increase hard currency earnings to pay for increased grain purchases and the desire to reduce external debt in the light of increased interest rates and the world liquidity crisis) but was also stimulated by Soviet and western predictions of potential Soviet energy shortages if production did not keep pace with the growth of Soviet and East European consumption. A study by the CIA in 1977, which predicted a fall in Soviet oil output in the early 1980s, indicated that unless domestic consumption growth decelerated, the Soviet Union would become a net oil importer by the early to mid-1980s (for an assessment, see Goldman 1980).

Although the CIA forecasts proved to be excessively pessimistic about Soviet production levels in the mid-1980s, they provided an indication of the problems the Soviet hard currency balance of payments would face, if the growth of Soviet and East European oil consumption outpaced Soviet production. Soviet energy policy in the early 1980s was directed towards reducing total CMEA oil consumption by boosting conservation and by substituting other forms of primary energy for oil in the Soviet and East European energy balance (particularly natural gas, which was the fastest growing energy source in the Soviet Union) in order to preserve available supplies of crude oil and products for sale in western markets. The major reasoning behind the policy of substitution was that oil exports that were delivered by sea (predominantly from ports in the Baltic Republics and the Black Sea) required little or no additional expenditure for the provision of transportation and storage facilities. Furthermore, crude oil could be sold relatively easily in the existing world spot markets (even if this required accepting a lower price to boost sales) which made it a more flexible product than natural gas for covering short-term hard currency requirements (Gustafson 1989: 270).

The strategy of substitution, however, contained major environmental as well as economic risks. In addition to developing natural gas, which is a relatively clean fuel source, Soviet policy in the early and mid-1980s evolved towards developing cheaper and plentiful open-cast coal deposits in Kazakhstan and Siberia to meet local demand for power generation. The growth in demand for power in the industrial European republics of the Soviet Union (Russia, the Ukraine, Byelorussia and the Baltic republics) was to be met primarily from increased locally generated nuclear power, which would eliminate the need for either transmitting power or transporting coal over vast distances from the growing areas of production in Siberia to the consuming areas. Eastern Europe was expected both to increase the generation of nuclear power and to use domestic low-quality and brown coal and lignite in power generation, both of which caused highly polluting emissions.

Gustafson (1989: 272) demonstrates that the decision to pursue the strategy of substituting gas for oil in domestic consumption to release oil for export for hard currency was finally taken sometime in 1982–83 after considerable debate between Soviet energy specialists and central planners. The decline in oil exports to the OECD was reversed in 1982 when oil exports to the OECD rose by 16.5 million tonnes to 709 million tonnes. This was principally achieved by cutting exports to Eastern Europe by 10 million tonnes to 70 million tonnes (which was partly offset by increased supplies of natural gas) and by reductions in exports to developing countries, and only then by stabilising domestic oil consumption and eventually reducing it after 1982 as the policy of substitution started to bear fruit (Chadwick et al. 1987: 29; Smith 1987). As a result, although Soviet crude oil production initially peaked at 616 million tonnes in 1983, cuts in domestic consumption enabled further increases in the volume of export to the OECD in 1983 and 1984, which reached an initial peak of 81 million tonnes in 1984 (although this represented a fall in dollar income from a peak of $17.5 billion in 1983).

Soviet exports of natural gas to the industrialised West have remained relatively minor in comparison with exports of crude oil and products, particularly considering that by 1985 natural gas constituted 35.8 per cent of Soviet extracted energy (in terms of standard fuel equivalent) and by 1989 had overtaken crude oil to become the largest source of Soviet extracted energy, providing 40.5 per cent of the total (Narkhoz 1989: 377). The lower level of exports in relation to production mainly resulted from the greater technical and political difficulties associated with the delivery of natural gas, which contributed to the policy decision to expand oil rather than gas exports to the West in the early 1980s. This decision was partly justified by the oversupply of natural gas to the West European market from other sources which drove prices down in the 1980s. However, the economic importance of natural gas exports to the Soviet economy should not be underestimated as they still constituted the second largest single merchandise export to the industrialised West in the early 1980s and, as Stern argues (1987: 44), the Soviet Union had become a major actor in the West European natural gas market, with the ability to influence prices.

Although the expansion of Siberian natural gas exports represented one of the major possibilities facing the Soviet government, the economic and political implications of natural gas exports were far more complicated than those applying to oil exports. In order to generate a large volume of exports, natural gas must be delivered by pipeline from remote regions of Siberia either direct to the recipient or to a seaport and then be shipped by specialised vessels in the form of liquefied natural gases. This requires major capital expenditure before delivery can commence, which in turn requires the development of long-term stable economic (contractual) and political links between the supplier and the consumer and a considerable degree of inter-dependence, as it is difficult for either the customer to seek alternative sources of supply in the short run or for the supplier to find alternative markets.

Soviet negotiations concerning exports of natural gas followed three major avenues in the Brezhnev era (Goldman 1980: 78–83; Stern 1987: 31–34):

1   Natural gas imports from Iran for transit or substitution in exports to Western Europe

From 1970 until 1974 the Soviet Union was a net importer of natural gas with major supplies from Iran and Afghanistan supplying the Transcaucasian republics by a Soviet-built pipeline to Azerbaidzhan (IGAT I). Under a set of multilateral agreements reached in 1975 (Smith 1982: 123) the Soviet Union agreed to build a second pipeline (IGAT II) from Iran to the Soviet border in exchange for imports of crude oil and to deliver natural gas to Eastern and Western Europe. The Soviet Union planned to use the gas imported from Iran to supply the Caucasus, Central Asia and the Ukraine while meeting contracted supplies to Czechoslovakia, West Germany, Austria and France through the existing Orenburg pipeline, profiting by the major difference in prices paid to Iran and received from the European importers. The fall of the Shah of Iran in 1979 resulted in the cancellation of the project, while deliveries through IGAT I ceased in 1980 and were only recommenced in 1990. The cancellation of IGAT I forced the Soviet authorities to extend domestic gas pipeline networks into the Transcaucasian republics to meet their needs.

2   Liquefied natural gas (LNG) for export to Japan and the USA

In the early 1970s the Soviet authorities actively sought the cooperation of US and Japanese companies in the development and transportation of Siberian reserves for liquefaction and export by sea to the USA and Japan. The first of these projects, known as the North Star project, involved American companies in the construction of a pipeline from Urengoi in Western Siberia to the Russian port of Murmansk in the Barents Sea, east of Norway, together with a liquefaction plant at Murmansk from where LNGs would be shipped across the Atlantic to the east coast of America (Goldman 1980: 80). The second proposal involved US and Japanese companies in the development of a natural gas field in Yakutia in the east Siberian lowlands and the construction of a 2,000 mile pipeline (much of it close to the Chinese border) to the sea coast at Nakhodka for liquefaction and shipment to Japan and across the Pacific to the west coast of the USA. This would have been a major capital project costing nearly $10 billion at 1992 prices, which would have been principally dedicated to export earnings and consequently would have required a major commitment from all partners to deliver and receive large volumes of gas over a substantial period.

Neither of these proposals were put into practice for what at first sight appear to be political reasons. The sheer size of the projects would have required US government support in the form of Eximbank credits and risk insurance. The Jackson-Vanik and Stevenson amendments to the 1974 Trade Act limited US government support to $40 million and linked increases in US lending to freer emigration policies, leading to the USSR cancelling its trade agreement with the USA and effectively killing off US co-operation in the development of Soviet natural gas. The proposals also suffered from major logistical problems, including difficulties in ensuring supplies from ice-bound Soviet harbours (at the period of highest demand) which brought the economic viability of the project into question. Japan, however, has retained some interest in the Yakutia project which could be revived in the post-Soviet era, while American companies are again investigating the possibility of shipping oil and/or gas from West Siberia through Murmansk and developing offshore oil deposits in the Barents Sea. The best prospect for Russian supplies of LNGs to Japan remains with the development of the smaller offshore fields off Sakhalin Island in the Sea of Okhotsk, north of Japan.

## West Siberian gas to European Russia, Eastern and Western Europe

The abandoning of LNG proposals involving large-scale US and Japanese co-operation in East Siberia required the Soviet authorities to concentrate their attention on the fields in the Urals–Volga region and the West Siberian lowlands, from which gas could then be delivered by overland pipeline to the European Republics of the Soviet Union and then on to Eastern Europe before reaching Western Europe. This generated considerable economies of scale as the capital costs of exploration, exploitation and transportation of major projects could be offset by a far larger European market. It also reduced the political risk to the Soviet government as the Soviet republics and the CMEA countries offered a secure market. Soviet proposals to develop natural gas also included orders for West European pipe and pumping equipment and compressors, either as part of compensation deals involving deliveries of natural gas in exchange or as straightforward purchases. This would have intensified trade complementarity between the Soviet Union and Western Europe but also would have created divergent interests between Western Europe and the USA in trade relations with the Soviet Union. This came to a head in 1982 with the 'pipeline incident' when the Reagan administration, in part alarmed by what it perceived as the prospect of West European dependence on Soviet gas deliveries, but primarily intending to impose economic pressure on the Soviet government following the imposition of martial law in Poland, embargoed US exports of oil and gas equipment to the Soviet Union and extended this extra-territorially and retrospectively to the subsidiaries and licensees of US companies in Western Europe, some of whom had already concluded contracts for the delivery of compressors.

The ban, which remained in force until 1987, did not delay the scheduled completion of the pipeline, which was completed with the use of smaller Soviet-built (but apparently less-reliable) compressors and inflicted some considerable damage to European–US relations, although European governments effectively agreed to limit their dependency on Soviet gas to approximately one-third of total gas supplies to each country (Stern 1987: 33). By 1989 only four West European countries, the FRG, Austria, Italy and France imported significant volumes of gas from the Soviet Union, with Finland importing approximately 1 billion cubic metres. In 1980 these five countries imported 25.5 billion cubic metres from the Soviet Union at a cost of $2.8 billion, which had doubled in volume to 49 billion cubic metres in 1989 at the same cost (see Table 5.4). The East European CMEA countries (excluding the former GDR) imported 40 billion cubic metres from the Soviet Union in 1989 (with the GDR importing 8 billion cubic metres).

## EXPORTS OF ARMAMENTS AND MILITARY EQUIPMENT

Exports to developing countries of armaments, military equipment and civilian goods with military uses have grown in importance since the Arab–Israeli war of 1973 and the subsequent increase in world oil prices which significantly increased the purchasing power of oil exporting countries. The CIA estimates that Soviet arms transfers to the Third World amounted to $49.1

bn between 1974 and 1982 compared with a total of $10.4 bn in the entire period from 1955–73 (CIA 1980, 1984). Similarly, the Stockholm International Peace Research Institute (SIPRI) estimates that the volume of Soviet deliveries of major weapons to the Third World trebled between 1972 and 1980. Although there are major differences of opinion between western specialists about the absolute size of Soviet arms transfers (Efrat (1985: 34a) estimates that Soviet deliveries are between 50 to 125 per cent higher than the CIA estimates) and about Soviet motives for arms deliveries, the methods of payment and the contribution they made to the Soviet balance of payments, there is broad agreement that the above figures give an accurate impression of changing trends in arms exports over time and that the Soviet Union had become one of the four major arms exporters in the world by the mid-1970s, and was generally regarded as the second largest after the USA (Pierre 1982: 74).

## Soviet motives for arms sales

Pierre (1982: 73) argues that the 'Soviet motivation in supplying arms has traditionally been far more political and ideological than economic'. Given that the Soviet Union had little else to offer in the form of civilian technology transfer, arms supplies became the major vehicle for extending Soviet influence in the Third World. In the 1960s the Soviet Union offered arms to Third World countries on far more advantageous terms than western suppliers. These included large price discounts (up to 40 per cent) and long-term, low-interest (2.5 per cent) credits involving repayment in the form of local produce (Pierre 1982: 78). Arms supplies were largely concentrated on the newly emerging Marxist regimes and national liberation movements in the former British and French empires and Cuba.

This pattern changed in the second half of the 1970s, as more than half of Soviet deliveries were concentrated on the oil-rich Middle Eastern states, notably Iraq, Syria, Libya and Algeria, who were able to pay in cash. Valkenier (1983: 25) argues that 'regardless of whether political or economic motives predominate in Soviet arms trade, there is no doubt that it has netted vast profits for Moscow'. The prevailing view is that the Soviet Union took a far more commercial attitude towards arms deliveries following the oil price rise of 1973–74. This included a shift from aid to direct sales for cash, more stringent credit terms, including higher interest rates and shorter repayment periods and higher prices (Deger 1985: 160–1). Arms sales started to play a far more significant role in meeting the increased Soviet demand for hard currency, which enabled the Soviet Union to fund increased imports of grain and machinery and equipment in the mid-1970s without incurring major balance of payments problems. This reflected the practice of western suppliers who also pursued a more commercial approach to arms sales, reducing the proportion delivered on credit and concessionary terms during this period.

### The economics of Soviet arms sales

As the Soviet authorities did not publish data relating to the size of arms deliveries and methods of payments and prices, the profitability of arms sales and their contribution to the Soviet balance of payments has to be estimated from secondary sources. This is a hazardous process, which involves a number of assumptions and calculations that are subject to significant error. Ideally an estimate of the profitability of the arms trade would require an accurate estimate of the actual volume of arms deliveries; an estimate of the actual prices paid, including allowances for discounts, credit terms, etc.; an estimate of the means and timing of payments (hard currency, local produce, grant aid, etc.) and, finally, an estimate of the real opportunity costs involved in arms manufacture. As this is a highly complex task, it is not surprising that many serious writers in the field have been compelled to use the unclassified results of studies undertaken by intelligence agencies. Unfortunately the assumptions on which these estimates have been based have not always been clearly indicated, which leaves some studies of Soviet arms trade open to the accusation that they have 'proved' the unstated assumptions on which the original estimates of the data were based. I will argue that this has led to a serious overestimation of the actual contribution of arms sales to the Soviet balance of payments and especially to Soviet liquidity since the mid-1970s.

The CIA has attempted to estimate both the volume of Soviet arms transfers to the Third World and their contribution to Soviet hard currency earnings. The principal method used by the CIA to estimate the volume of Soviet arms sales to Third World

*Table 5.5*  Soviet exports of arms and defence equipment to non-socialist countries (million roubles)

| | Unidentified residuals | | | Identified trade: CTN digits | | | Totals | |
|---|---|---|---|---|---|---|---|---|
| | LDC | ICC | M&E | 191 | 193 | other | Roubles million | $ US million |
| 1975 | 1,370 | 310 | 114 | 122 | 87 | 23 | 2,026 | 2,720 |
| 1976 | 1,748 | 333 | 111 | 157 | 83 | 15 | 2,447 | 3,250 |
| 1977 | 2,869 | 567 | 187 | 175 | 77 | 15 | 3,890 | 5,285 |
| 1978 | 2,873 | 890 | 240 | 150 | 151 | 12 | 4,316 | 6,319 |
| 1979 | 2,847 | 955 | 314 | 134 | 145 | 9 | 4,404 | 6,725 |
| 1980 | 3,095 | 773 | 358 | 151 | 162 | 8 | 4,547 | 6,979 |
| 1981 | 3,550 | 1,393 | 274 | 154 | 348 | 34 | 5,753 | 7,984 |
| 1982 | 4,656 | 1,643 | 252 | 245 | 429 | 31 | 7,256 | 10,007 |
| 1983 | 5,230 | 1,139 | 273 | 280 | 450 | 21 | 7,393 | 9,957 |
| 1984 | 5,613 | 656 | 341 | 306 | 567 | 20 | 7,503 | 9,183 |
| 1985 | 4,289 | 727 | 278 | 382 | 584 | 15 | 6,275 | 7,497 |
| 1986 | 5,452 | 636 | 327 | 315 | 567 | 20 | 7,317 | 10,401 |
| 1987 | 5,308 | 518 | 242 | 430 | 603 | 9 | 7,110 | 11,225 |
| 1988 | 5,298 | 747 | 218 | 335 | 539 | 4 | 7,141 | 11,745 |
| 1989 | 5,528 | 944 | 225 | 244 | 542 | 7 | 7,490 | 11,889 |
| 1990 | 3,861 | 802 | 508 | 225 | 249 | 3 | 5,648 | 9,410 |

*Source:* All estimated from Vneshtorg (various years).
*Notes:* LDC residual: exports to developing countries that are not identified by country of destination.
ICC residual: exports to developing countries that are identified by country of destination, but not by commodity.
M&E residual: Exports of machinery and equipment that are identified by country of destination but not by item. CTN 191: heavy and specialised vehicles.
CTN 193: aircraft, helicopters and aviation techniques.
Other: other items with military uses.

countries was known as the 'estimated export prices method' which was said to attempt to estimate the actual prices charged to individual arms recipients in roubles and convert these into dollars at the official exchange rate (Efrat 1985: 4) but which produced surprisingly similar results to those obtained from an analysis of the residuals in Soviet trade statistics outlined in this chapter.

My own estimates of the level and development of Soviet exports of armaments and equipment with military and potentially military uses to non-socialist countries during the period from 1975–90 are shown in Table 5.5. The estimates are derived from the sum of the LDC residual, the intra-country commodity residual, the machinery and equipment residual and exports of aircraft, heavy vehicles and small amounts of ships and construction equipment (see above). These estimates necessarily include elements of non-military exports and therefore over-estimate the level of arms exports. However, an examination of residuals that arise from statistical under-reporting in other sections of the trade statistics indicates that this element is relatively small. The most critical problem concerns the LDC residual. There has been speculation among western specialists that the LDC residual included sales of gold, diamonds and other precious metals in addition to arms. However, the analysis above indicates that these exports (except gold) were concealed in other residuals. It is officially stated that gold sales are not included in export statistics, and the steady growth in the LDC residual is not consistent with the annual fluctuations in gold sales. It appears safe to conclude that the LDC residual is largely composed of arms sales. The estimates indicate that Soviet exports of military and related equipment grew steadily from $2.7 billion in 1975 (compared with $1.5 billion in 1972) to a peak of $10 billion in 1982 (before falling back to $7.5 billion in 1984) and amounted to a total of $52.1 billion between 1974 and 1982. These estimates are slightly higher than the CIA estimates for each year, which have probably made an allowance for the inclusion of non-military expenditure in the residuals.

A major problem concerns the estimation of the methods of payments for arms and their contribution to the hard currency balance of payments. The CIA has published estimates of the Soviet balance of payments on both current and capital account which revealed some of its methodology for estimating hard currency arms sales. Firstly, the CIA assumed that all exports (including arms), which could be identified from the data on exports to individual countries with whom the Soviet Union had agreements to conduct trade in hard currency, actually were exported for hard currency, while all exports to countries with whom the Soviet Union normally conducts trade on a clearing basis were not conducted in hard currency. This assumption may be suspect, as international arms trade is frequently conducted on a different basis from civilian trade, but it has the benefit of clarity. These exports were included in aggregate estimates of Soviet hard currency exports and were not specifically identified as arms. Secondly, exports were allocated according to the year of recorded delivery, without regard to credit terms or the timing of payments. Although this is the standard methodology for estimating the current account balance of payments on a trans-actions basis, it does not tell us when (or even whether) the Soviet Union was paid for arms sales and the contribution of arms sales to the Soviet cash flow which could then be used to alleviate short-term balance of payments problems and shortages in the domestic economy.

Finally, an estimate had to be made for the allocation of arms deliveries contained in the LDC residual between payment in hard currency and soft currency. CIA estimates of Soviet hard currency exports included a separate item for 'additional military deliveries to LDCs' which was derived from the LDC residual (Smith 1985a: 150–4). In a study published by Ericson and Miller in 1979, the proportion of 'additional deliveries' deemed to have been exported for hard currency in the 1970s was estimated to be 43 per cent (these estimates are shown as CIAa in Table 5.6). This ratio was obtained from intelligence estimates of the proportion of Soviet arms exports delivered on hard currency terms in 1977 which was then extrapolated to other years. A later CIA study by Zoeter (shown as CIAb in Table 5.6), published in 1983, indicates a substantially higher value for hard currency arms sales, under the description 'additional military deliveries to LDCs fob', with a footnote saying that 'this item excludes the value of arms related commercial exports included in Soviet reporting on exports to individual LDCs'. This indicates that the estimate was derived from the LDC residual and also indicates that the proportion of the LDC residual which was assumed to have been exported on a hard currency basis increased to between 81 and 96 per cent

Table 5.6 Estimated Soviet arms sales for hard currency 1975–81 ($ billion)

|  | 1975 | 1976 | 1977 | 1978 | 1979 | 1980 | 1981 |
|---|---|---|---|---|---|---|---|
| Smith | 1,142 | 1,365 | 2,220 | 2,654 | 2,825 | 2,910 | 3,335 |
| Portes | 1,000 | 1,250 | 2,300 | 2,500 | 2,750 | 3,500 | 3,700 |
| CIAa | 793 | 1,108 | 1,500 | 1,644 | na | na | na |
| CIAb | 1,500 | 1,850 | 3,220 | 3,965 | 3,855 | 4,200 | 4,200 |
| CIAb errors and omissions | −1,915 | −672 | −3,292 | −2,156 | −2,516 | −3,532 | −5,840 |

Sources: Smith, estimated from Table 5.5 with an allowance of 42 per cent for hard currency sales.
Portes, from Portes (1983).
CIAa from Ericson and Miller (1979)
CIAb Zoeter (1983).
For explanations see text.

(depending on the year) from 1975 and 1981. On this basis Zoeter concludes that Soviet hard currency earnings from arms sales came to $25.8 billion from 1973–81, in addition to items included in reports on trade with individual countries. If the same proportions were to be applied to other military deliveries included in the reports on trade with individual countries, total Soviet hard currency earnings from arms sales would rise to between $40 bn and $45 bn from 1974–82 and would have exceeded $8 billion in 1982, which would indicate that arms sales were a major source of Soviet hard currency earnings which any Russian government would be very reluctant to forgo.

How accurate are these figures? The CIA also estimated the Soviet balance of payments on capital account, principally from open western banking and government statistics. The major inflows on capital account were new borrowing from western banks and governments and gold sales, while capital outflows include repayments of loans, plus or minus changes in known Soviet financial assets held in western banks (the equivalent of reserves). According to standard accountancy practice any discrepancy between deficits (surpluses) on current account and surpluses (deficits) on capital account which should offset one another, were designated as net errors and omissions. A negative sign here indicated either that capital outgoings had not been included in the estimated accounts (e.g. the granting of credits or grants which could not have been included in the estimates because the information was not available) or the overestimation of hard currency receipts from export earnings.

In the Zoeter study this figure was negative in each year from 1974–81 and amounted to a total of $23.1 billion over this period, which implies that the methodology either consistently over-estimated export earnings and/or consistently underestimated grants and outstanding credits. This figure is comparable with Zoeter's estimates of hard currency receipts from 'additional' military deliveries (derived from the LDC residual) which came to $24.3 billion over the same period. This provides considerable support for the hypothesis that the Soviet Union did not secure payment in hard currency for a significant proportion of arms sales included in the LDC residual.

A more detailed estimate of the proportion of exports of arms and military equipment denominated in hard currency utilising recently published evidence is provided in Chapter 8. This provides further support for the argument that only 42 per cent of arms sales were designated in hard currency and that a significant proportion of that amount was delivered on the basis of extended credits, which did little to alleviate hard currency problems. Accordingly in Table 5.6 I have applied a factor of 42 per cent to the estimates of arms sales in Table 5.5 to arrive at an estimate of hard currency sales (including those delivered on credit). These estimates indicate that Soviet hard currency arms exports grew from $617 million in 1972 to $3.3 billion by 1981, rising further to $4.2 billion in 1982 and 1983.

On this basis Soviet arms sales for hard currency amounted to $31.5 billion between 1974 and 1984. Outstanding hard currency claims against the Third World amounted to approximately $12 billion at the end of 1984, indicating that hard currency receipts for arms (and/or repayments in hard goods such as oil, which were resold on western markets, and food) over the ten-year period were in the region of $19 billion. In addition, the Soviet Union delivered arms estimated at $43.5 billion dollars from 1974–84 on a bilateral or soft currency basis over the period for which it received goods to the value of $23 bn, which was largely accounted for by imports of oil (which were resold for hard currency), natural gas, cotton, foodstuffs, consumer goods and clothing. Thus, although the contribution of Soviet arms sales to overcoming Soviet liquidity problems may have been overestimated, arms sales did make a significant contribution to easing import constraints.

## EXPORTS OF GOLD

The Soviet Union did not publish any figures for Soviet gold production, consumption, sales and gold stocks until 1988 (when selective output figures for 1970, 1980, 1984 and 1985 were released as part of a bond issue). Sales of monetary gold are not included in Soviet foreign trade statistics and cannot be estimated from the trade residual, but were estimated by the CIA and other specialists from data provided by western intermediaries and financial analysts who largely base their estimates of Soviet gold sales on the differences between aggregate world gold supplies and supplies from known sources. The CIA and some western specialists (for example, Kaser 1984) have also attempted the far more complicated task of estimating production, consumption and stocks. As these estimates were undertaken with no co-operation from the Soviet authorities, they are necessarily subject to error.

The initial production figures released by the Soviet authorities in 1988 were slightly lower than CIA and other western estimates, indicating production levels of 202 tonnes in 1970, rising to 311 tonnes in 1980 but falling back to 300 tonnes in 1984 and only 271 tonnes in 1985. Later figures released by the Ministry of Finance in 1991 reduced the 1984 output figure to only 251.8 tonnes, the 1985 figure to 264.0 tonnes (*Moscow News* 1991, no. 46: 9). There is broad agreement from these data and western estimates that the Soviet Union remained the world's second largest gold producer in the 1980s (after South Africa), producing from 250–300 tonnes per annum. Soviet production levels did not respond to the higher world gold prices in the 1980s and had in fact fallen, in sharp contrast to output levels in the USA and Australia which grew 8–10-fold during the 1980s. As a result the Soviet share of world production fell from 25 per cent in 1980 to around 15 per cent in 1988–89.

The data 'unearthed' from the Ministry of Finance by the economist Grigory Yavlinsky and published in *Moscow News* contained a major surprise as they indicated that Soviet gold reserves were only 240 tonnes in October 1991 and that stocks had been run down in the thirty years following Stalin's death from

2,049.1 tonnes (on 1 January 1953) to only 577.2 tonnes at the beginning of 1984. This is in sharp contrast to CIA estimates that Soviet gold stocks stood at 2,391 tonnes at the end of 1983. *Moscow News* (1991, no. 46) commented that it was Stalin who had behaved like a true oriental despot, holding gold in awe and selling none of it, while under Khrushchev and Brezhnev annual sales exceeded production by hundreds of tonnes, and that the bulk of gold had been squandered to support pro-Soviet regimes. This claim is impossible to verify but, if true, could help to explain western overestimates of Soviet gold stocks as they would not have identified the true origin of any gold that was subsequently sold by client states on western markets.

The prevailing western view, analysed by Lavigne (1991a) and Nissanke (1987), is that the Soviet authorities boosted gold sales to meet short-term balance of payments pressures (largely generated by unanticipated grain imports) and then reduced sales below production levels to restore stocks. Soviet gold sales first commenced at moderate levels under Khrushchev in the mid-1950s, then averaged about 180 tonnes a year in the early 1960s (compared with production in the region of 125–150 million tonnes) but really gathered momentum following the major grain crisis of 1963 when gold sales averaged 450–500 tonnes a year from 1963–65, realising an average of $500–550 million to pay for grain imports. This clearly involved a substantial depletion of gold stocks and the Soviet authorities virtually removed themselves from the market from 1965–71 while stocks were built up. CIA estimates indicate a second surge of gold sales associated with grain imports at the end of 1972, which reached 300 tonnes in 1973, realising $962 million, rising to $1,175 million in 1974. Despite the high level of grain imports in 1975 and the related balance of trade deficit of $6.4 billion, gold sales fell to around 150 tonnes as stocks were again replenished. As Soviet imports of both grain and machinery and equipment soared in the mid-1970s gold sales were again increased to 325–30 tonnes in 1976 and 1977 (yielding $1.4 billion to $1.6 billion), peaking at 400 tonnes in 1978 when they yielded $2.5 billion. Despite the increase in world oil prices the Soviet authorities experienced further balance of payments difficulties and were forced to borrow nearly $10 billion in 1975–76. Gold sales again fell in 1979, and although gold prices approached $1,000 an ounce in early 1980, Soviet sales in 1980 were only 80 tonnes as reserves were again rebuilt and the second round of world oil prices boosted income from oil exports. The CIA estimates that sales were pushed back up to 200 tonnes in 1981, yielding $2.7 billion as grain imports from the West were again increased by just under $2 billion. Gold exports were again reduced to facilitate restocking from 1983 and 1984 and according to the Ministry of Finance figure were only 10 tonnes in 1984.

The Yavlinsky data provided further evidence that the decision of the Soviet leadership to cut imports of western machinery and equipment in the late 1970s and early 1980s was not purely based on a desire to limit dependence on western technology but was largely determined by acute problems of generating exports to pay for imports.

## CONCLUSION

The evidence in this chapter supports the argument that there was a significant bias against the export of Soviet manufactured goods to the industrialised West. In 1984, less than 4.4 per cent of Soviet exports to the industrialised West could be classified as manufactured goods and half of these comprised a low volume of cars which sold at the cheaper end of western markets. The presence of hard currency constraints which necessitated cuts in imports of machinery and equipment indicates that the low volume of manufactured exports was not purely a result of the latter being 'crowded out' by exports of energy, minerals and raw materials.

The Soviet Union did succeed in exporting significant quantities of arms to developing countries, although a significant proportion was not actually paid for in hard currency while the major recipients of Soviet arms may have chosen Soviet supplies on political as much as technical grounds. Nevertheless the quadrupling of the value of defence sector exports between 1975 and 1982 was a major success. The defence industry, however, was protected from many of the problems arising from supply constraints that bedevilled civilian industry: defence enterprises could commandeer the best inputs and enforce stricter quality conditions on suppliers, conduct their own R & D, offer attractive salaries and work conditions to the best engineers and managers, and were even reported to have overproduced as a matter of routine in order to be able to meet urgent export orders (Deger 1985: 164). The critical question is whether civilian exports could flourish to the same extent if the constraints on that sector were to be lifted.

# Chapter 6

# Soviet economic reforms and reform debates under Gorbachev

## THE RADICALISATION OF REFORMS

When Gorbachev became Secretary-General of the CPSU in March 1985 he indicated that the reversal of the post-war decline in economic growth was an urgent priority, both to satisfy the demands of the population for a steady improvement in living standards and to preserve the status of the Soviet Union as a superpower. Despite the priority attached to the improvement of economic performance, the pace of implementation of economic reform under Gorbachev was far slower than the pace of reform in domestic social policy, constitutional reforms and reforms to foreign policy. The failure to implement a coherent economic reform and to create a properly functioning economic system over a seven-year period was a major factor contributing to the deterioration in economic performance in 1990–91, which in turn contributed to the disintegration of the Soviet economy and the collapse of the Soviet Union itself at the end of 1991.

The slower pace of domestic economic reform resulted from a combination of economic, social and political factors. Firstly, it reflected the analysis of reformist advisers, who concluded from the experience of the failure of economic reforms in the Soviet Union and Eastern Europe since the 1960s that economic reforms would not succeed unless they were preceded by changes to the political and social system designed to create a more questioning and innovative environment and to replace officials who were hostile to the concept of reform. Although the selection of Gorbachev as party leader indicated that a majority of the Politburo had concluded that more vigorous reforms were unavoidable if further economic decline was to be prevented,

Gorbachev did not have the patronage to immediately appoint his own supporters to positions of authority (unlike many incoming leaders in western political systems) but had to work alongside conservative opponents in the Politburo and with a conservative majority in the Central Committee. Gorbachev also depended initially on the existing apparatus in the state economic planning hierarchy and management in enterprises to implement decentralising economic reforms which would, at best, lead to a considerable loss of their status and authority and, at worst, to the loss of employment.

Opposition to radical economic reforms was not confined to those who exercised control in the existing system or even the economic mafia who exploited the shortages resulting from the system to generate income from the secondary economy. Despite its growing problems the communist economic system provided a majority of the population with job and income security combined with stable prices and, until the 1980s, a gradual but steady growth in living standards. Some conservatives also argued that this had been achieved since the death of Stalin with a gradual, but progressive reduction in the use of authoritarian controls, coercion and terror in a culturally heterogeneous and potentially unstable multi-ethnic state. Thus, although economic reforms may have promised improved economic circumstances and living standards for a significant proportion of the population in the longer run, they inevitably created greater uncertainty for many sectors of the population in the short run (including the threat of unemployment and higher relative prices for basic consumption goods, following the reduction or removal of subsidies) with the possibility that the growing uncertainty could threaten social stability. This has to be set against the background of the continued deterioration in economic performance, with growing shortages in both retail and wholesale trade, rising budget deficits and personal savings, growing pressures on the balance of payments and, finally, falls in output.

Although there was a progressive radicalisation in debates on economic reform, particularly in academic circles (which later extended into the new parliamentary institutions) throughout the Gorbachev era, major gaps remained between firstly, the degree of radicalism in reform debates and proposals and the ensuing reform decrees (which were formulated by the bureaucracy) and more seriously between the decrees themselves and their implementation in the state sector of the economy. One interpretation of the gap between reform debate and reform implementation is that Gorbachev supported radical reforms from the start of his period of office, but his background in the Politburo had made him a shrewd but cautious politician, who would only publicly support proposals that would not provoke outright public opposition and which would be accepted by the political leadership. Consequently, he publicly espoused less radical reforms than he felt were necessary until such time as he had removed the opposition to more radical reforms from the Politburo and Central Committee and had convinced the public of the necessity for radical reforms. A more probable interpretation is that Gorbachev (and his advisers) drastically underestimated the seriousness of the economic situation facing the Soviet Union when he took power and found themselves forced into adopting increasingly more radical solutions with far greater political, social and economic consequences than had been initially intended. Gorbachev finally, baulked at political and social dangers presented by the more radical reform proposals presented in 1990 and found himself forced back into making concessions to conservative factions.

It must also be said that many of Gorbachev's policies betrayed a failure to appreciate quite basic economic principles and lacked consistency and coherence. On many occasions parts of the reform package were introduced without other complementary elements. Frequently, further legislation, consistent with a more radical stage of reform, was being discussed just as new legislation was coming into effect, thereby weakening the impact of the latter. Finally, in 1990, as the debate widened to embrace vastly different concepts of reform, Gorbachev attempted to combine mutually exclusive proposals into a single inconsistent reform package. Ultimately central control over basic magnitudes such as the money supply, the budget balance, the balance between the supply and demand for consumption and, finally, the balance of payments was lost completely.

The net effect was that by the time of the collapse of communism in Eastern Europe at the end of 1989, when radical (and on occasions former dissident) economists in Eastern Europe were drawing up and implementing framework proposals for the radical transition to an essentially capitalist market economy, the basic modus operandi of the Soviet economic system had not been substantially altered from that which Gorbachev inherited. The most discernible systemic change was that some new methods had been introduced into the old system, creating new sets of inconsistencies. While central controls had been weakened they had not been replaced by market disciplines, with the result that the system was operating with even more imperfections than before.

## THE FIRST PHASE OF REFORMS 1985–87

The progress of domestic economic reform under Gorbachev can be analysed in terms of three conceptually distinct (but over-lapping) periods. The first period, which started with Gorbachev's nomination as general-secretary in March 1985, effectively ended with the Party Plenum called to discuss the progress of economic reform in June 1987. Economic policy during this period was largely based on the resurrection of the measures to reform the economy and the system of economic administration which had been introduced by Andropov in 1983 (inner-system reforms) but which became partly stalled under Chernenko, until revived by Gorbachev, who took increasing control over economic policy throughout 1984 as Chernenko's health deteriorated. The conceptual basis of economic policies and reforms during this period was that central planning was a viable economic system which was working imperfectly, largely as a result of lax discipline, unambitious plan targets and the failure to modernise industry (and the engineering and machine tool industry in particular while investment and resources had been excessively concen-trated on the energy sector) during the Brezhnev era.

Gorbachev argued that these problems could be overcome by setting higher targets for economic growth (acceleration) combined with a crash investment programme to modernise and raise the technical level of industry, and by campaigns directed at increasing labour productivity in the short term, largely by increasing factory discipline. The most notable of the latter was the anti-alcohol campaign which drastically reduced the pro-duction and availability of alcohol and increased the penalties for drunkenness at the workplace. This measure was largely unsuccessful, partly because it led to an increase in illicit brewing, but also because the authorities failed to provide alternative consumption items to absorb the displaced purchasing power.

Consequently, the campaign removed a major source of budget revenue and increased excess demand in retail markets, causing the policy to be effectively abandoned during the second stage of reforms in 1988.

The administrative approach to overcoming problems of an economic-systemic nature can be illustrated by the operation of Gospriemka (the State Quality Control Board) which was established in 1986 and was charged with bringing 95 per cent of Soviet manufactured goods up to world quality standards by 1991–93 by rejecting poor quality output. In theory, the improvement of product quality should have alleviated pressures on the hard currency balance of payments in the long run by increasing the competitiveness of Soviet exports and reducing the demand for imported precision goods that could not be produced domestically. In practice, Gospriemka's inspectors set about their task with such enthusiasm that 15–18 per cent of production was reported to be rejected as substandard on first inspection. This both increased domestic supply bottlenecks and resulted in lost bonuses for workers, managers and officials, leading to a wave of strikes which were frequently settled in the workers' favour, contributing to the growth of wages at a time of stagnant output (IMF *et al.* 1991, vol. 1: 20–2; Cook, 1992: 46–8).

The policy of acceleration was typified by Gorbachev's rejection of the first draft of the perspective plan of development for 1986–2000, on the grounds that it was too unambitious, and its replacement by a programme which increased the rate of investment and economic growth. This was to be achieved by the more intensive use of energy, labour and raw materials, reflecting the view put forward by Aganbegyan that economic growth could only be achieved by increasing the proportion of GNP devoted to investment (Sutela 1991: 147). In practice, acceleration meant that enterprises were required to achieve higher gross output targets with a given supply of inputs which only aggravated the supply constraints and the problems associated with a seller's market.

## STREAMLINING THE ECONOMIC SYSTEM 1988–90

The first indications of a more radical approach to reform were contained in Gorbachev's speech to the 27th Party Congress in February 1986, which included proposals for a major reorganisation of the system of economic administration, which was intended to reduce the operational work of central economic organisations to leave them free to concentrate on long-term planning and guidance and to free enterprises from 'petty tutelage' (excessive interference in day-to-day operations by central authorities) and to link workers' pay more directly to 'work performed'. These proposals were intended to streamline the existing system of management, but left many of the basic principles of a centrally planned economy intact.

The second phase of the reform process is normally considered to have started with Gorbachev's speech to a Central Committee plenum convened to discuss the progress of economic reforms in June 1987 (Hardt 1990). Sutela (1991: 151) shows that the reform concepts approved at the plenum resulted from a conference of academic economists held in November 1986, at which an internally consistent reform programme commanding a wide degree of support from economists was drawn up. The programme combined a system of state controls over strategic and certain other goods (e.g. raw materials, production for the health sector, etc.) which would be put into effect through a system of state orders. Enterprises would have far greater autonomy to decide on the structure of other inputs and outputs, in response to predominantly market signals. At the same time the non-state sector (co-operatives, private firms and even foreign-owned firms and joint ventures) would be expanded and would be simultaneously complementary to and competitive with state enterprises.

The most striking feature of Gorbachev's speech to the plenum, however, was his statement that the economic problems facing the country necessitated more drastic solutions than had been realised. In a direct appeal to conservatives, Gorbachev argued that the economy was in a 'pre-crisis situation' which, if not averted, would threaten the status of the Soviet Union as a superpower by the end of the century. He attributed the economic crisis to the overcentralised system of management which had been established in the late 1920s and 1930s but which had proved resistant to attempts at reform under Khrushchev, Kosygin and Brezhnev as result of bureaucratic opposition. These problems could only be overcome by the 'creation of an efficient flexible system of managing the economy as a matter of priority' (*Pravda*, 26 June 1987).

Gorbachev's proposals were radical (in Soviet terms) in their vision of a new form of essentially market socialist economy, with strong similarities to NEP, which combined a large (but more efficient) state sector in large-scale industry with an increased role for the private sector, in services and small-scale industry and agriculture and the widespread use of leasing arrangements in agriculture and industry. Unlike the failed reforms of his predecessors, Gorbachev's proposals were holistic in that they were not restricted to changes in the system of enterprise success indicators but incorporated reforms to the systems of administration and planning, the banking system, the foreign trade system, the system of retail and wholesale trade and prices, the system of taxation and welfare, the system of labour organisation and experiments with the system of property rights. They retained strong elements of state control together with a (weakened) planning hierarchy. The proposals were in a direct line from the 'indirect centralisation' reform schemes of the mid-1960s (Gorbachev cited a paper by Nemchinov in the party paper *Kommunist* in 1964 in this tradition).

In practice many of the reform decrees that were enacted and implemented over the next eighteen months had already been discussed in general terms at the 27th Party Congress in February 1986 and had been circulated in draft form. The most important (and illustrative) of these was the State Enterprise Law which was adopted at the June plenum, but which had been outlined in Gorbachev's speech to the Party Congress in 1986 and had appeared in draft in February 1987. The basic provisions of the law (which was modified in a conservative direction from the original draft) were to make the enterprise respond to financial rather than physical indicators, while retaining state ownership. State orders in the sense of central instructions to produce a given amount of gross output were to be replaced by state orders in the financial sense, whereby the state would purchase a proportion of the plant's output at agreed prices. In theory the proportion of output subject to central orders was to diminish progressively as central controls were loosened and be replaced by wholesale trade agreements with suppliers and consumers.

Enterprises were to operate according to the principles of self-accounting, self-financing and self-management, which meant that enterprises would become autonomous financial institutions (rather than creatures of the state with no independent rights or assets) which would be expected to cover their variable costs from their revenues from the sale of output (self-accounting) and that investment would no longer be provided as a 'free gift' from the state, but would be financed by repayable bank loans on which interest would have to be paid (self-financing). The principle of self-management provided for greater enterprise democracy whereby workers would elect plant managers, supervisors and foremen, and workers' incomes would be directly linked to enterprises' net income (profits). This was intended as an appeal over the heads of the bureaucracy directly to the workers, who it was hoped would elect efficient managers who would increase enterprise income and thus wages. This would weaken the principle of enterprise subordination to ministerial authority, as enterprise managers would become responsible to workers who elected them. In practice, workers tended to elect managers who could play the existing system well and could continue to provide them with job security and guaranteed income.

## THE FAILURE OF GRADUALIST REFORMS

If the proposals initially enjoyed such widespread support from academic economists, why did the reform debate become increasingly radical over the next three years? Part of the answer lies in glasnost and greater democracy, which widened the area of public debate to those with more radical views who had not previously participated, but in the main can be attributed to a combination of weaknesses in the proposals themselves and inconsistencies in their implementation and in the sequencing of their implementation in particular. As these problems have reappeared in a more extreme form in the period of the transition from central planning to the market in Russia and Eastern Europe and are also crucially related to the problems of reform to the foreign trade sector it is appropriate to examine them now in greater detail.

The reforms started to operate from 1 January 1988, which brought them into direct conflict with the five-year plan which had established accelerated targets for investment and output and meant that in theory much of enterprise production potential was already committed. This conflicted with the advice of many economists, who thought that either a new, less directive plan should be introduced at the same time as the reforms, or alternatively that the introduction of the new system should be delayed until the next plan period in 1991. The process of transition to the new economic system was introduced gradually, which largely reflected a wariness of popular antagonism to unpopular economic measures. However, the gradualist approach also provided the 'new class' of middle-tier bureaucrats, who would potentially be most disadvantaged by the proposals, with an opportunity to form new alliances to oppose and delay reform (and to prepare themselves for the day when central planning collapsed). Equally critically, the gradualist approach meant that reforms were introduced in an ad hoc fashion which paid insufficient attention to the interrelationships between different parts of the economic system and thus extended the period over which parts of the old system had to co-exist with the new in a hybrid economic system. Furthermore, the proposals failed to establish new market mechanisms for regulating macroeconomic balances during the transition period to replace the old central controls that had been deliberately weakened. The combined effect was that the proposals exacerbated bottlenecks and imbalances in the economy which in the past had been regulated by central controls.

The most critical area was price reform. It is an economic axiom that if decentralisation and/or liberalisation of economic decisions is not accompanied by measures to make prices reflect genuine opportunity costs and utility (demand), profit-oriented enterprises will have an incentive to overconsume/underproduce/ export goods that have an artificially low domestic price and to overproduce/underconsume/import goods that have an artificially high domestic price. The 1987 plenum proposed that a radical reform of the whole system of wholesale and retail prices should be undertaken. Reform of the system of fixed and highly subsidised state retail prices, many of which had not been changed since the early 1950s in what has been interpreted as a form of unwritten 'social contract' between the rulers and the people, was considered to be highly sensitive politically and socially, particularly in the light of the public disturbances in Poland in 1970, 1976 and 1980 and riots whose suppression led to several deaths in Novocherkassk in 1962 following food price increases. In an attempt to overcome hostility to price increases, Gorbachev promised that living standards and purchasing power would be preserved by the payment of equivalent increases in the level of wages. As the state was simultaneously decentralising wage determination to the enterprise level, this commitment would have required the payment of a fixed per capita payment from the central budget. Furthermore, under conditions of excess consumer demand it was inherently inflationary.

Equally critical, there was the fear that in conditions of 'inflationary overhang' the elimination of central controls over state prices would trigger off hyperinflation as highly monopolistic producers and retail outlets (freed of central controls over the volume of output and with little incentive to improve efficiency or boost output) would simply increase prices as far as possible to increase revenues. This led to heated debates on whether prices should initially be increased from one level to another to eliminate subsidies and to reduce wasteful consumption, or whether an entirely flexible price system designed to equate supply and demand should be introduced immediately. The extreme sensitivity on the subject of retail prices, however, resulted in backtracking and postponements to proposals to change state retail prices. Although, *de jure*, retail prices remained centrally fixed throughout 1988, many retail outlets increased prices in response to deteriorating supply conditions, leading to growing signs of popular discontent (Cook 1992). By the beginning of 1989 splits between reformers on the issue of retail price reform were growing. Those favouring retail price reform argued that subsidies did not benefit the poor, who faced increasing difficulties in obtaining supplies in the state network, and that the major beneficiaries of food subsidies were the nomenklatura who had priority access to supplies through party stores (Kiselev, *Pravda*:18 January 1989). The state retail price of red meat, for example, which was more readily available in party stores than in the state retail market was estimated to be only 27 per cent of the production cost, while the retail price of bread was estimated to be 72 per cent of the cost to the state (estimated from IMF *et al.* 1991, vol. 2: 14). Nevertheless budget studies show that expenditure on food and clothing accounted for 50 per cent of the average working family's total income in the 1980s (Narkhoz 1989: 88), a proportion that would rise with lower incomes. Gorbachev's leading adviser, Aganbegyan, had become so alarmed by the potential social problems resulting from the removal of subsidies at a time of deteriorating supplies and escalating wages that he advocated that 'the question of price reform should be removed from the agenda for the next three to four years' and proposed doubling imports of consumer goods to stabilise the domestic market' (*Pravda* 6 February 1989).

## THE GROWTH OF INFLATIONARY PRESSURES
## 1988–1990

A reform of state wholesale prices, however, was introduced in January 1988, which together with the introduction of growing powers for enterprises to determine their output levels contributed to the growing disequilibrium in the state retail sector. According to the principles of the reform, wholesale prices were to fall into two basic categories. Firstly, prices of commodities subject to state orders (and basic inputs such as energy and raw materials) remained centrally determined but were subject to major increases. Enterprises had far greater powers to determine the wholesale prices of other goods on the basis of negotiations with customers (contract prices). Initially this largely extended to 'new goods' or higher quality goods for which state prices did not exist. These prices were still subject to central controls and limits on the permitted levels of markups on the price of goods they replaced.

The net effect was that enterprises used their increased powers to choose their production mix by diverting production to goods that carried high prices and were artificially more profitable and by increasing the output of 'new goods', which frequently embodied very minor alterations to existing products simply to achieve higher prices and revenues. This, combined with the relaxation of central controls on wages, permitted managers (who were increasingly elected by their workers) to increase wage payments in excess of their real growth in output. As retail prices were fixed, this unleashed hidden inflation (price increases that actually took place but were not recorded in official statistics) and suppressed inflation (the growth of involuntary savings) and a major growth of prices in legal and illegal secondary markets.

The problem was aggravated by the reforms to the banking system introduced on 1 January 1988, which involved the break up of the old monobank system and the creation of five specialised but state-owned banks, which fell under the general supervision of Gosbank. The banks were specialised by function (investment, housing, agriculture, savings and foreign trade) and appeared to operate more as sub-departments of Gosbank rather than as autonomous competitive entities. In addition, a number of small co-operative and commercial banks came into operation towards the end of 1988. The net effect of the changes was to weaken central control over the supply of cash and credit and to exacerbate inflationary pressures.

Critics of the banking reforms argued that the reorganisation of the state banking system meant that the functions of raising and disbursing credit had become separated and that Gosbank's control over the aggregate supply of money and credit had been considerably weakened as the new banks (which could not go bankrupt) operated a lax credit policy. More critically, the development of commercial and co-operative banks facilitated the expansion of economically unjustified credit. The major source of deposits was the excess liquidity of enterprises which under the old system would have been effectively appropriated by central authorities as tax revenues. Demand for credit largely came from enterprises with cash problems which could not obtain credit from more regular channels. Commercial banks, therefore, effectively stimulated inter-enterprise credit, in the safe knowledge that it was unlikely that the borrowing enterprise would be allowed to go bankrupt and that the loan would not be repaid. This was akin to a form of internal capital flight whose main function appears to have been to ease liquidity problems of enterprises paying wage increases and which further aggravated inflationary pressures.

The net effect was that total disposable incomes (incomes from all declared sources minus personal taxes) rose by 9.2 per cent (39 billion roubles) in 1988 (compared with 3.8 per cent in 1987) to 457 billion roubles, while total consumption rose by 7.2 per cent (28 billion roubles) to 415 billion roubles. The stock of personal savings rose by 42 billion roubles; deposits in the State Savings Bank rose by 33 billion roubles to 297 billion roubles and cash in hand by 9 billion roubles to 88 billion roubles. This implies that the stock of uncapitalised personal savings (cash plus saving bank deposits, including time deposits) at the end of 1988 stood at 93 per cent of total annual consumption and 84 per cent of annual disposable income, while individuals continued to save 29 per cent of additional income. The state budget deficit rose to 81 billion roubles, equivalent to 9.3 per cent of GDP. Macroeconomic disequilibrium continued to deteriorate in 1989 and 1990. Disposable money incomes grew by 13.1 per cent in 1989 to 515 billion roubles, consumption rose by 9.5 per cent to 454 billion roubles, personal savings deposits rose by 45 billion roubles to 338 billion roubles and cash holdings by 17 billion roubles to 105 billion roubles, taking personal savings to the equivalent of one year's personal consumption. The budget deficit remained at 80 billion roubles, equivalent to 8.5 per cent of GDP (IMF *et al.* 1991, vol. 1: 53–9 and 121–32).

## THE STRUGGLE FOR REFORM 1989–90

By the middle of 1989 the economic situation had deteriorated from 'pre-crisis' to a full-blooded crisis. However, there was no longer a clear consensus among economists on the best method of dealing with the crisis. A major cause of the accelerated decline in economic performance was the mixture of the old system with the new and the loss of control over basic macroeconomic aggregates. An increasing number of economists had begun to recognise that the 1987–88 reform concept was basically flawed. This raised critical questions. Macroeconomic stabilisation had clearly become an urgent priority, but should this be achieved by an initial return to administrative methods to stabilise the domestic retail market before liberalising prices, or should it be achieved by accelerating the introduction of the reforms? Would not price liberalisation under conditions of both inflationary overhang and loss of control over the money supply and escalating budget deficits trigger off hyperinflation, while stabilising prices through monetary controls alone would generate a major recession with mass unemployment? Furthermore, if reforms were to be introduced more quickly, did this mean accelerating the 1987–88 concept or the more rapid introduction of a full market economy?

### The Abalkin plan of November 1989

Reform proposals from the end of 1989 until the collapse of the Soviet government were marked by this lack of consensus over both the ends, and the means to achieve those ends. The first set of proposals was produced by the economist Leonid Abalkin (who in August 1989 had been appointed as a deputy prime minister with responsibility for economic reform). His proposals, which were published and discussed in November 1989, contained a far more radical concept of a mixed market economy as the end goal than had previously been seen in any Soviet reform proposals, but they involved a gradual transition incorporating an initial stabilisation programme which would last for two to three years. The legal framework for the transition to a market economy was to be established in 1990, together with an initial stabilisation package which included a gradual reduction of budget deficits and subsidies. The macroeconomic stabilisation programme was to continue from 1991–93 with the partial liberalisation of prices, together with wage indexation and the development of a social security system. The deeper transition to a market economy was to take place from 1993–95 with the break-up of state monopolies, the abolition of enterprise subsidies, the creation of capital markets and the development of a conventional two-tier banking system incorporating a national bank and entirely separate commercial banks (see *European Economy* 1990: 81–104; Jeffries 1992: 34–5; Sutela 1991: 164–7).

The official government version of the Abalkin plan was presented to the Congress of People's deputies by prime-minister Nikolai Ryzhkov on 13 December 1989 (*Izvestiya*, 14 December 1989). The Ryzhkov plan was considerably more conservative than Abalkin's initial proposal and placed far greater reliance on 'rigid directive measures' to stabilise the domestic consumer market from 1990–92, including proposals for an immediate increase in the output of consumer goods (which were planned to grow by 66 billion roubles (17.6 per cent) in 1990 and by 140 billion roubles (38 per cent) over the three years to the end of 1992. This was to be achieved largely by converting military plants to the production of consumer goods and by proposals to defer or cancel large-scale investment projects and other structural changes to reduce the importance of heavy industry. Central controls over prices and wages were to continue while the budget deficit and the growth of the money supply were to be gradually reduced. Ryzhkov dismissed proposals for the introduction of private property and widespread denationalisation. A stage-by-stage price reform would be introduced in 1991–92 after 'nationwide discussion'. The proposals for the transition to a market economy which, like the Abalkin plan, would not really get under way until 1993–95, were far more circumscribed and less detailed. To many observers the proposals sounded very much like acceleration all over again, but with the emphasis shifted from investment to consumption causing reformers like Bogomolov to vote against the programme on the grounds that it was not sufficiently radical (Bogomolov 1990: 34).

## The deterioration of economic performance in 1990

The reform debate grew progressively more radical during the first quarter of 1990 as economic performance continued to deteriorate. For the first time in peacetime, official statistics admitted that GNP and industrial output had fallen in the first quarter of 1990. Money incomes, however, grew by 13.3 per cent in the first quarter of 1990 compared with the corresponding period for 1989 and a plan target for the whole year of 7.3 per cent and deposits in state savings banks continued to grow. Although the value of consumer goods production was reported to have grown by 6.3 per cent, growing shortages of basic consumer goods including soap led to increased public dissatisfaction, reflected in strikes and work stoppages which had a knock-on effect on production, creating further shortages (Ekonomika i Zhizn 1990, no. 14). This also aggravated the popular (and probably correct) perception that goods were being diverted from state stores to secondary markets for purposes of profiteering, thereby creating hostility to the idea of a market economy.

By the time Gorbachev was elected President by the Congress of People's Deputies in March 1990 it had become apparent that the Ryzhkov strategy of 'macrostabilisation through increased production before reform' was unworkable. At the same time far more radical reforms were being introduced in Poland and discussed elsewhere in Eastern Europe, and Gorbachev indicated in his inaugural speech on 15 March 1990 that reforms would be accelerated. Leading Soviet reform economists expected that a package of 31 reform decrees, leading effectively to the creation of a market economy and including the establishment of retail, wholesale and capital markets, and the introduction of a form of currency convertibility, would be submitted to the Supreme Soviet on 1 May (personal discussions). This amounted to little less than a shock therapy programme, similar to that being implemented in Poland. A resurrected version of the Abalkin plan was discussed by the newly established Presidential Council on 18–19 April, but was sent back for revision. A major dispute centred on the relationship and sequencing of price increases and privatisation. It appears that the latest version of the Abalkin plan was rejected by reformists in the Presidential Council (including Petrakov, Shatalin and Arbatov) as being insufficiently radical in the pursuit of the goal of establishing a market economy and placed too great an emphasis on a monetary and fiscal squeeze on popular purchasing power and too little emphasis on cutting back on defence expenditure and investment in heavy industry (Arbatov, *Financial Times* 2 May 1990). Petrakov also argued, that unlike Poland, the government enjoyed little popular support, which extended to hostility to market reforms and in particular to policies that necessitated price increases which in turn threatened social stability. Consequently prices should, and could, be stabilised during the transition period and reforms should start with destatisation of the economy (i.e. the removal of state control and authority over enterprises). The government view (expressed by Abalkin) was that there was no alternative to an early and drastic macroeconomic stabilisation programme, which under conditions of widespread subsidisation and inflationary overhang would inevitably result in price increases for basic goods, but that such price increases should be administered by the state rather than left to market forces alone.

The accelerated version of the Abalkin plan, which proposed an immediate trebling of the price of bread and additional two-threefold increases in the state retail prices for foodstuffs and household goods (compensated for by increases in wages and allowances) from 1 January 1991, as part of a tough macro-economic stabilisation package which would precede a structural transformation of the economy, was presented to the Supreme Soviet by Ryzhkov on 24 May 1990 but was rejected (*European Economy* 1990: 85). This in effect marked the beginning of the end, not just of the Soviet economic system which was already in a state of collapse but of the Soviet economy as a single economic union. Although central planning was no longer working it was now clear that no consensus could be found on what should replace it and how to effect the transformation or on the nature of economic relationships within the Soviet Union.

## THE RUSSIAN GOVERNMENT AND THE SHATALIN PLAN

On 29 May 1990, Boris Yeltsin was elected as chairman of the newly established Russian Supreme Soviet on the third ballot. During his electoral campaign he had advocated his support for the transition to a market economy, and the campaign of one of his opponents, the Russian prime minister Alexander Vlasov, was damaged by his support for price increases contained in the second Ryzhkov–Abalkin plan (Morrison 1991: 146). Economists working for the Supreme Economic Council of the RSFSR, an advisory body established by the Russian government, had been preparing a series of proposals for the rapid transition to a market economy. The latest plan produced by the head of the Council, Mikhail Bocharov, based on a proposal initially drawn up by Grigory Yavlinsky for the entire Soviet Union, but rejected by Abalkin, contained a detailed set of proposals for the transition to a market economy in 500 days (Morrison, 1991: 164). At Yeltsin's behest and with Gorbachev's agreement a group of experts representing both the Russian and Soviet governments was established in August 1990 under the chairmanship of Shatalin to construct a plan for the transition to a market economy, based on the Russian version. Abalkin withdrew from the group and headed a rival commission, which drew up more comprehensive and detailed proposals for the gradual transition to a 'socially-oriented market economy' (Morrison 1991: chapter 14).

As a result, two competing and mutually exclusive programmes for economic reform were published at the beginning of September against a background of growing acrimony. Ryzhkov made it quite plain that acceptance of the Shatalin plan implied the break up of the Soviet Union and its effective disintegration into independent republics. Gorbachev attempted to bridge the two proposals by instructing Aganbegyan to prepare a compromise plan. This was virtually impossible and Aganbegyan's plan was effectively a modified version of Shatalin's proposals. In the meantime the Shatalin plan was approved by the Russian Supreme Soviet and was officially scheduled to come into effect in the RSFSR only on 1 October. Three plans (Abalkin, Shatalin and Aganbegyan) were all presented to the USSR Supreme Soviet for approval but were all rejected on 24 September 1990. The USSR Supreme Soviet then empowered Gorbachev to prepare a single programme known as the 'Basic Guidelines for the stabilisation of the national economy and the transition to a market economy', which was conceptually far nearer to the government (Abalkin) plan and which was approved by the USSR Supreme Soviet on 15 October and then became official government policy. This effectively brought the Russian government (which had delayed its proposal to implement its own plan based on the Shatalin plan to 1 November) into direct conflict with the Soviet government.

Yavlinsky resigned as deputy premier of the Russian Republic in protest, arguing that the Gorbachev stabilisation programme and the Russian 500–day plan could not coexist on the same territory.

The distinguishing economic feature of the Abalkin plan was its continued emphasis on measures to reduce inflationary overhang including a fiscal and monetary squeeze and price liberalisation which were scheduled to commence in 1990 before other measures designed to improve the supply side of the economy (including privatisation and destatisation) got under way. The Shatalin plan was a radical, highly detailed programme for the rapid transition to a full market economy, with vastly reduced powers not just for the state but for Soviet institutions themselves, which was to be achieved within 500 days (Shatalin 1990; see also Lavigne 1991b; Jeffries 1992; *European Economy* 1990). Its critical distinguishing features were the speed and sequencing of the transition process; the nature of the relationship between the republics and Soviet authorities and the strength of commitment to a free market economy based on private initiative. The most radical political feature of the Shatalin plan was its almost minimalist concept of the role of the Soviet Union itself. The underlying concept was that of an economic union of independent republics with common external tariffs and customs, which would maintain a single currency and a two-tier banking system with an independent central bank modelled on the USA federal reserve system. The republics should have the sole authority to raise taxes and would decide on the criteria for allocating revenues to the central budget to finance (external) defence policy, state-wide social welfare programmes, statistical services, etc. Federal authorities would also be responsible for the management of power supplies, nuclear power, telecommunications and pure research. Republican authorities would control their own mineral wealth and resources and property awaiting privatisation. Republican law would take precedence over Soviet law.

The plan also contained a detailed, itemised timetable for the transition to a market economy. The Shatalin plan proposed that measures for privatisation and liberalisation would be introduced at the same time as (and would therefore contribute to) macroeconomic stabilisation. The first hundred days of the programme (to the end of 1990) were to be devoted to enacting the legislation for reform, some smaller-scale privatisation of small businesses, retail outlets, cafes, restaurants, hotels, etc., and sales of housing which it was hoped would both mop up some of the inflationary overhang and create an immediate improvement in supplies, helping to win support for the programme in the initial stages. The programme of macrostabilisation would be completed in the first 250 days. There would be no growth of the money supply in 1991 and the budget deficit would be reduced to 2.5 per cent of GDP in 1990 and eliminated altogether in 1991, which would be achieved by the elimination of virtually all enterprise subsidies and by major cuts in government expenditure on foreign aid, defence and the KGB, and cuts in investment. There would be a rapid liberalisation of wholesale prices (except fuel and raw materials) and state retail prices for 75–80 per cent of household goods (virtually all goods except basic necessities) would be liberalised by the end of 1991. Rapid privatisation of large-scale industry would be concentrated in the 250–500 day period, so that 70 per cent of large-scale industry would have been privatised by day 500.

The strengths of the Shatalin proposals lay firstly in their de facto recognition that the Union was already in the process of disintegration and that it was necessary to transfer greater authority to the republics, if only to prevent an accelerated collapse and to preserve some elements of Union authority where this was desirable. Secondly, the establishment of a detailed timetable did at least cope with the problem of continued delay and debate that had bedevilled earlier reform proposals and which resulted in the coexistence of hybrid systems. Its sheer speed, however, was also a weakness as it seems impossible that privatisation of large-scale industry could be completed in such a short period.

## GORBACHEV'S ATTEMPTED COMPROMISE

The Abalkin plan and the Presidential Guidelines were by comparison far less radical documents. Both wished to preserve a strong role for the Union government with a single currency, a single market with a Union budget funded by federal taxes but with some tax authority devolved to the republics. Union ownership and control would be maintained over energy production and distribution, transport, communications, defence production and defence installations. Both plans aimed at achieving macroeconomic stabilisation before liberalisation and privatisation. This was to be achieved by reducing the budget deficit by a combination of cuts in expenditure on defence and the KGB and on investment and enterprise subsidies. Wholesale prices would be liberalised, but retail prices would be subject to an administered price increase and would then be held constant throughout 1992, before being determined by market forces. Pensions would be 100 per cent indexed but wages and salaries would only be indexed by 70 per cent according to the Presidential Guidelines (as in the Shatalin plan and against 100 per cent in the Abalkin plan) to reduce the threat of a hyper-inflationary wage–price spiral. The sections on privatisation in both plans were not very specific, referring to multiple forms of ownership and appearing to place greater emphasis on destatisation as on private ownership, per se.

## THE DETERIORATION OF ECONOMIC PERFORMANCE IN 1991

The failure by the leadership both to recognise the seriousness of the economic problems facing the Soviet Union and to implement a consistent economic programme was a major factor contributing to the collapse in economic performance in 1991, which combined an accelerated fall in output with incipient hyperinflationary pressures as the government lost control over the central budget and the money supply. These problems were aggravated by the arbitrary stabilisation measures introduced by the new premier, Valentin Pavlov, who was one of the original participants in the attempted coup.

According to official statistics National Income fell by 10 per cent in the first quarter of 1991, accelerating to 12 per cent in the first six months, and 13 per cent for the first nine months and 15 per cent for the year as a whole. The fall in output was widespread with official statistics recording falls for 127 out of 156 reporting products in the first six months. Industrial output fell by 17.8 per cent and agricultural production by 17 per cent. Energy production was badly affected with oil and coal production both falling by 10 per cent, contributing to domestic energy shortages and export shortages (see Chapter 8). Although production of consumer goods only fell by 4.5 per cent, the total is biased upwards by the growth of alcohol production (which grew by 5 per cent, with spirits up by 10 per cent) while food production fell by 8.8 per cent and production of industrial consumer goods by 8.1 per cent. The reduction in imported consumer goods (see Chapter 9) resulted in a fall in consumption of 13 per cent.

Supply problems contributed to the growing disequilibrium in the consumer sector, which resulted in accelerating inflationary pressures as the government failed to control demand and income growth accelerated. Two emergency measures to stabilise the retail sector were implemented in the Spring of 1991. Firstly, all 100 and 50 rouble notes were recalled, with citizens only allowed the right to change small amounts if they could not explain how they obtained them. This measure was theoretically aimed at confiscating the incomes of black marketeers who operated in large denomination notes, many of whom were rumoured to have anticipated the measure and reduced their holdings of large denomination notes. Secondly, price rises for basic products, including food in state stores, were implemented on 2 April. These were officially estimated as equivalent to an increase in the cost of living of 70 per cent, but were reported as being equivalent to at least a doubling of prices (Khanin 1991: 17). Money incomes were increased by an average of 69 per cent and personal savings in the State Savings Bank were supplemented by compensation accounts that could not be drawn on in the short term. Price increases for the year as a whole were officially given as 96 per cent for the state retail network and 140 per cent for the economy as a whole, including free markets.

Although these measures helped to reduce the level of consumer subsidies and increased the relative price level for basic goods purchased in the state network, they failed to eliminate the underlying inflationary pressures as the government was unable to control either the money supply or the State budget deficit (as republican authorities failed to make their contributions to the state budget in addition to more generalised problems, of raising revenue as the tax base was eroded). Furthermore, confiscatory measures and the fear of future price increases destroyed any remaining confidence in the rouble. The Union budget deficit for 1991 was estimated at 150 billion roubles or between 12–14 per cent of GNP compared with 4 per cent in 1990. Additional cash in circulation (new emissions) increased by 4.8 times to 127.3 billion roubles. Credit investments doubled to 762 billion roubles. Total money incomes of the population grew by 89.8 per cent from

654.4 billion roubles in 1990 to 1,242.2 billion in 1991. Incomes exceeded consumer expenditure by 281.3 billion roubles or 23 per cent of income for the year as a whole. By 1 January 1992 personal savings in the State Savings Bank amounted to 526.7 billion roubles or 656.7 billion roubles including compensation accounts (see below) and total savings, cash bonds and other personal securities were estimated at 976 billion roubles. (Statistics in this section from Ekonomika i Zhizn 1991: nos 5, 17, 44, and 1992: no 6.)

## CONCLUSION

The Soviet economy had entered the stage of accelerated collapse by the time of the collapse of the Soviet Union itself at the end of 1991. While the institutions that manipulated the visible hand of central planning had lost authority and had effectively ceased to function, they had not been replaced by the invisible hand of the market. Although suppressed inflation became open inflation during the course of 1991, latent inflationary pressures were not brought under control. The growing loss of confidence in the monetary system contributed to the deterioration in inter-republican trade as republics increasingly failed to meet contracted deliveries outside their own territory. Given the highly monopolistic and interrelated structure of Soviet industry this created bottlenecks which had a multiplied (downward) effect on production.

# Chapter 7

# The reform of foreign economic relations under Gorbachev

## GORBACHEV'S INHERITANCE: THE BACKGROUND TO TRADE STRATEGY

It was shown in Chapters 4 and 5 that Soviet economic growth in the late 1970s and early 1980s was constrained by the inability to generate a sufficient volume of hard currency exports to finance the level of imports of machinery and equipment which were necessary for industrial modernisation and capital formation, foodstuffs which were largely required to compensate for deficiencies in the structure of agriculture and food distribution, and consumer goods which were required to stabilise the domestic market.

Despite these pressures the Soviet Union had pursued a relatively conservative borrowing policy in international financial markets and had avoided the indebtedness problems that had beset the East European economies in the early 1980s as a result of the failure of the import-led growth strategy, which required them to make substantial cuts in their imports from the industrialised West in the early 1980s as credit facilities were withdrawn. Soviet gross hard currency debt was estimated by the OECD at $23 billion ($12 billion net of Soviet assets in western banks) at the end of 1984, a figure that was considered to be moderate in relation to the country's earning capacity, by many western bankers.

The Soviet Union had been protected from the full impact of its inability to export manufactured goods for hard currency during the latter half of the Brezhnev era by the 13-fold increase in world oil prices between 1973 and 1984 and the doubling of oil exports to the OECD over this period. However, the cost of the strategy of developing the energy sector and energy exports was increasingly attacked by Soviet economists. The energy sector absorbed 30.1 per cent of industrial investment and 10.5 per cent of all investment in the economy during the tenth five-year plan (1976–80) rising to 36.2 per cent and 12.9 per cent respectively in the 1981–85 plan period (Narkhoz 1917–87: 330). These figures exclude investment in pipelines and exploration (Gustafson 1989: 39) which, if added to the above, would take the share of energy investment to 38 per cent and 46 per cent of industrial investment in the 1976–80 and 1981–85 plan periods respectively. Not surprisingly this led to accusations that the development of the energy and the armaments sectors had contributed to the failure to modernise other industrial sectors (including machine tools and engineering), which in turn had contributed to the poor quality and low level of manufactured exports. More surprisingly, in view of its high priority, the oil industry did not receive a high priority for imported equipment and was forced to rely on domestic equipment, two-thirds of which was produced in the Baku region of Azerbaidzhan, which was the original major source of Soviet oil production. This equipment was the subject of constant complaints concerning low quality and its unsuitability to Siberian and Arctic conditions (Gustafson 1989: 189–93).

Relations with the West and with the USA in particular remained a major source of concern. The attitudes of the Reagan administration towards trade and economic relations with the Soviet Union in the wake of the Soviet invasion of Afghanistan in 1979 and the imposition of martial law in Poland in 1981 (for which it held the Soviet Union responsible) had increasingly been influenced by the concepts of linkage and economic warfare. Hanson (1988) has described this rationale in the following terms: the Soviet Union was seen as an inherently expansionist power whose foreign policy interests conflicted with those of the West. It was therefore prudent to limit the ability of this adversarial power to engage in measures that were inimical to western interests, by increasing the cost of those measures themselves (e.g. trade denial in response to specific policy measures which the West opposed, even if this also damaged Western economic interests) and by taking general economic measures which were designed to limit the economic and thus the military capacity of the Soviet Union to the greatest possible extent in relation to that of the West.

There was also a perception in the USA administration that the

Soviet Union in the last years of Brezhnev's life was increasingly isolating itself and its CMEA partners from economic contacts with the West (which was reflected in the decline in orders for western machinery and equipment in the late 1970s and early 1980s) and was limiting its purchases of equipment from the West to those that offered the greatest economic and military advantage (Kaufman 1991: 48–9). It was argued in Chapter 5, however, that the reduction in orders for western equipment did not result from a deliberate policy of favouring CMEA suppliers on strategic grounds, but from far more severe pressures on the hard currency balance of payments than were appreciated at the time. This was combined with the need to increase imports of machinery and equipment from Eastern Europe to balance intra-CMEA trade following the rising price of oil exports which the Soviet Union was contractually obliged to deliver.

US administrations attempted to utilise trade pressures to influence Soviet policy on three separate occasions in Brezhnev's last years. Firstly, President Carter placed an embargo on US grain exports (over and above deliveries included in long-term contracts) following the Soviet invasion of Afghanistan. In April 1991 President Reagan honoured a campaign pledge to lift the embargo on the grounds that it was causing greater damage to US farming interests than to the Soviet Union, which had found alternative (but more costly) sources of supply. Secondly, the Reagan administration focused its attention on western exports of technology to the Soviet Union, which it was argued made a greater contribution to Soviet growth and development than to western well-being. US policy initiatives in this respect were largely concentrated on tightening CoCom controls on the export of militarily useful technology and dual-use items that were civilian in origin but had potential military applications. In 1982 the US administration proposed, with limited success, to strengthen western export controls over a range of products including computers, fibre optics and other electronic goods (Bertsch and Elliot-Gower 1991a: 19). Finally, following the imposition of martial law in Poland, the US government imposed further trade sanctions on the Soviet Union, including the suspension of licences for the export of equipment for use in the oil and gas industry. In June 1982 this restriction was extended retrospectively to overseas subsidiaries of US firms and to foreign licensees of US firms. This effectively involved extra-territorial legislation to induce West European companies and subsidiaries to break existing contracts to supply compressor stations and large diameter pipes for the Urengoi pipeline project (Stern 1987: 33).

In practice, the Reagan administration had been exerting pressure on western governments and companies to deter them from participating in the construction of a major gas pipeline from Urengoi in western Siberia to Eastern and Western Europe before the imposition of martial law, on the grounds that the supply of Soviet natural gas to Western Europe (and particularly to the FRG) would lead to dependence on Soviet supplies which would limit the power (or willingness) of west European governments to take political and economic actions against the Soviet Union in the future. It was also felt that the supply of Soviet natural gas to Western Europe would enhance Soviet export earnings, which would be used to purchase technology from the West. It was also argued that US exports of grain to the Soviet Union would draw down Soviet hard currency earnings and limit purchases of technology, an argument that had been used in 1962–63 when the Kennedy administration was attempting to sell grain to the Soviet Union while simultaneously attempting to prevent west European participation in the construction of an oil pipeline which would have increased Soviet oil exports to the West (Stent 1981: 93–126).

The US government dropped its objections to West European participation in oil and gas projects in November 1982, following strong West European protests (and the death of Brezhnev), and Soviet imports of equipment for the gas industry rose from 5 million roubles in 1981 to 942 million in 1983 (Vneshtorg 1981, 1983) with Italy, the FRG and France the major western suppliers. This was not a major defeat for US foreign policy as West European governments agreed to strengthen controls over technology transfer and export credits to the USSR, which were both major US policy objectives and which significantly influenced the trade background against which Gorbachev came to power.

## GORBACHEV'S INITIAL TRADE STRATEGY

Gorbachev's advisers argued that Soviet participation in international trade was too low and was excessively dependent on exports of energy, raw materials and unprocessed goods. They also argued that Soviet imports were excessively biased towards grain and metal manufactures including pipelines, and that imported machinery and equipment were frequently inappropriate for Soviet conditions and were used wastefully (see Aganbegyan 1988: 141–56). This implied that the Soviet Union should both increase its level of participation in world trade and alter the structure of imports and exports. There was a growing appreciation that the problem extended beyond the level and structure of trade to the lack of openness of the economy, including the isolation of domestic producers from world markets and foreign competition, the lack of experience of Soviet managers and workers of foreign markets and work practices, the absence of foreign capital and investment in the Soviet economy, the inconvertibility of the currency, the separation of the domestic price system from the influence of world prices, the total lack of responsiveness of enterprises to changes in world market conditions, and the non-participation of the Soviet Union in international economic organisations which had been seen as tools of the capitalist international monetary system.

However, if the Soviet economy was to be integrated with the world economy, this would have to be achieved against a background of international mistrust and even hostility. The speeches of Gorbachev and Ryzhkov to the 27th Party Congress, in March 1986, gave no indication that they were considering a major opening up of the domestic economy to the capitalist West and placed greater emphasis on reducing Soviet and CMEA vulnerability to economic sanctions and trade embargoes. The prime minister, Ryzhkov, who was regarded by many radicals as a representative of heavy industry and the military–industrial complex, stressed the need to strengthen the world socialist system to 'increase our technical and economic invulnerability to imperialist actions' (*Pravda*, 4 March 1986). Gorbachev's opening speech to the Congress gave greater priority to the improvement of trade relations with the Third World (which he saw as a cheaper source of industrial components and consumer goods) than to trade relations with the industrialised West.

Ryzhkov's speech gave some clear indications of the trade strategy which was to facilitate the programme of acceleration. Firstly, he argued that it was necessary to 'change the raw material bias of exports' and stimulate the competitiveness of exports of manufactured goods, but admitted that this would take longer than a single five-year plan period. Secondly, he indicated that although the draft five-year plan implied a 'considerable expansion of economic relations ... directed towards scientific and technical progress ... cooperation with socialist states would be determinant in this respect.' (*Pravda*, 4 March 1986). He also confirmed his faith in Soviet science and technology, praising the 'outstanding achievements of the USSR Academy of Sciences' and attributing the poor performance of Soviet equipment to the 'headlong pursuit of imported technology'. Ministerial officials displayed 'remarkable activity in obtaining machinery and equipment from abroad, which could be ... produced by our own efforts ... which had a demoralising effect on our own scientists'.

This did not mean that the Soviet Union intended to cut itself off from western technology, but involved a shift in emphasis in the structure of imports of machinery and equipment away from budget allocations to large-spending ministries (which were used to overcome short-term bottlenecks) towards an import policy that was geared towards overcoming longer-term strategic economic problems and industrial modernisation. The policy of acceleration also required greater emphasis on investment in the machine tools industry and on the modernisation of plant and equipment in place of expenditure on large-scale civil engineering projects and complete installations, leading to a switch in emphasis to a greater number of imports of smaller items of machinery and equipment within a given value of imports.

However, the state monopoly of foreign trade was largely designed to cope with a centrally determined import and export structure, concentrated on a small number of relatively homogeneous products, and was ill-suited to implement a more diverse structure of imports and exports. Firstly, if machinery and equipment imports were to be geared towards the technical modernisation of existing plants, end-user enterprises would need to play a far greater role in selecting and determining the technical specifications of imported equipment. Secondly, economic comparisons between domestic equipment and foreign equipment and estimates of the rate of return on investment in energy or labour-saving equipment would require more rational methods for comparing domestic and international production costs and for assessing the real cost of earning foreign exchange.

## REFORMS TO THE FOREIGN TRADE SYSTEM UNDER GORBACHEV

Gorbachev's reforms to the foreign trade system incorporated three major aspects: administrative and structural reforms to the operation of the foreign trade system; measures to rationalise the system of exchange rates with the ultimate goal of introducing a form of convertibility and measures to attract foreign investment, including legislation to permit the establishment of joint ventures on Soviet territory and the introduction of free enterprise zones. In addition, a series of diplomatic initiatives directed towards improving Soviet relations with (and ultimately membership of) international economic organisations including the IMF and GATT were undertaken.

The reform of foreign trade relations, which ran in parallel with domestic economic reforms, also involved a progressive radicalisation of the reform debate and major gaps between proposals to reform the foreign trade system, the ensuing legislation and its implementation. Attempts to reform the foreign trade system were also conducted against a background of deteriorating terms of trade and an escalating hard currency crisis. The conduct of reforms to the foreign trade sector supports the argument that Gorbachev and the Soviet authorities were forced to undertake progressively more radical reforms (and ad hoc adjustments) to the trade system as a result of bureaucratic resistance to the reform process and the failure of the reforms as originally conceived to overcome the problems confronting the Soviet economy, rather than as a result of the implementation of a deliberate strategy. It is also important to note that many of the reforms which are discussed below, which created greater powers for some enterprises and other local bodies to conduct foreign trade relations, operated in conjunction with the old centralised system, not as an immediate and comprehensive replacement for the old system.

## THE FIRST PHASE OF REFORMS

Initial legislation, which was enacted on 19 August 1986, was subsequently published as a resolution of the Central Committee and the Council of Ministers entitled 'On measures to improve the management of foreign trade' *Ekonomicheskaya Gazeta* 1987, no. 4),

which came into effect on 1 January 1987. The basic logic of the
proposals was to introduce more efficient methods of economic
management into the existing trade system and to weaken the
control of the planning bureaucracy by introducing major
changes to the structure of administration and organisation of
foreign trade.

This involved the creation of a super-ministry (directly
responsible to the USSR Council of Ministers) called the State
Foreign Economic Commission, which was responsible for
coordinating the work of all state bodies involved in foreign trade.
This was a major downgrading of the authority of the Ministry of
Foreign Trade, which was also deprived of its sole right to conduct
foreign trade relations, which were decentralised to 21 industrial
ministries and 70 large enterprises, predominantly in the areas of
machine tools and chemicals, which absorbed the appropriate
FTOs. At the same time, retention quotas were introduced which
allowed enterprises to retain specified proportions of their hard
currency earnings for their own use, instead of surrendering them
in their entirety to the state budget. Hard currency was held on
the enterprises behalf by the foreign trade bank which, however,
frequently did not release it to the enterprise until a year had
elapsed. The Ministry of Foreign Trade retained control over
trade in fuel and raw materials, foodstuffs and 'other goods of
statewide significance' (including arms sales). Consequently the
major sources of hard currency earnings remained centralised
and enterprises remained heavily dependent on central
allocations of hard currency to conduct imports.

A resolution of the Council of Ministers was also passed on 13
January 1987, permitting the establishment on Soviet territory of
joint ventures involving the participation of firms from western
and developing countries (details of which were published in
*Pravda* on 27 January 1987). This made the Soviet Union the last
CMEA country (except East Germany) to permit joint ventures on
its territory. In practice, the legislation was more restrictive and
less attractive to western partners than legislation that had been
introduced in Poland and Hungary. Surprisingly, Soviet joint
venture legislation bore more similarities to Romanian legislation
which was first enacted in 1972 and which had only succeeded in
attracting a total of six joint ventures.

Firstly, all joint ventures had to be approved by the USSR
Council of Ministers. Secondly, the Soviet share in the joint

venture had to be a minimum of 51 per cent. Thirdly, the chairman of the board and the enterprise director had to be Soviet citizens. Fourthly, the enterprise would be detached from the internal Soviet planning process. Although this meant that it would not receive compulsory plan targets or state orders, it also meant that the enterprise would experience major difficulties in obtaining inputs from Soviet suppliers and in selling finished or intermediate goods on the Soviet market. Relations with the domestic Soviet suppliers and receivers were to be organised through FTOs and would be conducted at 'agreed' prices which took world market conditions into account (which would then be converted into roubles at the official exchange rate), not domestic prices. Finally, the enterprise would operate with separate accounts for transactions in hard currencies (lodged with Vneshekonombank) and in roubles (lodged with the State Bank). The western partner could only repatriate profits (after payment of additional taxes) out of its share of profits which accumulated in hard currency from exports. As profits designated in roubles could not be converted into western currencies and could only be used to make limited purchases in the Soviet market, these offered no real economic benefit to western partners. The Soviet authorities also firmly indicated that they were not willing to consider sales to the Soviet market which substituted for hard currency purchases as 'hard currency earnings', despite representations from western companies who felt that import substitution provided the best prospects for mutually advantageous trade. Soviet economists insisted that the hard currency rules were principally designed to ensure that the produce of joint ventures met world market specifications and to prevent them from being equipped with obsolete technology. Many western firms, however, felt that this indicated that the Soviet authorities were primarily interested in establishing joint ventures which would stimulate hard currency exports and not in satisfying the domestic market and/or creating competition for domestic producers.

These arrangements put the western partner at a considerable disadvantage. At worst it appeared that the western partner would have to put its trust in the Soviet management of the venture to negotiate questions concerning the quantity, quality and price of inputs, and possible markets for outputs in the Soviet Union with monopolistic/monopsonistic Soviet organisations who had little incentive to meet the demands of either the venture or the domestic market. Many of the major western companies operating in the Soviet market were primarily involved in large-scale engineering projects and were principally interested in expanding sales to the Soviet Union, not in establishing production bases in the Soviet Union for export to the West. Finally, the lack of western control over such factors as manning levels, and the prices and quality of inputs and outputs, meant that Soviet joint ventures offered western partners a far less easily controlled and less competitive environment than wholly owned subsidiaries in many Third World countries.

It was clear from discussions with senior Soviet officials immediately following the publication of the law that they regarded this legislation as complete in itself and not as a framework for further negotiation with western partners on a case by case basis. Despite claims in the Soviet press that large numbers of western companies were interested in establishing joint ventures, only 23 ventures with a total (Soviet and foreign) capital value of 159 million roubles were established in 1987 (IMF *et al.* 1991, vol. 2: 102) and modifications to the legislation to make joint ventures more attractive to western partners were announced in September 1987. These modifications, inter alia, decentralised the right to approve a joint venture to individual Ministries at the all-Union or republican level, allowed joint ventures to operate through the internal supply system (Gossnab) instead of through the FTOs, extended the range covered by joint ventures to services, and facilitated accounting in hard currency for import substitutes.

## THE ACCELERATION OF REFORMS TO THE FOREIGN TRADE SYSTEM

An acceleration of the reforms to the foreign trade system, in line with the radicalisation of domestic economic reforms announced at the June 1987 Plenum, was already under way. Aganbegyan (1988: 155) indicates that radical proposals for the long-term introduction of full currency convertibility were discussed at the June 1987 Plenum. The reforms to the foreign trade system continued to reflect the reforms to the domestic planning system in that they attempted to combine elements of the old centralised system (now reflected in state orders for exports) with greater autonomy for enterprises to determine their participation in foreign trade over and above these levels. It was also hoped that greater openness to foreign trade, including the right of co-operatives to conduct foreign trade and giving greater scope to joint ventures would expose state enterprises to international competition (Sutela 1991: 152). The most obvious initial changes, however, involved a further restructuring of the administrative apparatus and a wholesale turnover of personnel involved in foreign trade. Dissatisfaction with the operation of the Ministry of Foreign Trade was frequently expressed in the Soviet press, and tensions between the new technocrats from the Foreign Economic Commission and the older personnel in FTOs and trade missions overseas were obvious to anyone who attended meetings involving Soviet trade officials in the early Gorbachev years.

On 17 January 1988 the Ministry for Foreign Trade and the State Committee for Foreign Economic Relations (GKES) were formally merged into a single unit known as the USSR Ministry for Foreign Economic Relations (MVES), which was headed by Konstantin Katushev, who had been the Chairman of GKES since 1986. The new ministry remained subsidiary to the State Foreign Economic Commission. Geron (1990: 19–20) argues that this amounted to the abolition of the Ministry of Foreign Trade and involved the loss of 5,000 jobs. Bykov (1991: 38) views the changes more charitably as a merger, which was (unsuccessfully) intended to overcome administrative duplication. Following the reorgan-isation, the new ministry administered the work of 25 FTOs responsible for 70 per cent of exports and 50 per cent of imports. At the same time (as part of the banking reforms introduced in January 1988) the State Foreign Trade Bank (Vneshtorgbank) was renamed the State Bank for Foreign Economic Relations (Vneshekonombank) but retained its monopoly over transactions in foreign currency and extended its functions to include the supervision of foreign currency operations of enterprises, including granting foreign currency credits and the management of foreign currency receipts.

Further administrative changes were approved by the USSR Council of Ministers on 2 December 1988, as part of a more radical set of proposals to move from the administrative regulation of foreign trade towards the greater use of economic measures that involved the gradual introduction of limited forms of convertibility and the gradual exposure of domestic enterprises to world market prices. In practice, these reforms foundered on the inability or unwillingness to reform the domestic price system. The most significant change introduced by the decree (which was published in *Vneshnyaya Torgovlya* 1989, no. 2) was the extension of the right to conduct foreign trade operations to all enterprises, associations and co-operatives from 1 April 1989, subject to the granting of a licence by the Ministry for Foreign Economic Relations. Although the legislation resulted in a major expansion of the number of organisations empowered to conduct foreign trade (14,000 licences had been granted by the end of 1989), direct budget allocations of hard currency to ministries and other organisations which were not held financially responsible for the efficient use of imports still remained the predominant method of financing imports in 1990–91, resulting in the continual wastage of hard currency on unutilised equipment (Bykov 1991: 39). Licensed organisations could conduct import and export operations either through specially created independent foreign trade firms or through other specialised trade intermediaries on the basis of 'self-recoupment' in foreign currency and on the understanding that the state was not responsible for their obligations. Organisations could also obtain hard currency credits to finance investments and to support current operations that required hard currency expenditure, provided that these would be recouped and repaid by the receipts from hard currency revenues in the (strictly specified) future. The Council of Ministers and the State Foreign Economic Commission also maintained quotas on items whose import and export was either banned or restricted on economic or political grounds.

The efficient decentralisation of foreign trade decisions to enterprises and co-operatives required that the latter should be able to make an accurate comparison of domestic production costs and scarcities with world market prices, which meant that domestic prices needed to reflect relative domestic production costs and scarcities, and the rate of exchange needed to be set at the level which would balance the supply and demand for foreign exchange in the aggregate. Under these circumstances domestic producers could be left to choose to export goods that were relatively cheap to produce at home and to import goods that were relatively expensive to produce domestically. The more open and exposed an economy is to international competition, the more domestic relative prices will resemble world market prices as international competition drives out high-cost domestic producers and low-cost domestic producers seek more profitable foreign markets. The entirely arbitrary nature of Soviet wholesale prices and exchange rates meant that central controls and regulation needed to be maintained over exports and imports that had been nominally decentralised, in order to prevent enterprises from attempting to profit from differences between domestic and world market prices, that did not reflect genuine differences in costs (e.g. the subsidisation of energy, which made exports of energy-intensive goods appear profitable).

Arbitrary differences between the structure of Soviet relative prices and world market prices also meant that a single exchange rate could not be used to evaluate the profitability of imports and exports. To combat this a system known as differentiated valuation coefficients (DVKs) had been introduced at the time of the introduction of the first limited decentralisation of foreign trade rights in 1987, to convert exports and imports of goods traded in world markets into domestic roubles for purposes of enterprise accounting. The system applied only to decentralised trade (chiefly exports of manufactured and engineering goods) while the preisausgleich system continued to operate for centralised trade which still involved the majority of imports as well as exports of raw materials and some manufactured goods. Manufactured goods traded on a decentralised basis were converted from foreign exchange roubles into domestic prices by ratios that reportedly ranged from 0.1 to 15.9. Provided that the system was operated efficiently, this should have allowed the state budget to continue to appropriate the rental earnings resulting from differences between domestic production costs and world market prices. The system became exceedingly complicated, however, as exporting enterprises attempted to negotiate favourable coefficients and the number of coefficients increased from 1,600 at the beginning of 1987 to 10,000 in 1988 (IMF *et al.* 1991, vol. 2: 47).

The system would have been unable to cope with the extension of decentralised trading rights to all enterprises and co-operatives, which would have necessitated the estimation of an exceedingly large number of coefficients. The decree of December 1988 proposed to overcome this in the long term by the gradual introduction of limited rouble convertibility (article 38), while Vneshekonombank was instructed to organise currency auctions whereby enterprises or co-operatives would be able to bid for hard currency by payment in roubles (article 16). This measure, however, would only help to address the problem of the artificial exchange rate of the rouble, not that of the irrationality of the domestic relative prices, which was a far greater barrier to the genuine decentralisation of trade. This was effectively admitted by article 12 of the decree, which proposed to 'change over to the use of a new exchange rate in settlements in convertible currencies beginning from 1 January 1991', which was the date then scheduled for the introduction of new wholesale prices. In the interim, article 13 proposed to 'abandon the application of differentiated currency coefficients' and, before the new rate came into force, to apply from '1 January 1990 a 100 per cent addition to the exchange rate of hard currency to the rouble'. This proposal, as western observers indicated at the time, was ambiguous. Lavigne argued that the most logical interpretation of the legislation was that the Soviet authorities intended to replace DVKs at the beginning of 1990 with a single coefficient that was double the rate of the existing official exchange rate (similar to a devaluation of 50 per cent), which would provide enterprises with a greater incentive to export and to cut back on imports than that provided by the existing overvalued exchange rate (see Lavigne 1991a: 143–51). This was to be a stepping stone to the introduction of a single exchange rate in 1991, the level of which would be in part determined by the experience of currency auctions.

This scheme suffered from two major drawbacks. Firstly, would the implicit devaluation of 50 per cent be sufficient to stimulate exports? Secondly, the problem of irrational relative prices would remain if a single coefficient were to be introduced before domestic price reforms had been initiated. Unless the Soviet authorities were willing to contemplate substantial foreign exchange losses as part of the price that had to be paid for arriving at a rational domestic price structure linked to world market prices, the central authorities would be required to re-impose export controls on goods that were priced too cheaply on domestic markets or to impose import controls, or selective tariffs, on goods that were overpriced on the domestic market.

In practice, the authorities issued decrees in March and December of 1989 imposing export and import licences for a wide range of goods (Geron 1990: 25) and DVKs remained in force until November 1990, when they were abolished as part of the

Presidential guidelines of 26 October 1990 which replaced them with four separate exchange rates. Firstly, the official exchange rate remained at what was by that time a highly overvalued rate of 1 rouble being equivalent to $1.79. This rate was still to be used for official statistical purposes and, more critically, for evaluating Third World debt to the Soviet Union, which was denominated in roubles, where a devaluation could have had the effect of depreciating the real value of Soviet claims. Secondly, a new commercial rate of 1 rouble to $0.56 was introduced from 1 November 1990 to replace DVKs in enterprise accounting as outlined above. This rate was established at a level that made the world market price for over 90 per cent of exports higher than the domestic wholesale price, to provide an incentive to exporters (IMF *et al.* 1991, vol. 1: 426). At the same time, import taxes were reduced and export taxes were imposed on raw materials to compensate for subsidies and irrationalities in domestic wholesale prices. Thirdly, the rate for personal transactions for Soviet and non-Soviet citizens (tourist rate) of 1 rouble to $0.18, which had been introduced in October 1989, remained in force. This had been introduced largely to undermine black market operations, including those whereby Soviet citizens with the freedom to travel abroad used the possibility to exchange roubles into hard currency at the official exchange rate to buy consumer durables which were resold in the domestic market at substantially higher prices. Although this rate nominally made the majority of Soviet goods very cheap to western tourists, the impact of this was reduced by the necessity for western visitors to conduct the majority of personal transactions in hard currency. Finally, hard currency auctions remained where the rouble was exchanged for between $0.03 and $0.05. The presidential decree extended the right to trade in currency auctions (or to buy from banks at the effective auction rate) to all enterprises and co-operatives from 1 January 1991. The auction rate, however, was a highly marginal (thin) rate which reflected the oversupply of roubles in relation to the supply of goods in the domestic retail market and the virtual absence of wholesale and capital markets. Consequently, the auction rate did not reflect the value of the nation's land and natural resources or capital stock, which could not be bought for roubles. This factor posed a major question about the ability to sustain the commercial rate over the long term.

## REVISIONS TO JOINT VENTURE REGULATIONS

The decree of December 1988 also contained specific measures to make joint ventures more attractive to western partners, which indicated that the Soviet authorities had paid considerable attention to complaints from potential western partners. The most significant measure was the abolition of the requirement that the Soviet partner(s) had to hold a majority share and that participation levels should be determined by the agreement of the parties concerned. Similarly, the requirement that the chairman of the board of the venture and the enterprise director had to be Soviet citizens was rescinded. The joint venture was also granted greater powers of hiring and firing, which gave Soviet workers in joint ventures (who frequently earned 2–3 times the average wage) less security and rights over management than workers in Soviet enterprises. Other, more technical concessions included improved tax breaks for foreign investors and permission for foreign employees of joint ventures to pay for housing and other services in Soviet roubles instead of hard currency. Finally, the legislation made additional tax concessions to attract joint ventures to the Soviet Far East.

Despite these concessions and the publicity given to some high profile agreements, joint ventures made only a marginal contribution to the Soviet economy, contributing to less than one half of one per cent of GNP in 1990. By June 1990 a total of 1,754 joint ventures had been registered with a starting capital of 4 billion roubles, of which it is estimated that 40 per cent consisted of foreign contributions, a quarter of which was in the form of hard currency. Between a third and half of ventures had started operating by June 1990, employing a total of 62,532 workers. Only 8 ventures employed more than 1,000 workers and the majority had less than 50 employees. Furthermore, the average size and capital value of joint ventures continued to fall during 1989 and 1990, particularly as co-operatives established a number of relatively small-scale ventures. Only 285 ventures were operating in industry with personal computer production and programming and construction the most important sectors (IMF *et al.* 1991, vol. 1: 76, and 102–5, Bykov 1991: 41). Approximately half of joint ventures were registered in Moscow, reflecting the preponderance of low capital ventures servicing the tourist industry and foreign businesses. Joint ventures were heavily concentrated in the Russian republic, followed by the Baltic Republics. The creation of free economic zones (the first of which were approved by the Russian Supreme Soviet in July 1990) was intended to create greater incentives to attract foreign investors to both border and inland regions apart from Moscow but has been of limited economic impact. The relative lack of success in attracting foreign investment stimulated the announcement in the Presidential decree of 26 October 1990 establishing the possibility of 100 per cent foreign ownership. However, the major anxiety felt by potential foreign investors concerns the political stability of the region more than the more mundane questions of ownership and taxation.

## CONCLUSION

Gorbachev's attempts to open the economy to foreign investment through the creation of joint ventures and free enterprise zones were limited in concept and gradualist in implementation. Attempts to decentralise foreign trade decisions to the enterprise level, without at the very least exposing them to either domestic or international competition, hard budget constraints and scarcity prices failed to generate the sustained development of manufacturing industries that was required to reduce Soviet dependence on exports of energy and raw materials.

# Chapter 8

# Problems in exporting under Gorbachev

## THE NEED TO REDUCE DEPENDENCE ON ENERGY EXPORTS

The need to reduce Soviet dependence on energy exports was made more urgent by three critical factors in the first fourteen months of Mr Gorbachev's tenure of office. Firstly, a major fall in Soviet crude oil output, which started in the first quarter of 1985 (just before Gorbachev came to power), resulted in production falling by 18 million tonnes in 1985 to 595 million tonnes (compared with a five-year plan target of 620–645 million tonnes). Secondly, the world market price of crude oil collapsed from an average of $27 a barrel in 1985 to $14 a barrel in 1986. Finally, the accident at the Chernobyl nuclear power station in April 1986 raised serious doubts about the safety of maintaining production in similar graphite-moderated nuclear reactors (which accounted for 58.6 per cent of existing nuclear capacity and approximately 5 per cent of electric power generation in the European republics of the Soviet Union) and the planned expansion of nuclear power (from 28,000 megawatts in 1986 to 69,000 in 1990), which was intended to meet two-thirds of the increased demand for electricity over the five-year plan period so that oil could be diverted from power generation to exports.

The impact of falling world oil prices was far more serious (and far less amenable to domestic solutions) than falling production, particularly as the marginal cost of Siberian oil was substantially higher than the world average cost of oil production, which raised questions about the long-term profitability of Soviet oil production in a satiated world market. This was aggravated by the Soviet Union's position as a marginal supplier of crude oil to western markets, heavily dependent on sales in spot markets which were more volatile than supplies based on longer-term contracts. By April 1986 Urals crude oil was trading at only $12.60 a barrel on west European spot markets. At the 1986 level of net exports for hard currency (54 million tonnes) each dollar fall in the price of a barrel of Soviet oil cost the Soviet Union $400 million directly in lost hard currency revenue. In addition, the Soviet Union suffered from a deterioration in its terms of trade with Finland (who imported 13 million tonnes of crude oil and products from the Soviet Union), India (5 million tonnes) and Yugoslavia (6 million tonnes) with whom it traded on a bilateral (clearing) basis. The net effect on the terms of trade was equivalent to an additional indirect cost of approximately $150 million for each dollar per barrel fall in the oil price. Finally, a significant proportion of Soviet oil imports from OPEC countries (which were directly re-exported and have been netted off in the above estimates) was made as repayment for arms deliveries made on credit. As these countries could not boost export volumes to the Soviet Union to compensate for falling prices, the Soviet Union effectively lost a further $100 million in hard currency earnings for each dollar fall in the oil price. In sum, therefore, each dollar fall in the price of a barrel of oil cost the Soviet Union directly and indirectly approximately $650 million. In addition, the fall in the world market price of oil also contributed to a fall in the price of natural gas, the other major source of Soviet hard currency earnings, and by affecting the revenues of Middle-Eastern importers of Soviet arms, reduced their ability to service arms-related debt denominated in hard currency.

## ENERGY EXPORTS TO THE INDUSTRIALISED WEST 1985-91

Soviet trade balances with the industrialised West and developing countries from 1984–90 are summarised in Table 8.1. The major features of Soviet production and exports of oil (1985–90) and gas (1985–91) are shown in Tables 8.2 and 8.3. Estimates of the commodity structure of Soviet exports to non-socialist countries are shown in Table 8.4 and an estimate of the commodity structure of Soviet exports for convertible currency for the period 1984–90 measured in $US is shown in Table 8.5. The fall in the value of Soviet hard currency exports measured in roubles is

*Table 8.1*    Soviet trade with non-socialist countries 1984–89
(million roubles)

|  | 1984 | 1985 | 1986 | 1987 | 1988 | 1989 |
|---|---|---|---|---|---|---|
| **Exports** | 32,277 | 28,196 | 22,686 | 23,942 | 24,231 | 26,515 |
| **Imports** | 27,107 | 26,937 | 20,748 | 18,620 | 21,667 | 27,483 |
| balance | +5,170 | +1,259 | +1,940 | +5,322 | +2,567 | −969 |
| **Trade with industrialised West:** | | | | | | |
| Exports | 21,349 | 18,581 | 13,136 | 14,186 | 14,666 | 16,392 |
| Imports | 19,574 | 19,294 | 15,853 | 13,873 | 16,320 | 20,497 |
| balance | +1,775 | −713 | −2,717 | +313 | −1,646 | −4,105 |
| **Trade with developing countries** | | | | | | |
| Exports | 10,928 | 9,615 | 9,551 | 9,757 | 9,567 | 10,122 |
| Imports | 7,533 | 7,643 | 4,894 | 4,747 | 5,346 | 6,986 |
| balance | +3,395 | +1,972 | +4,657 | +5,010 | +4,221 | +3,136 |
| LDC residual | | | | | | |
| | 5,613 | 4,289 | 5,451 | 5,308 | 5,294 | 5,528 |
| Overall balance minus residual | | | | | | |
| | −443 | −3,030 | −3,511 | +14 | −2,727 | −6,497 |

*Sources:* Estimated from Vneshtorg (various years).
*Note:* Components to not sum to totals due to rounding.

considerably more severe than the fall in the value of exports measured in dollars because of the appreciation of the official rouble exchange rate against the dollar over the period up to 1989, which in turn largely reflects the depreciation of the dollar against European currencies including the Deutschmark. As the majority of Soviet imports of machinery and equipment were purchased in western Europe in European currencies, the value of energy exports expressed in roubles provides an indication of the fall in Soviet purchasing power in European markets, resulting from the combination of falling oil prices and dollar depreciation.

The major burden of equating supply and demand for Soviet oil following the fall in output in 1985 fell on exports to the OECD (including Finland) which were cut by 14 million tonnes to 67 million tonnes, resulting in a fall in the value of Soviet exports of crude oil and products to the OECD from 13.6 billion roubles ($16.6 billion) in 1984 to 10.6 billion roubles ($12.7 billion) in

*Table 8.2*   Soviet oil production and trade 1985–90 (million tonnes)

|  | 1985 | 1986 | 1987 | 1988 | 1989 | 1990 |
|---|---|---|---|---|---|---|
| **Production** | **595** | **615** | **624** | **624** | **607** | **570** |
| **Exports total** | **167** | **186** | **196** | **205** | **184** | **159** |
| Crude | 117 | 129 | 137 | 144 | 127 | 109 |
| Products | 50 | 57 | 59 | 61 | 57 | 50 |
| **Exports for** | | | | | | |
| **hard currency** | **60** | **69** | **76** | **90** | **62** | **68** |
| Crude | 29 | 32 | 38 | 49 | 27 | 35 |
| Products | 31 | 37 | 38 | 41 | 35 | 33 |
| Imports | 14 | 17 | 16 | 22 | 15 | 11 |
| of which: | | | | | | |
| hard currency | 12 | 15 | 15 | 20 | 14 | 10 |
| **Domestic use** | **442** | **446** | **444** | **441** | **438** | **422** |
| **Net exports** | **153** | **169** | **180** | **183** | **169** | **148** |
| of which | | | | | | |
| crude oil | 105 | 114 | 123 | 124 | 114 | 101 |
| products | 48 | 55 | 57 | 59 | 55 | 47 |
| **Hard currency** | | | | | | |
| **net exports** | **48** | **54** | **61** | **70** | **48** | **59** |
| of which | | | | | | |
| crude | 17 | 18 | 24 | 30 | 14 | 26 |
| products | 30 | 36 | 37 | 40 | 34 | 33 |

*Sources:* 1985–89 Rows 1–9 (Narkhoz 1989: 377, 644, 653).
1990 rows 1–4 (Ekonomika i Zhizn 1991, no 5). Rows 5–9 (see text).
Rows 10–16 (estimated from above data).

*Table 8.3*   Soviet natural gas: trade and production 1985–91
(billion cubic metres)

|  | 1985 | 1986 | 1987 | 1988 | 1989 | 1990 | 1991 |
|---|---|---|---|---|---|---|---|
| Production | 643 | 686 | 727 | 770 | 796 | 815 | 810 |
| Exports | 69 | 79 | 84 | 88 | 101 | 109 | 104 |
| of which | | | | | | | |
| hard currency | 31 | 37 | 39 | 41 | 47 | 54 | |
| soft currency | 38 | 42 | 45 | 47 | 54 | 58 | |
| Imports | 2 | 2 | 2 | 1 | – | – | |
| Consumption | 576 | 609 | 645 | 683 | 695 | 706 | 706 |

*Sources:* 1985–89 Narkhoz 1989: 377 and 644.
1990 Ekonomika i Zhizn 1991, no. 5.
1991 Ekonomika i Zhizn 1992, no. 6.

*Table 8.4*   Soviet exports to non-socialist countries 1984–89
(million roubles)

|  | 1984 | 1985 | 1986 | 1987 | 1988 | 1989 |
|---|---|---|---|---|---|---|
| Total | 32,277 | 28,196 | 22,686 | 23,942 | 24,231 | 26,515 |
| Machinery | 2,561 | 2,622 | 2,444 | 2,650 | 2,468 | 2,449 |
| Fuel and energy | 18,906 | 16,128 | 9,498 | 10,514 | 9,558 | 10,157 |
| of which: oil | 13,567 | 10,623 | 5,522 | 7,103 | 6,282 | 6,686 |
| Ores and metals | 977 | 959 | 1,084 | 1,327 | 2,045 | 2,821 |
| Chemicals, etc. | 1,046 | 1,100 | 748 | 726 | 927 | 976 |
| Wood and paper | 904 | 845 | 1,000 | 1,055 | 1,234 | 1,350 |
| Textiles | 93 | 113 | 135 | 182 | 216 | 255 |
| Foodstuffs | 442 | 395 | 454 | 427 | 498 | 509 |
| Industrial consumer goods | 413 | 479 | 590 | 622 | 592 | 563 |
| Unspecified | 6,937 | 5,554 | 6,733 | 6,437 | 6,693 | 7,435 |

*Sources:* Vneshtorg (various years).
*Notes:* Estimated from percentage breakdowns of Soviet exports to all
destinations minus exports to socialist countries.
Components to not sum to totals due to rounding.

1985, while Soviet and CMEA consumption was virtually
maintained at 1984 levels. Exports for hard currency (excluding
Finland) fell from $14.7 billion to $11.2 billion. As demand for hard
currency imports exceeded the supply of hard currency exports,
the failure to restore oil production to 1984 levels would have
required the Soviet authorities to either increase borrowing from
the West, and/or make painful cuts in imports from the West
and/or cut supplies to the domestic and East European markets.
Under Chernenko's leadership the value of imports from the
industrialised West continued to grow by 10 per cent in the first
quarter of 1985 (compared with the first quarter of 1984) despite
a 28 per cent fall in the value of exports to the West, resulting in
a deficit in trade with the industrialised West of 1.7 billion roubles
($2.0 billion) for the first quarter of 1985 alone, which was
equivalent to the deficit incurred in the whole of 1984. This was
financed by running down Soviet hard currency deposits in
western (BIS) banks from $11.3 billion at the end of 1984 to $8.8
billion at the end of March 1985.

The annual seasonal improvement in energy exports in the
second quarter of 1985 (as domestic demand for heating oil fell)
still resulted in a quarterly deficit in trade with the industrialised
West of 730 million roubles ($0.9 billion) as imports were allowed
to grow by more than 10 per cent. Gorbachev responded with a
major cut in imports from the OECD in the second half of 1985,

*Table 8.5*    Soviet hard currency exports 1984–1990 ($ million)

|  | 1984 | 1985 | 1986 | 1987 | 1988 | 1989 | 1990 |
|---|---|---|---|---|---|---|---|
| **Total** | **28,361** | **23,694** | **21,802** | **25,756** | **27,826** | **29,412** | **33,500** |
| **Energy** | **18,895** | **15,401** | **10,898** | **13,268** | **12,745** | **12,690** | **16,370** |
| of which: |  |  |  |  |  |  |  |
| oil | 14,710 | 11,240 | 6,851 | 9,925 | 9,528 | 9,329 | 11,600 |
| gas | 3,736 | 3,797 | 3,694 | 2,725 | 2,538 | 2,648 | 3,602 |
| **Machinery (civil)** | **1,009** | **820** | **846** | **1,156** | **1,363** | **1,595** | **1,475** |
| **Arms and military** | **3,868** | **2,937** | **4,384** | **4,626** | **4,798** | **4,707** | **3,799** |
| of which: |  |  |  |  |  |  |  |
| LDC | 2,855 | 2,151 | 3,251 | 3,521 | 3,662 | 3,686 | 2,770 |
| ICCR | 388 | 380 | 437 | 286 | 450 | 460 | 567 |
| Machinery |  |  |  |  |  |  |  |
| residual | 144 | 104 | 131 | 101 | 71 | 155 | 287 |
| vehicles | 122 | 97 | 162 | 251 | 240 | 89 | 80 |
| aircraft | 324 | 205 | 378 | 456 | 375 | 317 | 95 |
| **Diamonds and** |  |  |  |  |  |  |  |
| **precious metals** | **1,730** | **1,715** | **2,228** | **2,829** | **4,162** | **4,866** | **5,935** |
| of which: |  |  |  |  |  |  |  |
| cut | 362 | 418 | 660 | 723 | 708 | 656 | 798 |
| uncut | 663 | 631 | 697 | 755 | 1,063 | 1,167 | 1,147 |
| other pms | 705 | 666 | 871 | 1,351 | 2,391 | 3,043 | 3,990 |
| **Other ores** |  |  |  |  |  |  |  |
| **and metals** | **240** | **284** | **500** | **392** | **537** | **843** | **800** |
| Chemicals | 1,018 | 1,061 | 873 | 917 | 1,289 | 1,370 | 1,775 |
| Wood, etc. | 905 | 720 | 1,105 | 1,337 | 1,692 | 1,717 | 1,895 |
| Textiles | 103 | 112 | 189 | 300 | 337 | 412 | 278 |
| Furs |  | 131 | 130 | 216 | 148 | 117 | 85 |
| Food | 462 | 419 | 560 | 611 | 663 | 719 | 948 |
| Other |  | 94 | 89 | 104 | 92 | 376 | 140 |

*Source:* Vneshtorg (various years)
*Notes:* Identified exports (energy, oil, gas, machinery, chemicals, wood [wood paper and cellulose, textiles, furs and food) derived by aggregating data on exports to individual countries. Unidentified residuals for military goods, diamonds and precious metals derived by methodology outlined in Chapter 5. See notes to Tables 5.4 and 5.5. Pms = precious metals.

which restored the surplus in trade with the industrialised West and provided a hint of the conservative policy towards imports from the West that was to dominate his trade policy until 1988. Imports from the industrialised West were pruned by 34 per cent in the third quarter of 1985 (compared with the second quarter), allowing the Soviet Union to achieve a surplus in its trade with the industrialised West in the second half of 1985 of 1.75 billion roubles ($2.1 billion). This was not sufficient to create a surplus in trade with the industrial- ised West in 1985 as a whole (see Table 8.1) and net debt with western banks for the remainder of the year was stabilised at its end-June level of around $9.5 billion.

Soviet oil production was restored to 615 million tonnes in 1986 and Soviet oil exports to the OECD recovered to 1984 levels in 1986, reaching 78 million tonnes. However, Soviet hard currency earnings from oil exports of 69 million tonnes (i.e. excluding Finland) fell further to $6.9 billion, under the impact of falling oil prices, a fall of $7.9 billion from the 1984 level, when export volumes were similar. In 1987 Soviet oil production recovered to 624 million tonnes permitting an increase in Soviet oil exports for hard currency to 76 million tonnes which, assisted by an improvement in world oil prices, increased the value of Soviet hard currency oil revenues to $9.9 billion. Despite the continued growth in the volume of natural gas exports for hard currency (see Table 8.3) the value of natural gas exports to the West fell by 28 per cent in 1987 to $2.7 billion compared with $3.8 billion in 1985. Oil and natural gas prices weakened again in 1988 and, although oil output stabilised in 1988 at the 1987 level of 625 million tonnes, the Soviet authorities increased the volume of hard currency oil exports by 14 million tonnes (9 million tonnes net of imports) to a record level of 90 million tonnes (70 million net) in an attempt to maintain hard currency revenues (an example of an increase in supply in response to a fall in price). The value of hard currency oil exports, however, fell to $9.5 billion and natural gas to $2.5 billion while total energy exports fell to $12.7 billion.

Soviet energy production hit serious problems in 1989 as oil output fell to 607 million tonnes and continued unrest and strikes in the mining regions of Siberia and the Ukraine contributed to a fall in coal production (which was officially reported to be 4 per cent, but was believed to have been considerably greater). Only the growth in natural gas production kept the fall in fuel extraction (measured in standard fuel equivalent) to below 1 per cent according to official statistics (Narkhoz 1989: 377). Even if these figures are accepted as accurate, they understate the economic disruption caused by seasonal fluctuations in energy production and supply. As energy production continued to fall from 1989 onwards, the maintenance of export volumes placed a growing strain on the domestic economy. Hard currency oil exports fell to 62 million tonnes in 1989 (Narkhoz 1989: 644), although foreign trade statistics indicate deliveries of 67 million tonnes, but improved oil prices reduced the impact on revenues, which fell to $9.3 billion, and a continued growth in the volume of natural gas exports helped to sustain energy exports to the West at $12.7 billion.

In 1990 oil output fell by a further 6 per cent to 570 million tonnes, the lowest level since 1977 (compared with an original five-year plan target of 635 million tonnes), coal production also fell by 5 per cent and, although natural gas production rose by 2 per cent, total fuel extraction fell by a further 2 per cent placing further strain on domestic availability (Ekonomika i Zhizn 1991, no. 5). Exports of crude oil and products to all destinations were cut by 25 million tonnes to 159 million tonnes. Although the analysis of the fall in oil exports on hard currency earnings in 1990 is complicated by the amalgamation of data on trade with the former GDR in trade with the Federal Republic of Germany, there is strong evidence to suggest that the Soviet authorities concentrated available oil supplies on exports to hard currency markets at the expense of deliveries based on clearing agreements in order to maximise hard currency receipts. Exports to the CMEA (including Cuba, Mongolia and Vietnam but excluding the former GDR) were cut by 17 million tonnes, of which exports to the remaining East European CMEA members accounted for 13 million tonnes and exports to Finland were cut from 11 million tonnes to 8 million. Oil exports to Germany as a whole were cut by 6.9 million tonnes from 30.6 million tonnes in 1989 to 23.7 million tonnes, while data provided by Goskomstat to the IMF indicate that exports to the former GDR fell by 5.8 million tonnes, a figure that is consistent with Soviet data on trade in the first nine months of the year before German unification took place (IMF *et al.* 1991, vol. 1: 181). As a result exports to the industrialised West (excluding Finland) remained at 66–67 million tonnes.

In 1991 oil production in the CIS republics (which accounted for all but 0.03 per cent of Soviet production of oil and gas) fell by a further 10 per cent to 515 million tonnes. Total exports of crude oil (to all destinations) were cut by 57 million tonnes (52 per cent) to 52 million tonnes and exports of refined oil products fell by 9 million tonnes (18 per cent) to 41 million tonnes (estimated from Ekonomika i Zhizn 1992, no. 6). Consequently, total Soviet exports of crude oil and products in 1991 amounted to only 98 million tonnes, less than half the peak level of 205 million tonnes realised in 1988. Declining energy production also affected exports of other energy products. Natural gas production fell by 0.5 per cent to 810 billion cubic metres, leading to a fall in exports of 4.5 billion cubic metres to 104 billion cubic metres. Coal output in the CIS republics (which accounted for 99.8 per cent of Soviet production) fell by a further 10 per cent to 629 million tonnes leading to a further 32 per cent reduction (11.5 million tonnes) in the volume of coal exports to 24 million tonnes (compared with a peak of 39 million tonnes in 1988). Exports of metallurgical coke and electricity, which were largely directed to the CMEA countries, also fell substantially.

## EXPORTS OF DIAMONDS AND PRECIOUS METALS

Diamonds, precious metals and other ferrous and non-ferrous metals offered the Soviet authorities one of the few potential sources of hard currency exports that could be expanded quickly to compensate for the loss of energy revenues. The estimates of exports of these items in Table 8.5 have been largely based on the methodology outlined in Chapter 5. In addition, Soviet data for 1988 and 1989 provide improved information on the country distribution of exports of 'minerals, earths and clays' (CTN 25), which include cut diamonds and which supports the analysis of the specification of residuals outlined in Chapter 4 and indicates a near doubling of exports of uncut diamonds over the period. The estimates indicate that exports of diamonds and precious metals grew in value from $1.7 billion in 1985 to $4.9 billion in 1989. The major part of this growth is attributed to increased exports of unspecified non-ferrous metals which include nickel, aluminium, copper, zinc, lead, platinum and possibly even uranium. Unfortunately it is not possible to identify these by examining trade partners' statistics. The largest residual in Soviet exports to individual countries occurs in exports to the UK. However, UK trade statistics, regularly record lower levels of imports from the Soviet Union than are recorded in Soviet data on total exports to the UK, the difference between the two figures roughly coinciding with the unspecified residual in Soviet exports. Some, but not all of this, can be explained by Soviet exports of diamonds, the remainder is presumably composed of exports of other precious metals which are not identified by country of origin in UK data. Other western estimates of Soviet exports of non-ferrous metals provide some evidence of a growth in Soviet exports of lead and nickel in the late 1980s.

The analysis of the data for 1990 in Table 8.5 is complicated by the inclusion of exports to the former GDR in the statistics for exports to Germany. This does not have any significant effect on the data for exports of diamonds, but some exports of non-ferrous metals to the former GDR will have been included in unspecified exports to the united Germany. If an allowance of 200 million roubles is made for this trade, Soviet exports of diamonds and non-ferrous metals to the industrialised West rose to approximately $5.9 billion in 1990, making them a significant source of hard currency earnings. In 1990 the Soviet government concluded an agreement with the South African company, De Beers, for the sale of diamonds worth $5 billion over the period from 1990–94 against the wishes of the Russian government (Bradshaw 1992: 426).

## EXPORTS OF ARMS AND GOODS WITH MILITARY USES

It was argued in Chapter 5 that exports of armaments and military-related goods (which are produced in specialised defence factories which did not suffer to the same degree from the systemic problems which confronted the civilian economy) were the major source of Soviet exports of manufactured goods to non-socialist countries, but that there were major doubts about the methods of payment for these and their contribution to Soviet hard currency earnings. Estimates of Soviet exports of arms and military goods denominated in hard currencies from 1984–90 are shown in the estimates of Soviet hard currency exports in Table 8.5. Estimates of Soviet arms exports to developing countries were shown in Table 5.5, which indicated that, following a fall in total arms sales (for convertible and non-convertible currency) from 7.5 billion roubles ($9.2 bn) in 1984 to 6.3 billion roubles ($7.5 billion) in 1985, the value of Soviet arms sales was restored to over 7 billion roubles in each year from 1986–89, rising to 7.490 million roubles ($11.9 billion) in 1989. In 1990 the volume of Soviet arms sales fell back to only 5.6 billion roubles ($9.4 billion), with reductions in trade that cannot be identified by destination (the LDC residual) as well as in recorded data for exports of aircraft and heavy transportation equipment. These figures show that Soviet armaments exports continued to be of major significance during the Gorbachev era, although the problem of identifying the method of payment remains, particularly for arms sales that cannot be identified by country of destination, if we are to estimate their importance to the Soviet economy.

Further light on this problem has been shed by the provision of Soviet data on their outstanding claims against developing countries, provided by the Soviet Ministry of Finance to the IMF (IMF *et al.* 1991, vol. 1: 117), which indicate both that a significant proportion of deliveries of armaments and related equipment to developing countries was supplied on the basis of extended credits, and that more than half of these credits were designated in inconvertible currencies. Total Soviet claims against developing countries reached $34.8 billion at the end of 1985 and grew by a further $32.6 billion to $67.4 billion by the end of 1989. Exports that cannot be identified by country of destination (the LDC residual) amounted to $33.2 billion over this period, while Soviet trade with developing countries that can be identified by partner country in the Soviet trade statistics was actually in deficit over the period from 1985–89 by 6.8 billion dollars. Therefore, a significant part (or possibly all) of the growth of claims against developing countries must have arisen from trade that cannot be identified by country of destination and was included in the LDC residual.

At the same time Soviet claims denominated in inconvertible currencies grew from $25.2 billion (57.6 per cent of the total) at the end of 1986 to $38.9 billion (57.7 per cent) at the end of 1989, indicating that roughly 57 per cent of Soviet credits to developing countries from 1985 to 1989 were denominated in inconvertible currencies, while Soviet claims denominated in convertible currencies only grew by $10.1 billion from $18.4 to $28.5 billion. The breakdown of Soviet claims against individual developing countries at the end of October 1989, which was provided by the Soviet Ministry of Finance to the IMF (IMF *et al.* 1991, vol. 1: 118), also indicates that approximately 57 per cent of claims are held against countries that conduct trade relations in inconvertible currency and that the growth of Soviet claims cannot be explained by trade that is recorded in the data on trade with individual countries. These figures are shown in Table 8.6 together with the total Soviet visible trade balances with the countries concerned from 1975 to the end of September 1989, estimated from Soviet trade statistics. The choice of 1975 is arbitrary, but includes a sufficiently long period to allow for the repayment of credits in the form of products (e.g. oil) to be reflected in the trade statistics. The difference between Soviet accumulated surpluses or deficits over this period and Soviet claims against individual countries is also shown.

In the case of trade with India, Libya, Egypt and Cameroon, Soviet statistics on visible trade indicate that the Soviet Union

Table 8.6   Soviet trade surpluses and outstanding claims against
Third World countries (million roubles)

| Country | Soviet claims | Cumulative trade balance | Difference |
|---|---|---|---|
| Hard currency trade partners | | | |
| Iraq | 3,514 | +237 | 3,277 |
| Algeria | 2,448 | +226 | 2,222 |
| Angola | 1,930 | +1,144 | 786 |
| Yemen PDR | 1,836 | +1,093 | 743 |
| Libya | 1,641 | −5,319 | 6,960 |
| Cameroon | 956 | −203 | 1,159 |
| Yemen Arab Republic | 955 | +430 | 525 |
| Nicaragua | 837 | +1,242 | (405) |
| **Total – hard currency** | **14,117** | **−1,150** | **15,267** |
| Clearing trade partners | | | |
| India | 8,907 | −617 | 9,524 |
| Syria | 6,515 | −30 | 6,545 |
| Afghanistan | 2,899 | 2,057 | 842 |
| Ethiopia | 2,850 | 1,499 | 1,351 |
| Egypt | 1,711 | −798 | 2,509 |
| **Total – soft currency** | **22,882** | **2,111** | **20,771** |
| **Total – hard plus clearing** | **36,999** | **961** | **36,038** |
| Others | 3,645 | | |

*Sources:* Soviet external claims against developing countries from IMF *et al.* 1991,
vol. 1, p 118, reconverted from dollars into roubles at official exchange rate at 1
October 1989. Cumulative trade balances from 1975–October 1989 estimated
from Vneshtorgs (various years) and Vneshnyaya Torgovlya 1989, no 12.

incurred a cumulative trade deficit over the period, not a surplus.
Thus although the debt figures also include unpaid interest on
fixed interest loans as well as principal, this cannot explain how
the Soviet claim originated in the first place, as claims against
those countries can only have arisen from invisible exports or
exports that were not identified by country in Soviet export data.
For example, Soviet outstanding claims against India amounted
to 8,907 million roubles, whereas Soviet data on visible trade with
India indicate that the Soviet Union actually incurred a deficit in
its trade with India of 617 million roubles between 1975 and

September 1989. This indicates that Soviet claims against India, which are known to be associated with arms trade, must be largely attributed to exports that were not included in the statistics on trade with India, but were included in the LDC residual. The other countries that show a major difference between their outstanding debt to the Soviet Union and the accumulated trade deficits/surpluses over the period from 1975 to end September 1989 are Libya (7.0 billion roubles), Syria (6.5 billion roubles), Iraq (3.3 billion roubles), Egypt (2.5 billion roubles), Algeria (2.2 billion roubles), Ethiopia (1.4 billion roubles), Afghanistan (0.8 billion roubles), Angola (0.8 billion roubles) and the Yemen PDR (0.7 billion roubles), all of which have been identified by SIPRI as recipients of Soviet arms at some time and who also account for 85 per cent of Soviet exports of arms and military equipment that can be identified by country of destination.

Finally, the total difference between the claims against developing countries and aggregated trade balances for all the countries identified in Table 8.6 over the period from 1975–88 amounts to 36 billion roubles, while the aggregate LDC residual over that period amounts to 54.2 billion roubles, indicating that a significant proportion of the country destination of trade concealed in the LDC residual can be identified from the debt figures. There is therefore a considerable body of evidence to suggest that a major proportion of arms exports concealed in the LDC residual was delivered on extended credit terms and that approximately 58 per cent of these were denominated in inconvertible currencies and made no contribution to Soviet hard currency earnings or claims in hard currencies.

Further evidence comes from an estimate of the Soviet balance of payments in 1990 and 1991, published by a group of experts under the direction of the Committee for Foreign Economic Relations of the Russian Federation in *Ekonomicheskaya Gazeta* in March 1992 (hereafter referred to as Sarafanov *et al.* 1992), which attempts to break down Soviet trade and payments relations between trade with CMEA, trade in convertible currencies and trade conducted on a clearing basis. Soviet exports conducted on a clearing basis were given as $18.1 billion, which is equivalent to 10.6 billion roubles at the official exchange rate, which was used to convert all data from roubles to dollars in the study. Soviet exports to countries with whom trade is identified in the study as conducted on a clearing basis in 1990, however, only amounted to

8.4 billion roubles in 1990 according to data in the Soviet trade handbook. This indicates that exports amounting to 2.2 billion roubles over and above those included in the export data to individual countries were designated as clearing. As this sum is equivalent to 58 per cent of the LDC residual, this provides further evidence to indicate that a proportion of the residual was denominated in inconvertible currency. Consequently, in the estimates of Soviet arms sales for hard currency, I have only allocated 42 per cent of the LDC residual to the hard currency category. Other exports of militarily related exports that can be identified by country of destination from Soviet trade data have been allocated between hard and soft currencies according to the prevailing nature of the trade agreements with the individual countries.

These estimates indicate that Soviet exports of arms, designated in hard currencies, fell from $3.8 billion in 1984 to $2.9 billion in 1985, but then stabilised at $4.4–4.7 billion between 1986 and 1989 before falling back to $3.8 billion in 1990. Approximately 75 per cent of these deliveries appear to have been made on credit.

## HARD CURRENCY EXPORTS OF PROCESSED GOODS

The attempt to increase exports of manufactured goods for hard currency was unsuccessful. Although the rate of growth of the dollar value of hard currency exports of civilian machinery and equipment, chemicals, textiles and wood products between 1985 and 1989 shown in Table 8.5 may look impressive, at first sight, a number of major qualifications must be considered. Firstly, the figures are biased upwards by approximately 25 per cent between 1985 and 1989 by the depreciation of the dollar, and estimates of the growth in volume of exports of manufactured goods to non-socialist countries in Table 8.7 reveal a less spectacular rate of growth; secondly, the growth is from a very low starting point and the trade volumes involved remained insignificant by world market standards; thirdly, a more detailed analysis of the commodity structure of exports indicates that the growth in exports that did take place was largely confined to relatively unsophisticated products.

All these points can be illustrated by Soviet exports of passenger cars to the industrialised West. The dollar value of Soviet hard

*Table 8.7*    Commodity structure of Soviet exports to non-socialist
countries in comparable (1985) prices (million 1985
roubles)

|  | 1985 | 1988 | 1989 | 1990a | 1990 as % of 1985 |
|---|---|---|---|---|---|
| Total | 28,196 | 36,687 | 35,942 | 29,272 | 103.8 |
| Machinery | 2,622 | 2,331 | 2,228 | 1,786 | 68.1 |
| Fuel and energy | 16,128 | 22,992 | 21,278 | 18,120 | 112.4 |
| Ores and metals | 959 | 1,690 | 2,264 | 2,430 | 253.3 |
| Chemicals, etc. | 1,100 | 1,346 | 1,402 | 1,522 | 138.3 |
| Wood and paper | 845 | 1,217 | 1,114 | 937 | 110.9 |
| Textiles | 113 | 324 | 325 | 146 | 129.2 |
| Foodstuffs | 395 | 587 | 539 | 615 | 155.7 |
| Industrial consumer goods | 479 | 616 | 503 | 585 | 122.1 |
| Unspecified | 5,554 | 5,584 | 6,289 | 3,132 | 56.4 |

*Sources:* Vneshniye Ekonomicheskiye Svyazi SSSR (Vneshtorg) 1989 and 1990.
*Notes:* Estimated from percentage breakdowns of trade by commodity
group/region in 1985 prices. Total trade estimated from volume indices.
Components to not sum to totals due to rounding.
a) Data for 1990 do not include the former GDR and are consistent with data for
earlier years.

currency exports of cars to the OECD (excluding Finland) grew
2.2-fold from $123 million in 1985 to $275 million in 1989.
However, this only involved an increase of 31 per cent in volume
from 87,000 to 114,000 cars (equivalent to a growth in sales of
6,750 cars per annum). Furthermore, this relatively small volume
of cars which were sold at the bottom end of western markets
constituted 42 per cent of total Soviet exports of machinery to the
entire OECD region (excluding Finland) in 1989.

Estimates of the volume of exports of machinery and equipment to the entire non-socialist world (including exports for
non-convertible currencies and military goods included in that
category) indicate a decline of 32 per cent in the volume of
machinery exports between 1985 and 1990 (see Table 8.7). The
growth in the dollar value of exports of chemicals from $1,061
million to $1,775 million from 1985–90 reflects a 38 per cent
growth in volume as well as price changes, but remained relatively
insignificant in the world market and was concentrated on

unsophisticated products (basic fertilisers, ammonia, caustic soda, etc.). Similarly, 80 per cent of Soviet hard currency exports of wood and wood products in 1989 comprised basic timber and sawn wood amounting to $1.4 billion, while hard currency exports of textiles were predominantly composed of cotton fibres (produced in the Central Asian Republics) and raw wool, not finished products.

## SOVIET GOLD EXPORTS

One of the more startling economic revelations of the era of glasnost was the interview (in *Moscow News*, October 1991, no. 46) with Grigory Yavlinksy, who announced that data provided by the USSR Ministry of Finance indicated that Soviet gold reserves had fallen to only 284 tonnes at the at the beginning of October 1991 and were expected to be only about 240 tonnes by the end of the year. On this basis Soviet reserves would be worth about $3.4 billion, compared with CIA estimates which put Soviet gold reserves at 2416 tonnes in 1989 worth about $34 billion at world market prices. Although the absolute size of Yavlinsky's estimates has been disputed, it is widely accepted that these estimates provide a reasonable approximation to the real size of Soviet gold reserves.

Although western estimates of Soviet annual gold production vary substantially, ranging from 340 tonnes in 1980 (Kaser 1984) to a low of only 125–175 tonnes in the 1980s (according to some private, commercial estimates), the overestimation of Soviet reserves results more from underestimates of domestic consumption (of around 100 tonnes a year) and exports since 1953 than overestimates of production. Yavlinsky, who indicates that Soviet reserves were only 577 tonnes at the end of 1983, provides new data for the export of gold between 1984 and 1991 (see Table 8.8). These indicate that following heavy sales of 297 tonnes in 1985 (worth $3.3 billion at world market prices) the Soviet Union restricted sales between 1986 and 1988 in an attempt to rebuild gold stocks. Gold sales on a large scale resumed in 1989, as balance of payments problems intensified, and reached 475 tonnes in 1990. A further 319 tonnes were exported in the first nine months of 1991. Estimates of the dollar value of gold exports derived from these volumes differ substantially from other western estimates, including those provided by the IMF, which were prepared

*Table 8.8* USSR Ministry of Finance estimates of Soviet gold stocks and sales (tonnes)

|  | 1984 | 1985 | 1986 | 1987 | 1988 | 1989 | 1990 | 1991 |
|---|---|---|---|---|---|---|---|---|
| Exports | 10.1 | 297.0 | 75.0 | 48.0 | 96.0 | 245.5 | 474.6 | 319.1 |
| Production | 251.8 | 264.0 | 271.3 | 260.0 | 277.6 | 304.0 | 302.0 | 230.0 |
| Stocks (end year) | 719.5 | 587.4 | 680.9 | 785.3 | 850.4 | 784.0 | 484.6 | 240.0 |
| Estimated value sales $m | 127 | 3,295 | 965 | 747 | 1,469 | 3,301 | 6,413 | 4,466 |

*Sources:* Exports, production and stocks from *Moscow News* 1991, no. 46.
*Notes:* Data for 1991 are to 1 October. Sales estimated by multiplying volumes by average world market price for year.

without the cooperation of the Soviet authorities (see Chapter 9). This may in part reflect problems of timing; Yavlinksy indicates, for example, that a significant volume of exports negotiated or used as collateral in 1989 were not actually delivered until 1990. It is clear, however, that significant amounts of gold were sold in the late 1980s and early 1990s to finance balance of payments problems and that there has been a substantial rundown of Soviet reserves. This is also consistent with anecdotes that claimed that gold bars bearing Tsarist markings appeared on the market in the late 1980s.

**CONCLUSION**

The structure of Soviet hard currency exports at the end of the Gorbachev era indicates that reforms to the domestic economy and the system of foreign trade did not help to overcome the systemic inability to export processed and more sophisticated manufactured goods which constitute the main area of growth in western markets. It is noticeable that, in sectors where there is a growth in export volume, this can largely be attributed to relatively unprocessed goods (crude oil not refined oil products; uncut diamonds not cut diamonds). This in part reflects the lack of processing capacity but also provides further confirmation of an inability to export processed goods to the industrialised West.

Despite the stated intention to increase the volume of manufactured goods, Soviet exports of manufactured goods fell from 0.3 per cent of OECD imports of these items in 1985 to only

0.2 per cent in 1988, compared with a growth from 2.0 per cent to 3.0 per cent for South Korea over the same period (IMF *et al.* 1991, vol. 2: 69). Soviet exports of processed goods to OECD countries from 1986–91 were characterised by both a low level of domestic value added and a low level of product sophistication. It is also noticeable that two of the major sources of exports of manufactured and processed goods to the OECD originated in the case of passenger cars from a plant which was entirely constructed on the basis of western technology, and in the case of chemicals from an industry that had received priority imports from the West.

Exports of arms and military equipment were the major exception to the inability to export manufactured goods to non-socialist countries, reaching an estimated $11.9 billion in 1989. However, approximately $7.1 billion of these were delivered for inconvertible currency and possibly as much as 80 per cent of the remainder were delivered on the basis of long-term credits.

# Chapter 9

# Soviet balance of payments pressures 1985–91 and their impact on the economy

## BALANCE OF PAYMENTS PRESSURES UNDER GORBACHEV

The first official estimates of the Soviet balance of payments produced with the co-operation of the Soviet authorities were published in the IMF study (IMF *et al.* 1991, vol. 1) for the period from 1985–89. These data were disaggregated into trade in convertible currencies and trade in clearing currencies. The Soviet authorities did not provide the IMF with data on gold sales and the IMF had to rely on its own estimates. Semi-official Russian estimates of the Soviet balance of payments on a transactions basis (which records all merchandise imports and exports at the time they take place, regardless of means of payment) for 1990 and 1991 were also prepared by the Sarafanov study (Sarafanov *et al.* 1992). These estimates of the hard currency balance of payments on a transactions basis have been summarised in Table 9.1.

The IMF estimates of hard currency exports on a transactions basis (which also include hard currency exports to socialist countries) are substantially higher than those given in Table 8.5. Comparison with trade data in the Soviet Foreign Trade year-books indicates that none of the LDC residual has been allocated to clearing accounts and, consequently, that the entire LDC residual has been included in hard currency exports. This gives a substantial upward bias to hard currency exports and, as a result, the Soviet Union appears to have run a surplus in its trade denominated in convertible currencies in each year from 1985–89, with the surplus reaching $8.2 billion and $4.8 billion in 1987 and 1988 respectively. Although this was partly offset by a deficit in trade in services and other invisibles (including interest on outstanding

*Table 9.1*  Official estimates of Soviet balance of payments in convertible currencies on a transactions basis 1985–91 ($ billion)

| | 1985 | 1986 | 1987 | 1988 | 1989 | 1990 | 1991 |
|---|---|---|---|---|---|---|---|
| Exports | 27.5 | 26.8 | 31.3 | 33.4 | 35.2 | 33.5 | 31.8 |
| Imports | −26.3 | −23.2 | −23.1 | −28.7 | −35.4 | −35.1 | −30.7 |
| **Trade Balance** | **+1.3** | **+3.6** | **+8.2** | **+4.8** | **−0.1** | **−1.6** | **+1.1** |
| **Services balance** | **−1.8** | **−1.8** | **−1.7** | **−3.3** | **−3.8** | **−6.2** | **−6.7** |
| of which: | | | | | | | |
| net interest | −0.7 | −1.4 | −1.8 | −2.0 | −2.9 | −4.0 | −3.7 |
| Gold sales | 1.8 | 4.0 | 3.5 | 3.8 | 3.7 | 2.7 | 3.8 |
| **Current a/c balance** | | | | | | | |
| excluding gold | **−0.5** | **+1.8** | **+6.6** | **+1.6** | **−3.9** | **−7.8** | **−5.6** |
| including gold | **+1.3** | **+5.8** | **+10.1** | **+5.4** | **−0.2** | **−5.1** | **−1.8** |
| **Capital a/c balance** | **−2.8** | **−5.2** | **−12.4** | **−6.1** | **−3.5** | **+2.3** | **+5.4** |
| of which: | | | | | | | |
| inflows | +6.5 | +4.8 | +3.1 | +6.4 | +9.5 | +11.4 | +13.9 |
| outflows | −9.3 | −10.0 | −15.4 | −12.5 | −13.0 | −9.1 | −8.9 |
| of which: | | | | | | | |
| trade credits | −4.8 | −4.1 | −8.0 | −7.0 | −6.9 | na | na |
| amortisation | −4.3 | −5.4 | −6.1 | −5.2 | −5.6 | −8.2 | −8.2 |
| **Financing requirement** | **1.5** | **−0.6** | **2.3** | **0.7** | **3.7** | **2.8** | **3.6** |

*Sources:* 1985–89: basic data from IMF *et al.* (1991) p. 116. 1990–91: from Sarafanov *et al.* (1992).
*Notes:* Export data for 1990–91 are not strictly comparable with those for 1985–89 (see text).
Components do not sum to totals due to rounding.

debt) the Soviet Union apparently still made a surplus on the current account balance of payments denominated in convertible currency from 1986–88 even before taking estimated gold sales into account. The deterioration in economic performance in 1989, however, led to a hard currency trade deficit of $146 million, the first to be reported in the Gorbachev era. The deficit in services of $3.8 billion (of which net interest payments accounted for $2.9 billion) pushed the current account deficit to $3.9 billion, but estimated gold sales of $3.7 billion reduced the estimated deficit to only $203 million. When estimated gold sales are added to export receipts for the years from 1985–88 the surplus on current account on a transactions basis apparently rises to comfortable levels, reaching a peak of $10.1 billion dollars in 1987.

Although the IMF estimates indicate that the Soviet Union ran an aggregate current account surplus of $22.6 billion between 1985 and 1989, the Soviet Union consistently increased its borrowing from the West. Soviet net debt to western financial institutions and governments grew from $10.2 billion at the end of 1984 to $37.3 billion at the end of a 1989 (see Table 9.2), a growth of $20 billion after allowing for dollar deprecation (of which $5 billion can be attributed to dollar depreciation which increased the dollar value of debt denominated in other currencies) and an upward revaluation of debt at the end of 1988, following a speech by Ryzhkov to the Party Congress in June 1989, which indicated that the level of debt was far higher than western estimates indicated. Ryzhkov argued that Soviet debt was 34 billion roubles (equivalent to $55 billion at the official exchange rate), but gave no indication of how this figure was obtained or what it referred to. Why did the Soviet Union get into debt and borrow on such a scale if it was running a current account surplus? The IMF largely explains the discrepancy between recorded exports and payments to export credits advanced by the Soviet Union to its trade partners, which it estimates amounted to $30.8 billion from 1985–89 (IMF *et al.* 1991: 116). However, the inclusion of the entire LDC residual (approximately 57 per cent of which was estimated in Chapter 8 to cover trade denominated in inconvertible currency) has contributed to a substantial overestimate of hard currency earnings, which makes the balance of trade and payments on current account appear far more healthy than it actually was. Secondly, the IMF estimates of gold

Table 9.2    Soviet hard currency balance of payments and indebtedness
1985–90 ($ million)

| | 1985 | 1986 | 1987 | 1988 | 1989 | 1990 |
|---|---|---|---|---|---|---|
| Exports | 23,694 | 21,802 | 25,756 | 27,826 | 29,412 | 33,500 |
| Imports | 25,662 | 23,056 | 22,882 | 28,362 | 34,562 | 35,100 |
| Trade balance | –1,968 | –1,254 | +2,874 | –536 | –5,150 | –1,600 |
| Services balance | –1,841 | –1,827 | –1,680 | –3,307 | –3,839 | –6,200 |
| Current account balance | –3,809 | –3,081 | +1,194 | –3,843 | –8,989 | –7,800 |
| Gold sales | 3,295 | 965 | 747 | 1,469 | 3,301 | 6,413 |
| Current account plus gold sales | –514 | –2,116 | +1,961 | –2,374 | –5,688 | –1,387 |
| Gross debt   a) | 27,979 | 33,061 | 36,653 | 40,856 | | |
|              b) | | | | 45,753 | 51,820 | 61,152 |
| Reserves at BIS | 13,062 | 14,769 | 14,134 | 15,288 | 14,500 | 15,797 |
| Net debt | 14,917 | 18,292 | 22,519 | 30,465 | 37,320 | 45,355 |
| Change in net debt | +3,747 | +3,375 | +4,227 | +3,049a | +6,864 | +8,035 |
| Valuation change | +2,316 | +2,585 | +2,332 | –1,466 | –612 | +2,927 |
| Adjusted change | +1,431 | +790 | +1,895 | +4,515 | +7,476 | +5,108 |
| Soviet hard currency claims | 14,650 | 18,400 | 22,800 | 25,100 | 28,500 | |
| Change in claims | | +3,750 | +4,400 | +2,300 | +3,400 | |

Sources: Exports from Table 8.5. Imports on a transactions basis estimated from
Soviet data on trade with countries which conduct trade in hard currency.
Services balance, IMF et al. 1991, vol. 1: 116; Gold sales from Table 8.8 ; gross
debt and valuation changes WEFA Group CPE Outlook for Foreign Trade and
Finance (various years); reserves at BIS, Bank of International Settlements data
(various issues). Soviet hard currency claims, Soviet claims against developing
countries denominated in hard currency from IMF et al. 1991, vol. 1: 117, except
1985, estimated from partial data in IMF et al.
Notes: Debt data was adjusted upwards by WEFA from 1988 to take account of
new information provided by Ryzhkov (see text).
Change in net debt a): change in 1988 is estimated from the unadjusted debt
figures;
Valuation changes account for the effect of exchange rate changes on dollar
evaluation of debt denominated in other currencies.

sales are for the most part substantially higher than estimates
derived from the volume figures released by the Ministry of
Finance in October 1991 (see Chapter 8).

I have attempted to re-estimate the Soviet balance of payments
on current account for 1985–90, using the estimates for hard
currency exports (including exports on credits) shown in Table
8.5 and the estimates of gold sales shown in Table 8.8. These
estimates are summarised in Table 9.2, which also contains estimates
of Soviet imports from non-socialist countries denominated in

hard currency. These indicate that the Soviet Union ran a deficit in its hard currency trade in each year except 1987 and that the deficit reached $5.2 billion in 1989. After the deficit in services is added to the trade deficit the current account deficit rises to $9 billion in 1989. The aggregate deficit from 1985–89 rises to $18.5 billion, which is partly offset by gold sales that have been estimated at $9.8 billion from 1985–89.

Table 9.2 shows that Soviet net hard currency debt grew by $22.4 billion from the end of 1985 to the end of 1989. Of this $4.9 billion can be attributed to the upward revision of debt data, $2.8 billion to currency movements, and $8.2 billion of new borrowing was required to cover estimated balance of payments deficits. A further $10.1 billion was accounted for by the growth in Soviet hard currency claims (credits minus repayments) in convertible currencies against developing countries between the end of 1985 and the end of 1989 (of which $2.9 billion reflected dollar depreciation against the rouble). The LDC residual denominated in hard currency (and included in the export figures) amounted to $14.1 bn over this period, again indicating that a considerable volume of Soviet arms exports which were nominally designated in hard currency continued to be conducted on the basis of trade credits granted by the Soviet government. Consequently the estimates of hard currency arms sales overestimate their contribution to Soviet hard currency earnings and to the Soviet balance of payments in both the long term and the short term, as these assets are completely illiquid in the short run and cannot be used to either finance imports or to service hard currency debt. Furthermore, it ignores the ability (or possibly even the willingness) of the recipient government to repay the debt in hard currency (or goods such as oil that could be re-exported for hard currency).

By 1990 Soviet balance of payments problems had become acute. The fall in energy production affected export earnings, while the general fall in domestic output increased the demand for imports to ease the most critical shortages and bottlenecks, and was accompanied by a growing loss of central control over imports following the extended decentralisation of trade rights to enterprises in April 1989. At the same time the Soviet Union faced a bunching of loan repayments, including an unusually high level of short-term loans, which pushed debt service requirements up to $13 billion in 1990 compared with an average of $6–8 billion from 1986–89. The transitional system, with inadequate central controls and without genuine decentralised responsibility, was simply incapable of withstanding the strains imposed on it.

According to the Sarafanov (1992) study the trade balance in convertible currencies was in deficit by $1.6 billion in 1990. However, this still overstated short-run hard currency revenues as it included hard currency exports delivered on credit to Third World countries (of which arms amounted to an estimated $4 billion). The services balance was in deficit by $6.2 billion (of which net interest payments accounted for $4.0 billion) resulting in a current account deficit in convertible currencies of $7.8 billion on a transactions basis. This was offset by gold sales which were estimated by Sarafanov at only $2.7 billion compared with estimates based on the Ministry of Finance figures of $6.5 billion (which could be explained by swap arrangements which were not included in the Sarafanov estimate but appear to reflect an unexplained difference of opinion). As a result, Sarafanov estimates the Soviet current account deficit in 1990 as $5.1 billion.

Although these figures were modest in comparison with the current account deficits of the UK or the USA at that time, the Soviet Union could (or would) not sell capital assets or claims against its natural resources to finance the deficit and was dependent on further credits for this purpose. The ability to finance the deficit was complicated by the growing loss of western bank confidence in the Soviet Union's ability to meet its debt service obligations (which was partly stimulated by nervousness about the future of the Soviet government following the collapse of communism in Eastern Europe), but more by the increasing difficulties encountered by exporters to the Soviet Union in securing payment. By the middle of 1990 arrears on Soviet debt amounted to $4 billion. Although some of this could be attributed to the decentralisation of trade rights to enterprises and co-operatives, which had very limited experience of foreign trade and which had undertaken agreements to import goods without ensuring they could obtain the hard currency to pay for them, it was becoming increasingly apparent that the Soviet Union was experiencing real problems in generating the volume of exports needed to finance desired imports as import controls were lifted. Consequently the Soviet authorities were forced to run down hard currency reserves at BIS banks by $6.2 billion in the first six months of 1990. At the same time the level of arrears on Third World debt to the Soviet Union denominated in hard currency was revealed to be $7.3

billion (equivalent to 25 per cent of Soviet claims against Third World countries in hard currency). The balance of payments situation was largely stabilised in the second half of the year by cutting back imports from the industrialised West and by diverting energy exports from CMEA partners to hard currency markets.

The Sarafanov study indicates that the Soviet Union only succeeded in attracting net capital inflows of $2.3 billion in 1990 (principally composed of credits of $10.9 billion while debt repayment amounted to $8.2 billion) resulting in a short-term financing requirement of $2.8 billion. This figure appears to have been partly arrived at by netting off increased (long-term) claims against developing countries against the short-term claims of western suppliers and banks. In order to finance its short-term obligations Vneshekonombank had to run down its hard currency reserves by an estimated $8.4 billion, while arrears on debt grew by $4.5 billion during 1990 (Sarafanov *et al.* 1992).

The analysis of the Soviet hard currency balance of payments in 1991 is complicated by the move to trade in hard currency with CMEA which resulted in its virtual collapse and the inclusion of trade with the former GDR in a single set of figures for the united Germany, which together with trade with Finland have been included in the data on hard currency trade in Table 9.1. However, the underlying situation did not change significantly in 1991 from that experienced in the second half of 1990, as the impact of external financial problems had to be borne by the domestic economy, contributing to the accelerated decline in performance. Although the Soviet Union succeeded in running an overall trade surplus this was largely achieved by a major compression of imports, which fell by 43.5 per cent in value while exports fell by 32.4 per cent. A surplus in hard currency trade (including arms) of $1.1 billion was offset by a deficit in services of $6.7 billion, resulting in a current account deficit of $5.6 billion. Gold sales were estimated at $3.8 billion, while net capital inflows, assisted by western government support, came to $5.4 billion.

## THE IMPORTANCE OF IMPORTS TO THE SOVIET ECONOMY

Balance of payments pressures resulted in renewed pressures to cut imports, which played a significant role in the deterioration of Soviet economic performance in 1990 and 1991. The static importance of imports to the Soviet economy is a subject of controversy among western analysts. The normal measure for assessing trade dependence in a market economy is the ratio of imports to GNP or GDP. This measure is difficult to assess for the Soviet economy for two principal reasons. Firstly, the Soviet measurement of national income (net material product or NMP) excludes the value of goods and services and depreciation and is not directly comparable with western GDP data. Soviet data provided to the IMF indicate that Soviet NMP in the late 1980s was equivalent to 73 per cent of Soviet GDP estimated by conventional methods. Secondly, the separate price systems used to evaluate domestic production and internal trade, trade with CMEA partners and trade with the rest of the world mean that comparisons between domestic production and foreign trade which must be based on a common price system must either attempt to re-evaluate domestic GDP and foreign trade at world market prices or to estimate imports in terms of domestic prices. Unfortunately the two methods lead to different results.

Most western studies indicate that the Soviet Union was less dependent on trade than would be expected for a market economy of equivalent size and development. The IMF study concluded that 'the USSR is a relatively closed economy as measured by the share of trade in GDP' (IMF et al. 1991, vol. 2: 68). The study followed the Soviet practice of estimating exports (not imports) as a proportion of GDP, which it gives as 6.8 per cent in 1988. Although the study argues that exports were measured in foreign trade prices, it is not stated how GDP, which is given elsewhere in the study as 875 billion internal roubles in 1988 (IMF et al. 1991, vol. 1: 166), was estimated. The export:GDP ratio is lower than the OECD average of 14.4 per cent, which as the report notes was in part to be expected for a country as large as the Soviet Union.

Substantially higher import:GNP ratios are reached when Soviet imports in internal prices are compared with national income in internal prices. Three major studies involving highly detailed attempts to estimate this relationship have been undertaken by Treml (Treml 1980, Treml and Kostinsky 1982 and Treml 1983). Treml (1980: 188) estimates that Soviet imports rose from 6.7 per cent of national income (excluding services) in 1959 to just over 8 per cent in the 1960s and reached 14.9 per cent in 1976, rising further to 19.98 per cent in 1980 (Treml 1983). Treml and Kostinsky argue that on this basis 'the long held notion that

Soviet Foreign Trade is unusually small for an industrialised nation should be discarded'.

Treml's estimates incorporate the fact that the Soviet authorities deliberately imported goods with a high domestic price (or production cost) and taxed the import to equate domestic with world market prices. Data provided by Goskomstat to the IMF (IMF *et al.* 1991, vol. 1: 85) indicate that the value of imports in domestic prices exceeded that of exports by 3.7 per cent of NMP in 1970, rising to 5.3 per cent in 1975 (after the first oil price increase) to 9.6 per cent in 1980 (following the second) and remained at 10.4–10.5 per cent from 1981–84 before peaking at 11.0 per cent of NMP (8.2 per cent of GDP) in 1985 and then fell steadily to 8.5 per cent by 1989, following the collapse in world oil prices in 1985. Soviet data (Narkhoz 1989: 634) show that total Soviet imports and exports in domestic prices in 1988 amounted to 97.62 billion roubles and 47.18 billion respectively. This is equivalent to 7.5 per cent and 15.5 per cent of national income (excluding services) respectively or 5.4 per cent and 11.8 per cent of Soviet GDP. The Soviet Union as a whole was a net importer of machinery and equipment by 20 billion roubles, foodstuffs by 16 billion roubles and industrial consumer goods by 23 billion roubles measured in internal prices (Narkhoz 1989: 638).

The evaluation of imports in domestic prices incorporates an approximation of the gains from trade which are not included in conventional western calculations of either GNP or the contribution of imports to GNP (e.g. North European countries evaluate imported tropical fruits at the actual import price, which reflects the overseas cost of production plus transportation not the cost of producing them domestically in greenhouses) and are not strictly comparable with western data (Lavigne 1991a: 15). They do give an approximation of the importance of imports to the Soviet economy, however, and the effect of a reduction in imports on domestic availability (subject to the irrationality of Soviet domestic prices).

## THE IMPACT OF BALANCE OF PAYMENTS PRESSURES ON THE DOMESTIC ECONOMY

### a) The supply side

The deterioration in the Soviet terms of trade following the fall in world oil prices in 1986 resulted in major reduction in the

*Table 9.3* Real volume growth of trade 1985–90: 1985 = 100

|  | 1986 | 1987 | 1988 | 1989 | 1990 |
|---|---|---|---|---|---|
| **Total exports** | **110** | **114** | **116** | **117** | **102** |
| **Total imports** | **94** | **93** | **98** | **106** | **105** |
| **Exports to socialist** | **na** | **na** | **107** | **110** | **101** |
| **Imports from socialist** | **na** | **na** | **101** | **104** | **100** |
| Exports to CME A | 104 | 105 | 106 | 108 | 94 |
| Imports from CMEA | 101 | 102 | 102 | 104/107 | 99 |
| **Exports to capitalist** | **116** | **122** | **130a** | **127a** | **104a** |
| **Imports from capitalist** | **86** | **83** | **93a** | **109a** | **113a** |
| Industrialised West: | | | | | |
| Exports | na | na | 140 | 136/126 | 112 |
| Imports | na | na | 87 | 100/98 | 101 |
| Developing countries: | | | | | |
| Exports | na | na | 109 | 111 | 88 |
| Imports | na | na | 106 | 137 | 141 |

*Sources:* All data from Vneshtorg (various years).
*Notes:* Different figures are given for trade with CMEA and industrialised West in 1989 in 1989/90 Vneshtorgs, which probably reflects the reclassification of GDR trade but this is not explicitly stated.
a: own estimate from data in rows 9–12.

resources available for use in the domestic economy as the authorities attempted to restore the trade balance. Estimates based on Soviet data on trade volumes show that the physical volume of Soviet imports from non-socialist countries fell by 14.7 per cent between 1984 (before oil output tumbled in 1985) and 1987, while the physical volume of exports to all non-socialist countries grew by 7.6 per cent over the same period. Recent Soviet data show an even stronger shift in the terms of trade with the industrialised West in the early Gorbachev period, with the physical volume of imports falling by 13 per cent between 1985 and 1988 and the physical volume of exports growing by 40 per cent in the same period. During the five-year plan period from 1986–90 Soviet imports from all sources grew by only 1 per cent a year in real terms, compared with 6 per cent a year in 1981–85, 5.8 per cent in 1976–80 and 10.4 per cent from 1971–75 (Vneshtorg 1990: 9). A breakdown of the change in physical trade volumes by trading region between 1985 and 1990 is provided in Table 9.3. The export growth figures are exaggerated by the use of 1985 (when oil export volumes fell) as a base year.

In a market economy a major deterioration in the terms of

trade would result in downward pressure on the exchange rate, which would drive up the price of imported goods in relation to domestic goods and simultaneously make exports cheaper on foreign markets. Government policy would have to combine devaluation, or depreciation, of the exchange rate with restrictive fiscal and monetary policies, to equate domestic demand to the reduced level of domestic availability to prevent inflation. In a smoothly working economy in which consumers and producers reacted quickly to price signals, importers would cut back on imports of the least desirable goods and exporters would increase exports of goods with the lowest domestic marginal cost in relation to foreign currency. The reaction of the Soviet economy (albeit in a stage of transition to a more decentralised system) to the deterioration in the terms of trade differed substantially from that of a market economy. Firstly, the combined impact of the preis-ausgleich, the overvalued and inflexible system of exchange rates and the reluctance of the Soviet leadership to reform domestic prices meant that both retail and wholesale prices did not reflect either the increased scarcity of imports or the need for greater exports and did not stimulate a response from importers or exporters. Consequently decisions on which imports should be cut and which exports should be increased and to whom to allocate available supplies of convertible currency had to be taken by central planners and foreign trade officials, who had very imperfect knowledge about the effects of their decisions on the domestic economy. Similarly, the relative failure to boost hard currency exports of manufactured goods forced the central authorities to divert raw materials and unprocessed goods to the export sector to sustain hard currency imports, which further contributed to supply bottlenecks in the domestic economy. Finally, the Soviet authorities pursued exceedingly lax fiscal and monetary policies, which contributed to domestic inflationary pressures and to the virtual collapse of the monetary system. These problems were aggravated by bad decision-making over the structure of imports which reflected central priorities.

The deterioration in the real terms of trade was felt in the form of unplanned reductions in imports, the diversion of energy and raw materials from planned domestic uses to the export sector and by a reduced ability to alleviate unexpected bottlenecks by imports. In an economy with unemployed resources the need to boost the volume of net exports would (*ceteris paribus*) lead to an

*Table 9.4*   Commodity structure of Soviet imports from non-socialist
countries ($ million current)

|  | 1984 | 1985 | 1986 | 1987 | 1988 | 1989 |
|---|---|---|---|---|---|---|
| Total | 33,188 | 32,105 | 29,492 | 29,396 | 35,666 | 43,623 |
| Machinery | 7,418 | 6,735 | 8,612 | 7,913 | 10,161 | 11,903 |
| Fuels | 3,803 | 3,465 | 2,903 | 2,542 | 3,211 | 2,089 |
| Ores, metals | 4,160 | 4,462 | 4,171 | 4,375 | 5,067 | 4,816 |
| Chemicals | 2,103 | 2,664 | 2,751 | 3,221 | 3,355 | 3,855 |
| Wood and paper | 772 | 1,251 | 918 | 952 | 1,070 | 1,162 |
| Textiles | 1,140 | 1,251 | 918 | 1,239 | 1,508 | 1,619 |
| Foodstuffs | 9,857 | 8,419 | 5,280 | 4,733 | 6,207 | 8,731 |
| Industrial consumer goods | 2,056 | 2,520 | 2,345 | 2,092 | 2,352 | 5,006 |

*Sources:* Estimated from Vneshtorg (various years).
*Notes:* Estimated from percentage commodity breakdowns of imports from all
sources minus commodity breakdowns of imports from socialist countries.
Figures for 1990 have not been included because of reclassification of trade with
former GDR as non-socialist.
Other miscellaneous exports have not been included in the table.

expansion of employment and output. In the supply constrained
and highly monopolised and interdependent Soviet economy the
reduction in the supply of resources available for domestic use
exacerbated existing shortages and bottlenecks and had a
multiplied impact on domestic production, which became more
acute after existing stocks and reserves had been used up. The
appropriate response to supply shortage would have been to slow
down the growth of industrial output to the rate permitted by the
lower level of supply constraints as well as to slow down the rate of
growth of investment to a rate that would permit equilibrium in
the consumer market.

Under these circumstances the policy of attempting to accelerate
the growth rate and boost investment to increase production
capacity in the long term without a deliberate strategy of increased
borrowing was a major error. The effects of this policy are
reflected in the structure of Soviet imports shown in Table 9.4.
The dollar value of Soviet imports of machinery and equipment
from non-socialist countries grew by 78 per cent from $6.7 billion
in 1985 to $11.9 bn in 1989, after an initial fall in 1985 as
Gorbachev attempted to reduce the trade deficit inherited from
Chernenko. Although the dollar value of imported machinery

*Table 9.5*  Commodity structure of Soviet imports in comparable (1985) prices (million 1985 roubles)

| | 1985 | 1988 | 1989 | 1990 | 1990 as % of 1985 |
|---|---|---|---|---|---|
| **From all countries** | | | | | |
| Total | 69,429 | 68,040 | 73,595 | 72,900 | 105.0 |
| Machinery | 25,758 | 25,243 | 25,390 | 27,920 | 108.4 |
| Fuels, energy | 3,680 | 4,899 | 3,753 | 3,937 | 107.0 |
| Ores, metals | 5,762 | 5,171 | 4,783 | 3,645 | 63.3 |
| Chemicals | 3,471 | 3,402 | 3,900 | 3,281 | 94.5 |
| Wood and paper | 903 | 748 | 810 | 656 | 72.6 |
| Textiles | 1,180 | 748 | 810 | 583 | 49.4 |
| Foodstuffs | 14,650 | 11,975 | 13,540 | 12,612 | 86.0 |
| Industrial consumer goods | 8,748 | 8,709 | 10,818 | 14,361 | 164.2 |
| Unspecified | 5,277 | 7,145 | 9,791 | 5,905 | 112.0 |
| **From non-Socialist countries** | | | | | |
| Total | 26,892 | 25,123 | 29,379 | 30,264 | 112.5 |
| Machinery | 5,647 | 5,802 | 6,551 | 7,778 | 137.7 |
| Fuel, energy | 2,931 | 3,955 | 2,703 | 2,088 | 71.2 |
| Ores, metals | 3,711 | 2,467 | 2,057 | 2,996 | 80.7 |
| Chemicals, etc. | 2,232 | 2,200 | 2,585 | 2,240 | 100.4 |
| Wood and paper | 699 | 619 | 646 | 545 | 78.0 |
| Textiles | 1,049 | 576 | 617 | 424 | 40.4 |
| Foodstuffs | 7,045 | 5,538 | 6,816 | 6,204 | 88.1 |
| Industrial consumer goods | 2,124 | 1,714 | 3,554 | 5,447 | 256.5 |
| Unspecified | 1,452 | 2,251 | 3,849 | 2,542 | 175.1 |

*Sources:* Estimates based on data for percentage breakdowns of trade by commodity groups in 1985 prices and physical volume data in Vneshtorg (various years).
*Notes:* Trade with non-socialist countries excludes trade with the former GDR in all years (i.e. GDR was not reclassified in 1990).
Components do not sum to totals due to rounding.

and equipment was cut in 1987 as part of the move away from the policy of acceleration, imports of machinery and equipment continued to grow in 1988 and 1989. This figure overestimates the real rate of growth as a result of the major increase in the dollar price of Soviet imports of machinery and equipment. Nevertheless, the estimates of the value of Soviet imports in comparable prices in Table 9.5 indicate that the volume of Soviet imports of machinery and equipment from capitalist countries grew by 37 per cent in real terms from 1985–89 and constituted a growing proportion of Soviet imports from capitalist countries. The expansion of imported equipment was once again partly linked to the chemical industry. Hard currency imports of chemical equipment grew from $0.4 billion in 1985 to $1.3 billion in 1989 and comprised 40.5 per cent of equipment supplied to the chemical industry compared with 23.5 per cent in 1985 (Narkhoz 1989: 653–8).

Other industries where the value of hard currency imports of machinery and equipment showed a significant expansion included sectors that were directed towards the long-term satisfaction of consumer demand and/or the creation of an export sector embodying a greater degree of value-added. These included equipment for the food industry, which grew from $131 million in 1985 to $429 million in 1989, and for textiles, which grew from $147 million to $513 million, while imports for the wood-processing and furniture industries also received greater priority (Narkhoz 1989: 653–60). Although import policy during this period indicated a more sensible set of priorities within the machinery sector, the policy of expanding imports of machinery and equipment in total remained suspect in view of the hard currency constraint.

The reduction in the value of imports of fuel and energy after 1985 principally reflected price changes and had little direct effect on supplies to the domestic economy, as it was largely composed of crude oil which was directly re-exported. This did have a direct impact on the short-run balance of payments as this was one of the methods of converting OPEC debt into hard currency which is reflected in the fall in value of energy exports. The real volumes of imports of chemicals and wood products were not significantly different in 1989 from their 1985 levels.

### b) The demand side

The impact of the deterioration in the terms of trade on domestic demand can be analysed from the perspective of its effects on balance in the domestic retail market and that of budgetary balance. The most straightforward method is to examine the effect on the balance between incomes and expenditure in the domestic retail market. In this case an increase in the volume of exports required to pay for a given volume of imports is equivalent to an increase in non-marketed expenditure, which creates money incomes for workers in export industries (and their suppliers) but does not add directly to the supply of goods available for consumption (and *ceteris paribus* needs to be offset by additional taxes to preserve equilibrium in the domestic consumer market). Similarly, a reduction in imported consumer goods constitutes a decrease in the availability of retail goods, which absorb money demand, with no consequent reduction in money incomes. A cut in imported components and equipment may also lead to a reduction in production of goods for the domestic retail market.

In addition to the direct contribution in the form of the 'special earnings of foreign trade', foreign trade also has a substantial indirect effect on both budget revenue (largely generated by imports) and expenditure (largely generated by exports). For example, losses arising from the additional expenditure associated with the high marginal cost of energy extraction to generate export revenues will normally be underwritten by the state budget. Similarly, additional turnover taxes on imported goods or from goods produced with imported components and/or enterprise profits generated by imported equipment made a direct contribution to the state budget that did not appear under the activities of foreign trade. These effects may be so large that the formal references to the contribution of foreign trade to state budget revenues and expenditure in the official budget statistics may considerably understate their real impact. The net effect was that the deterioration in the real terms of trade (i.e. the increase in the volume of exports required to pay for a given volume of imports) following the oil price increase required an equivalent cut in domestic investment or an increase in income or turnover taxes (or a reduction in wage rates) to prevent the generation of inflationary pressures in the domestic economy. The failure to recognise this was a factor which contributed to the growing budget deficits and growth of suppressed inflationary pressures in the second half of the 1980s, which were aggravated by cuts in imports of consumer goods.

It can be seen from Table 9.4 that the major burden of the attempt to restore equilibrium to the balance of trade between 1985 and 1987 fell on imports of foodstuffs, which fell by \$3.7 billion, and industrial consumer goods (\$428 million). Imports of textiles and clothing also fell by more than 20 per cent in real terms. The fall in value of foodstuffs was largely the result of reduced grain imports which was facilitated by improved harvests which (according to official statistics) averaged 196.5 million tonnes from 1986–89 compared with an average of 168.7 million tonnes in 1981–85, after adjustment for harvest losses (Ekonomika i Zhizn 1991, no. 5). The net effect was that in most years after 1985 the aggregate supply of grain (obtained by adding imports to the preceding year's harvest) exceeded 220 million tonnes and remained above the estimated levels of the late 1970s and early 1980s. There was, however, a marked reduction in hard currency imports of fresh fruit, which were cut from 329,000 tonnes in 1985 to 136,000 in 1989 which contributed to a decline in the availability of fruit. Similarly, hard currency imports of meat declined from 198,000 tonnes in 1986 to 77,000 in 1987 (compared with 653,000 tonnes in 1980) before growing to 218,000 tonnes in 1989. Imports of eggs and dairy products were also affected. Given the leadership's avowed concern with the problems of the Soviet diet and vitamin deficiency, these cuts (which also exacerbated the problems of consumer disequilibrium) displayed an unusual set of import priorities.

The government's reluctance to import consumer goods to help balance the domestic market was attacked by Nikolai Shmelev, a highly respected radical economist in a speech to the Congress of People's deputies in June 1989. Shmelev proposed that the government should immediately import $15 billion worth of consumer goods to absorb inflationary overhang, followed by additional annual imports of $5 billion a year to equate the flow of money incomes with the supply of consumer goods in order to avoid a financial collapse. His proposals were further outlined in an article published in *Kommunist* in 1990 (Spandaryan and Shmelev 1990). They argued that an expansion of imports of consumer goods could be financed by a combination of a reduction in wastage and overconsumption of raw materials, metals and intermediate inputs which would make these resources available for export; a reduction in imports of machinery and equipment particularly for the heavy and machine tools industries; a reduction in imports of grain and other agricultural products (which they argued could be produced domestically following radical agricultural reforms which would release hard currency to finance imports for investment in agrarian infrastructure); energetic measures to mobilise the potential of the population to generate hard currency, including the possibility of long-term leasing of land and buildings to foreigners; a reduction in overseas aid and the liquidation of existing debts to the Soviet Union and, finally, the move to hard currency trade in world market prices in relations with Eastern Europe and with the former East Germany in particular.

In practice several of the measures advocated by Spandaryan and Shmelev (including increased imports of consumer goods and the move to trade in hard currency with CMEA) were incorporated into Ryzhkov's emergency measures to improve supplies to the domestic retail market. The real volume of imported consumer goods rose from 8.7 billion roubles in 1988 to 10.8 billion in 1989 and was further increased to 14.4 billion in 1990 (see Table 9.5). Imports of consumer goods from non-socialist countries (excluding the former GDR), which had doubled in 1989 to $5 billion (largely as an emergency response to the need to improve consumer supplies to the coal mining and oil producing regions in response to industrial unrest), were increased by a further 53 per cent in real terms in 1990. Similarly, exports of non-ferrous metals were boosted to a record level of $4 billion (although it is not clear whether these came from unutilised reserves) and exports of arms (especially on credit terms) were substantially reduced. At the same time imports from India were substantially increased and exports to eastern Europe were curtailed. Critically, however, imports of machinery and equipment from the West (excluding the former GDR) grew by 18.7 per cent in real terms contributing to the crisis in the balance of trade and payments.

## THE COLLAPSE OF INTRA-CMEA TRADE

The Soviet Union had experienced major difficulties in meeting contracts to supply energy to Eastern Europe during 1989, leading to bitter complaints from Hungary, Poland and Czecho-slovakia in the autumn of 1989, which in turn led to attempts to restrict exports to the Soviet Union. The Soviet authorities attributed the failure to meet East European contracts to domestic supply problems not deliberate policy, a claim that appears justified in view of the falling domestic production which necessitated cuts in hard currency oil exports in 1989 (see Chapter 9), while (according to Soviet trade statistics) cuts in oil exports to Eastern Europe for the year as a whole were negligible.

The inability to sustain communist rule in Eastern Europe had been recognised by the Soviet leadership by the time of Ryzhkov's speech to the Congress of People's Deputies on 13 December 1989, in which he outlined his proposals to recentralise the economy and increase the production of consumer goods as part of a set of crisis measure to stabilise the retail sector. It was apparent from Ryzhkov's speech that the Soviet government was now aware of the depth of the economic crisis facing the country and was no longer willing to provide energy and raw materials on terms that were unfavourable to the Soviet Union to newly democratising, market-oriented and pro-western governments of Eastern Europe. Ryzhkov outlined his support for a 'proposal to transfer trade co-operation with them [the CMEA partners], to current world prices and to payments in freely convertible currencies' (*Pravda*, 14 December 1989). Although radical Hungarian and Czech economists had made similar proposals to reform the system of intra-CMEA trade and pricing on grounds of economic efficiency, Ryzhkov's proposals were clearly intended to ease the Soviet Union's hard currency problems by demanding payment for Soviet exports of energy and raw materials to Eastern Europe in hard currency or improved supplies of hard goods (including food, and better quality consumer goods and manufactures), not to pave the way for market reforms in CMEA. While Soviet exporters would be able to divert energy supplies to western markets if East European importers could not pay for them in hard currency, East European exporters' proposals would clearly be unable to divert manufactured goods that did not meet western quality specifications, while Soviet ministries and enterprises would be unlikely to continue to import these goods if they were required to pay for them in hard currency (see Smith 1989, 1992).

The value of Soviet exports to the CMEA (including trade with the former GDR which can be estimated for 1990 from the Sarafanov study) as a whole fell from 37.8 billion roubles ($60 billion) in 1989 to 30.7 billion ($52.2 billion) in 1990, while the rouble value of Soviet imports from the CMEA fell from 40.6 billion roubles in 1989 to 39.4 billion roubles in 1990, although this was equivalent to a small increase in the dollar value of Soviet imports from the CMEA as a whole from $64.4 billion in 1989 to $67.9 billion in 1990 as a result of movements in the official rouble:dollar exchange rate. More important, this represented falls of 13 per cent in the physical volume of Soviet exports and 7.5 per cent in the volume of imports. Exports to the five East European members of CMEA (excluding the GDR) fell by 16 per cent from 31.3 billion roubles in 1989 to 26.3 billion in 1990 and imports by 6.1 per cent from 33.4 billion roubles to 31.4 billion roubles (see Table 9.6). Thus, although the price terms of trade in CMEA moved against the Soviet Union in 1990, net resource flows moved in favour of the Soviet Union as the Soviet deficit in its trade with CMEA (including the GDR) grew from 2.8 billion roubles ($4.4 billion) in 1989 to 8.7 billion roubles ($15.7 billion) in 1990. The reduction in Soviet exports to the five East European countries was concentrated on energy, the value of which fell from 11.4 billion roubles in 1989 to 8.8 billion roubles in 1990. Although part of this was explained by price reductions, the volume of Soviet crude oil exports fell by 23 per cent from 51.3 million tonnes in 1989 to 39.3 million in 1990 as the Soviet Union attempted to maintain hard currency exports as domestic production declined. Soviet exports of natural gas to the five rose slightly from 39.8 billion cubic metres to 41.6 billion. The last formal session of the CMEA was held in Budapest on 28 June 1991. The collapse of Soviet trade with the former CMEA countries in 1991 was precipitate. Soviet imports from former CMEA members fell by 63 per cent and exports by 57 per cent, much of which was supported by crude short-term barter arrangements (Ekonomika i Zhizn, 1992, no. 6).

## THE COLLAPSE OF TRADE IN 1991

In 1991 the value of exports in total fell by 33 per cent and imports were cut by 44 per cent in current prices. This largely reflected the fall in trade with CMEA following the move to trade in hard currency. Exports to the developed West fell by 16 per cent and imports from the West fell by 32.6 per cent as the united Germany became by far the largest trade partner, accounting for 13 per cent of exports and 17 per cent of imports (*Ekonomicheskaya Gazeta* 1992, no. 6). Transactions for hard currency fell more sharply as barter transactions grew in importance. Hard currency exports fell to $31.8 billion while hard currency imports fell to $30.7 billion, according to the Sarafanov study. Critically these figures included trade with the former GDR and Finland and should be compared with exports of $43.6 billion and imports of $52.8

*Table 9.6*   Soviet energy exports to Eastern Europe (excluding GDR) in 1989 and 1990

|  | 1989 | 1990 | Difference |
|---|---|---|---|
| **Value data (million roubles)** | | | |
| **Total** | **11,371** | **8,812** | **−2,559** |
| Crude oil | 5,773 | 3,822 | −1,951 |
| Oil products | 686 | 479 | −207 |
| Natural gas | 3,373 | 3,131 | −242 |
| Volume data | | | |
| **Crude oil** | | | |
| (000 tonnes) | **51,361** | **39,269** | **−12,092** |
| Oil products | 5,032 | 4,087 | −945 |
| Natural gas | | | |
| (bn cubic metres) | 39,819 | 41,604 | +1,785 |
| Crude oil by country: | | | |
| Bulgaria | 11,463 | 7,801 | −3,662 |
| Hungary | 6,321 | 5,027 | −1,294 |
| Poland | 13,036 | 10,730 | −2,306 |
| Romania | 3,941 | 2,474 | −1,467 |
| Czechoslovakia | 16,600 | 13,237 | −3,363 |

*Source:* Vneshtorg 1990.

billion in 1990. Imports of consumer goods were especially badly affected, aggravating domestic shortages and fuelling inflationary pressures. Imports of coffee fell by 14 per cent, tea by 31 per cent, cocoa products 31 per cent, animal oil 25 per cent, sunflower oil 66 per cent, apples and pears 65 per cent, citrus fruits 46 per cent, cotton cloth 69 per cent, and leather footwear 71 per cent.

## CONCLUSION

Soviet import behaviour since the early 1960s indicates that cuts in imports of machinery and equipment from the West were largely caused by balance of payments pressures and emerging domestic shortages, particularly in the consumer sector. Gorbachev's attempts to boost imports of machinery and equipment in 1989 in apparent defiance of this principle contributed to the accelerated growth of both internal and external imbalances, which contributed to the breakdown of the monetary system. The significance of this conclusion for the future of the Russian economy is profound. To prevent the gap between Russian and western technology levels from widening, either the economy must become more capable of generating and diffusing domestic technology or a greater volume of imported equipment will be required to generate a given rate of growth. The centrally planned economic system was incapable of generating domestic innovation or the volume of exports required to sustain the required level of imports of technology. Radical economic and social reforms will be a necessary condition for Russian economic recovery. Can such reforms be implemented under Russian conditions and, if so, will they be sufficient to prevent further decline in Russia's relative economic position?

# Chapter 10

# The transition to a market economy in Russia

## INTRODUCTION

The Russian government approved a policy involving the rapid transition to a free market economy while the Soviet Union was still in existence. The economic policy of the Russian government was outlined by President Yeltsin on 28 October 1991 in a speech to the Russian parliament, which then passed a series of bills on 15 November creating the legal framework for the transition to a market economy. More specific detail was published in document called the 'Memorandum on the Economic Policy of the Russian Federation' (Memorandum 1992), which was approved by the Russian government on 27 February 1992 and which formed the basis of Russia's letter of intent to the IMF. The policies outlined in the memorandum (and other policy documents) incorporated the basic pillars for the rapid transition to a market economy (price liberalisation, removal of bureaucratic constraints on economic activity, privatisation of state industry and macro-economic stabilisation, together with an appeal for western economic assistance) developed by Jeffrey Sachs, Professor of International Trade at Harvard University, who has been a principal adviser to both the Polish and the Russian governments (Sachs 1991). The proposals, which had the broad support of the IMF, were largely modelled on the policies adopted by the Polish government in January 1990, which has been popularly referred to as a 'shock-therapy' programme. Yegor Gaidar, the first deputy prime minister, was given responsibility for implementing the reform programme.

## PRICE LIBERALISATION AND THE RUSSIAN STABILISATION PROGRAMME

The programme of the Russian government involved the immediate liberalisation of approximately 90 per cent of retail prices and 80 per cent of wholesale prices on 2 January 1992. Prices which remained under central control were increased by an average of 3.5 times. By the end of March 1992, price controls remained for only 12 basic staple foodstuffs, rents, public services and public transport. All remaining central government subsidies and price controls were scheduled to be eliminated by the end of 1993, by which time fuel prices were to be equated with world market prices at the market-determined exchange rate.

However, Russian industry, operating under highly monopolistic and protected conditions, responded to price liberalisation initially by increasing prices and cutting production to boost profits. According to official statistics (Ekonomika i Zhizn 1992, no. 17) industrial output fell by 13 per cent in the first quarter of 1992, while national income fell by 14 per cent, retail prices grew sixfold (following a 2.2-fold increase in the last three quarters of 1991) and were 13 times higher than at the end of March the preceding year. Prices of meat, poultry, sausage meat, butter, cheese, confectionery, children's items and clothes, shoes and other basic goods rose by between 5 and 8 times on average throughout the Russian Federation, although price increases in the major cities including Moscow and St Petersburg were substantially higher. Prices for fruit, vegetables and potatoes rose 2–3 times. The cost of public services remained controlled, but housing prices were three times higher than a year earlier, public transport between 5 and 8 times higher and certain health charges rose tenfold. Retail turnover fell by 51 per cent in real terms in the first quarter of 1992 compared with the corresponding period of 1991. Although this figure was affected by consumers running down stocks that had been built up before price liberalisation, consumers also shifted purchases away from more expensive items to cheaper goods, indicating the presence of tighter budget constraints. More seriously, food production fell by 28 per cent, partly because of supply difficulties but also indicating that the impact of price increases on household incomes and savings had led to an excessive reduction in demand for food and consumer goods. On the positive side the greater part of the sixfold increase in retail prices took place in January and were given officially as 245 per cent inflation (a price index of 345) as prices jumped up to new levels, followed by inflation rates of 38 per cent and 30 per cent in February and March (all figures in this section from Ekonomika i Zhizn 1992, no. 17).

Price liberalisation restored household savings to more 'normal' levels in relation to GNP and personal consumption by the simple expedient of converting repressed inflation into open inflation. A rough estimate indicates that the purchasing power of personal savings plus cash more than halved during the first quarter of 1992. Although higher relative prices for staple goods, together with the prevailing economic uncertainty, also provided households with a greater incentive to save out of current income, tight monetary and fiscal policies were still required to equate the flow of money income with the available supplies of goods and services. Monetary policy was complicated by the absence of financial instruments to fund government borrowing, as a result of which budget deficits could only be financed by expanding the money supply and by the fact that the Central Bank of Russia, which had de facto become responsible for monetary control, had no powers to prevent the central banks of the non-Russian republics from issuing rouble credits, although by historical accident the printing presses were all located in Russia and the Russian authorities could control the supply of cash itself. At the same time the shift to a tax system based on (ex ante) personal and enterprise taxes (including income taxes, value added taxes and profits taxes) in place of (ex post) budgetary expropriations of enterprise profits and arbitrary turnover taxes as the chief source of central budget income had (as was to be expected) a considerable adverse effect on government revenues, before the necessary regulatory controls and collection agencies could be established. In the interim, import duties and export taxes were required to play a major role as a source of budget revenue in the period before domestic prices had been brought in line with world market prices.

The Russian government initially approved a balanced budget for the first quarter of 1992 with planned revenues and expenditure at 420.5 billion roubles. The memorandum on economic policy (Ekonomika i Zhizn 1992, no. 10) projected a budget deficit for 1992 as a whole equivalent to 0.9 per cent of GNP, compared with an estimated deficit in excess of 20 per cent of Russian GDP in 1991 (including an estimate of Russia's share of the all-Union budget deficit). The scale of the proposed reduction in the budget deficit can be seen by comparison with Poland, where it had been planned to reduce the budget deficit from 7 per cent of GDP in 1989 to 1 per cent in 1990. The major part of the reduction was to be achieved by cuts in government expenditure on subsidies on basic goods including food, enterprise subsidies, expenditure on defence and internal security and economic administration. Budget revenues were expected to improve in the remainder of the year as taxes on oil and gas were gradually increased to bring domestic prices in line with world market prices and VAT revenue collection improved. The other major sources of planned revenue were import taxes (1.3 per cent of GNP in 1992 as a whole) and export duties (8.2 per cent of GNP) which were imposed in April to cover the difference between domestic prices of exportables (including oil, gas and precious metals) and the world market price.

The success (or lack of success) with which the government pursued a tight budget policy in the first quarter of 1992 was a matter of considerable debate, which in part reflects the inadequacy of the statistics available to the government itself. The government initially claimed that the budget deficit in the first quarter was only 1.5 per cent of GDP and that the collection of VAT revenue had improved dramatically in March (*Financial Times*, 13 May 1992). Hanson (1992) estimates from data published in *Izvestiya* that the real deficit may have been nearer 8–10 per cent of GNP. His estimates show that export revenues were only 9 billion roubles compared with a planned level of 228 billion, while parliamentary opposition forced reductions to the proposed 28 per cent value added tax which contributed to a further loss of 44 billion roubles of planned revenue. Similarly, parliamentary pressure for increased social expenditure added to difficulties in controlling government expenditure. In his bitter critique of government policy, Yavlinsky (1992) argues that government revenues, particularly from foreign trade activities, were far below planned levels and that revenue figures had been artificially boosted by the inclusion of foreign credits and borrowing from local budgets, while expenditure had been artificially reduced by deliberately slowing down expenditure from March to April. It appears that under conditions of definition and redefinition it was virtually impossible to estimate with any certainty one of the key variables on which government policy was based.

A major problem threatening macroeconomic stability was the rapid growth of credit and especially inter-enterprise credits which the Russian Central Bank estimated had reached a gross figure of over 1.4 trillion roubles (the equivalent of three months' GNP) by the end of April 1992. Inter-enterprise credits largely resulted from the failure, or inability, of enterprises to pay their suppliers and is in part a continuation of practices pursued under central planning when enterprises simply passed on their output to customers according to plan instructions without needing to check on the customer's solvency. There is some evidence to suggest that this problem is most acute in the arms manufacturing industries where enterprises are maintaining former output levels despite the loss of internal and foreign markets. This practice protected enterprises from the rigours of tight monetary policy and the need to shed labour on a large scale or cease production.

A considerable proportion of this sum can be explained by gross debt (enterprise A fails to pay enterprise B, which in turn is unable to pay enterprise C, etc.) and indicates an increase in the velocity of circulation of money. It also implies an effective subsidy to industries that receive interest-free credit at a time of rapid inflation. Some of the net debt appears as bank credits when supplying enterprises that cannot cover their current needs by delaying payment of bills simply increased bank borrowing. The growth of credit has been facilitated by the rapid growth of private and co-operative banks (some of which are little more than glorified loan institutions, incapable of or unwilling to assess the long-term viability of their creditors) and which are subject to few central controls, and has meant that enterprises with liquidity problems managed to find a relatively easy source of credit. Investment credits on Russian territory grew from 439 billion roubles at the end of 1991 (of which the commercial banks were responsible for 409 billion roubles) to 856 billion roubles by 1 April 1992 (*Ekonomicheskaya Gazeta* 1992, nos 6 and 17).

The implementation of a tight monetary policy will require the government to take firmer measures to limit the growth of credit including the maintenance of positive real interest rates, which could have the effect of bankrupting enterprises and creating open unemployment. The situation has also been aggravated by technical problems, which led to delays in processing inter-enterprise payments through the banking system. As a result, perfectly viable enterprises have been caught up in debt chains and it is exceedingly difficult to ascertain the long-term prospects for an enterprise by looking at its short-run cash position. There is a fear that a single enterprise bankruptcy could lead to a major chain of bankruptcies, which would result in the collapse of viable enterprises, in addition to the social problems involved. The government responded to the problem in May 1992 by easing monetary controls and expanding credits to industry by 200 billion roubles and by introducing clearing arrangements administered by local (oblast) governments.

A second problem has resulted from the failure of the printing press to keep up with the demand for cash, which has meant that many workers have not been paid, with some delays stretching back for three months and non-payment of wages and pensions totalling 40 billion roubles in March. As what has become a major social problem could be technically solved by the issue of high denomination banknotes, there is a suspicion that this is a crude method of limiting the money supply and the growth of cash demand in an economy that is unusually dependent on cash settlements in the sphere of personal consumption. At the same time the Russian Central Bank has restricted the supply of banknotes to other republics, which may accelerate the move towards the creation of new currencies, but has also reduced the scale of the problem of rouble cash holding outside Russia itself.

## MACROECONOMIC STABILISATION AND THE STANDARD OF LIVING

Given that money wages had consistently grown faster than the monetary value of consumer goods during the Gorbachev era, the elimination of inflationary overhang and the subsequent restoration of balance in the consumer market required that retail prices should grow faster than money incomes. The government target was that the population should be compensated for between 65 and 70 per cent of price increases. In principle, pensions, child benefits and teachers' salaries were increased broadly in line with this objective, although there were frequent complaints about delays in payment and that the government had underestimated the real rate of inflation. Similarly, although industrial wages were deregulated in January 1992, the government attempted to keep the growth of wages below that of prices by means of a progressive tax levied on any growth of the total wage fund of state enterprises above a government-determined norm. According to a report in *Izvestiya* (21 February 1992) real incomes fell by 40 per cent in January 1992 following price liberalisation. However, the impact of the fall in real incomes was widely dispersed, with those starting on low incomes and who lacked political or economic influence badly affected by the increase in prices for food and other staple goods. The average money wage in the first quarter of 1992 was 1,950 roubles a month with average per capita incomes of 1,250 roubles a month. However, more than nine million workers (11 per cent of the total employed) received less than 900 roubles a month and a third of the population (50 million) lived on basic per capita income of less than 900 roubles, which was estimated by the Ministry of Labour and Employment to be the basic minimum necessary for subsistence for an adult worker in April (Ekonomika i Zhizn 1992, no. 17). Other government estimates (Ekonomika i Zhizn 1992, no. 4) considered that the minimum consumption basket for a family of four cost from 1,300–1,500 roubles per head in February 1992. These figures imply that unless economic performance improves, the standard of living of those receiving below average incomes will be below what is considered to be the minimum acceptable. Consumption of carbohydrates grew at the expense of protein and 60 per cent of families consumed less than three kilos of meat per head per month, while economic crimes, including burglaries grew by 70 per cent (Yavlinsky 1992).

## PRIVATISATION

Detailed government proposals for the privatisation of state and municipal enterprise and facilities for implementation in 1992 and preparations for privatisation to be conducted after that date were published in a Presidential decree of 29 December 1991 (*Ekonomicheskaya Gazeta* 1992, no. 2). The proposals distinguished between the privatisation of trade, services and small-scale industry, which had been conducted relatively quickly in the majority of East European countries and had been one of the more successful aspects of reform, and the far more complicated and lengthy process of privatising large-scale industry. Furthermore, 'small' privatisation was expected to bring immediate benefits to the population in the form of increased competitiveness and provision of trade and services during the period of price liberalisation and to reduce inflationary pressures by absorbing personal savings and increasing budget revenues, which would be used to finance social expenditure.

The decree proposed the compulsory privatisation of all wholesale and retail trade, catering and other services, and industries supplying those sectors, including small enterprises (employing up to 200 people) in food and light industry and agricultural services, together with enterprises in the transport and construction industries. The programme established detailed targets for the proportion of enterprises in each industry scheduled for compulsory privatisation that had to be completed in 1992 (largely between 50 and 70 per cent) and broke these up into targets that had to be fulfilled by each autonomous republic and region in the course of the year. 'Small' privatisation was to be achieved by auction and was expected to raise revenue amounting to 92 billion roubles in 1992. The progress of 'small privatisation' in the first quarter was slow, with only 1,194 (0.7 per cent) businesses in retail trade, 962 (0.7 per cent) in public catering and 662 (0.5 per cent) in services privatised and only 58,000 (20 per cent) enterprises in retail trade, public catering and services actually registered as independent commercial entities by 1 April (Yavlinksy 1992).

The problem of privatising large-scale industry has proved to be far more complicated throughout Eastern Europe and involved the development of complicated voucher schemes in Poland and Czechoslovakia. These schemes were largely motivated by the desire to stimulate widespread ownership of industry, which it was hoped would win popular support for private ownership and make the transition to a market economy irreversible. This also means that the population receives some compensation for the creation of the privatised capital stock against which they have no other formal claim (e.g. in the form of pension funds). It was also hoped that this would limit 'spontaneous privatisation' whereby the nomenklatura (including managers and former party officials with inside knowledge) and the economic mafia transferred state property into their own hands at prices below those that reflected their true value and in some cases stripped them of their more profitable, or readily fungible, assets. A considerable part of the decree specified different categories of large-scale industry for which privatisation could only take place with the permission of the Russian government (e.g. higher education, publishing houses, production of tobacco and spirits) or the appropriate local authority (taxis, hotels, municipal services) or was prohibited altogether in 1992 (natural resources, water, television and radio). This part of the decree appears largely intended to prevent 'spontaneous privatisation', but there is considerable evidence to indicate that the provisions of the law were simply being ignored by local officials.

The decree proposed that the privatisation of large-scale industry would be mainly completed in 1993 and 1994 when assets worth an estimated 350 billion roubles and 470–500 billion roubles respectively would be privatised. Initially all state enterprises employing more than 200 workers were to be converted into public corporations, which was intended to strengthen financial discipline by at least subjecting enterprises to hard budget constraints and exposing them to market forces. These would then be converted into private corporations by the sale and distribution of shares on the basis of a combination of the issue of vouchers to the public, preferential (non-voting shares) to workers in the enterprise and ultimately the straightforward purchase of shares by Russian and foreign citizens.

The proposals for the privatisation of large-scale industry suffer from a number of problems. The idea of communal ownership predates communist power and remains strong in many parts of Russia, especially in rural and former rural areas. Furthermore, Gorbachev attempted to strengthen enterprise democracy and give workers greater power in the management of enterprises in the first years of his tenure. Consequently there have been demands inside and outside the Russian parliament for the creation of worker-owned enterprises or at the least for greater worker participation in plant ownership and management. At the end of May 1992 the Russian parliament proposed that workers should receive 51 per cent of shares in their enterprises. The microeconomic counter argument to this proposal (which is partly based on Yugoslav experience) is that, if worker-owners have more to gain from their function as workers in the plant than as owners of capital, they will have little incentive to use capital efficiently and will vote for increased wages rather than investment, use capital inefficiently and even sell off assets to generate short-term income.

The government proposals allow for a significant distribution of shares to workers and managers. Enterprise workers will be given 25 per cent and managers 5 per cent of the capital value of the enterprise in the form of non-voting shares (subject to an individual maximum of 20 times the minimum wage) and workers and retired employees will be able to buy a further 10 per cent of shares at a 30 per cent discount. The principle behind this is that, by restricting worker ownership to non-voting shares, workers will be given a financial interest in the efficient operation of the enterprise but not a controlling interest. It is hoped that this will be sufficient to win the support of industrial workers for the principle of privatisation. However, workers in unprofitable and potentially bankrupt industries will be exposed to the double jeopardy of the possible loss of employment and the value of their shares, while others may benefit, somewhat arbitrarily, from secure employment and increasing capital wealth.

Like 'small' privatisation, the proposals are to be implemented by local administrations on the basis of targets established by the central government which are to be implemented within a very short period of time, while the receipts from privatisation are expected to make a major contribution to government income in 1993 and 1994. Polish and Czechoslovak experience indicates that the general public displayed little initial enthusiasm for buying shares and had very little information on how to make sensible share purchases. The Czechoslovak scheme for rapid privatis- ation, which is being closely studied by some Russian economists, involved the sale of coupons to the public which could be exchanged for shares in an auction process. The scheme attracted few investors before it was salvaged by the emergence of financial intermediaries, who offered to take up vouchers from individuals (or exchanged them for shares in investment funds), sometimes promising tenfold returns within a year. This carries a great risk that investors will submit enterprises to extreme pressure for short-term returns rather than long-term profits. The problem of obtaining accurate information about the longer-term prospects of enterprises will be greatly magnified in the vast Russian economy. Local and bureaucratic opposition to the privatisation of large-scale industry is likely to be considerably stronger, and conflict between the government and local government agencies (particularly in the large cities and autonomous republics) makes the proposed timetable for the sale of shares look optimistic. If this is the case the government will be confronted with major difficulties in both raising budget revenue and bringing external pressures to bear on enterprise performance.

## THE CREATION OF AN OPEN ECONOMY

The creation of a fully open economy means that domestic consumers should be able to choose between imported and domestically produced goods and services on the basis of relative prices, not availability; producers should choose between selling to and buying from domestic and foreign markets on the basis of price criteria, and capital and labour should be free to move in and out of the economy according to price and profit criteria. A fully open economy involves allowing domestic relative prices to be determined by world market prices, while the price level is determined by the exchange rate which in turn is determined by the supply and demand for the currency in international currency markets. In the short term, however, while domestic prices continue to be affected by subsidies and price controls and while domestic shortages and undeveloped capital markets result in a lack of confidence in the domestic currency, reinforced by low international confidence in the ability of the country to both service debt and create an export sector, the exchange rate will be held below its long-term equilibrium value. Under these circumstances controls over the free movement of goods and factors of production may be justified on the grounds that they are necessary to prevent an irreversible outflow (or change in the ownership) of resources that carry subsidies or whose price may be undervalued at the current exchange rate.

### The introduction of convertibility

The lack of currency convertibility was a major factor contributing to the failure of Gorbachev's attempts to open the economy to foreign investment and to decentralise foreign trade rights to enterprises and co-operatives. The absence of external convertibility meant that the rouble had no value outside the Soviet Union and foreign trade activities had to be conducted either in convertible currencies or on the basis of bilateral agreements. Foreign investors had no incentive to produce for the Soviet market, as rouble earnings could not be converted into hard currency to pay for imported capital and inputs, or for the repatriation of profits. Domestic producers could not exercise their legal rights to import equipment and materials because of their lack of access to hard currency to pay for them.

The Russian government inherited a complicated mixture of multiple exchange rates, import and export licences and quotas, differentiated retention quotas and limited foreign currency reserves to defend a convertible currency. Retention quotas, which required exporting enterprises to surrender a proportion of their hard currency earnings (normally 40 per cent) to the central authorities at the official exchange rate, contributed to capital flight by giving exporters an incentive to (illegally) keep hard currency earnings overseas or to fail to declare hard currency earnings, and contributed to a two-tier system for the allocation of hard currency which artificially devalued the market rate for the rouble by restricting the supply of hard currency to currency auctions. Similarly, a ban was imposed on barter trade which was used by enterprises to avoid retention quotas, or to avoid restrictions on exports of subsidised or underpriced scarce goods. In the transitional period the Russian government was obliged to maintain these restrictions on trade until the source of the economic distortion had been eliminated. The first act of the Russian government in the field of foreign trade was to pass a resolution (dated 29 December 1991) banning the export of consumer goods in short supply, which listed 60 goods whose export was prohibited and which was mainly directed at preventing the export of goods to other former Soviet republics.

### The introduction of convertibility in Poland

The introduction of forms of internal convertibility played an important role in the transition to a market economy in Poland and Czechoslovakia by exposing domestic enterprises to international competition, thereby restricting their monopoly position on the domestic market, and introducing world market relative prices, which required enterprises to examine the profitability of export and imports at an early stage in the reform process. Trade liberalisation also facilitated an increase in the supply of imported consumer goods (including well-known western branded goods), the import of which had been suppressed or neglected by communist governments. This won some popular support for government policies and helped to alleviate suppressed inflation and provided a kick-start to the development of an entrepreneurial retail trade sector.

In Poland, the communist government initially introduced a

limited form of internal convertibility in March 1989. This initially permitted Polish citizens to exchange zlotys for hard currency at a rate that tracked the black market rate. This could be used to purchase goods and services in the domestic economy or at hard currency stores. Foreigners were obliged to change a minimum daily amount of hard currency into zlotys at the official rate, which was approximately ten times less favourable than the market rate. Legal private exchange offices mushroomed during 1989, but loss of control over the money supply resulted in accelerating inflation and shortages, leading to loss of confidence in the zloty which drove the exchange rate down to a third of its October value in December (Milanovic 1992: 521). The Balcerowicz government introduced a more extensive form of current account convertibility in January 1990, at the beginning of its stabilisation programme. This permitted individuals and enterprises to exchange currency at a fixed rate of 9,500 zlotys to the $US (compared with the December rate of 5,200 zlotys to the $US) for current account transactions (i.e. including all import and export activities). It remained illegal to export the currency or change it outside the country. Other forms of current account convertibility (e.g. Hungary) did not immediately give all citizens the right to freely change currency, but gradually liberalised import controls and permitted licensed importers to obtain currency.

The chief advantage of a fixed rate system was that it gave a minimum value to the zloty and restored some confidence in the monetary system. Furthermore, the preservation of a fixed rate acted as a constraint to the growth of the money supply, as holders of excess zlotys could demand payment in dollars. A fixed rate provided a clearly definable ceiling to the level of prices domestic producers could charge, beyond which they would incur competition from imports. Finally, it gave a clear message to the population of the government's commitment to sustain an open economy and the stabilisation programme. A fixed rate also has disadvantages. Firstly, it is difficult to establish what the real rate should be under highly volatile external circumstances combined with hyperinflationary pressures. In the Polish situation the determination of the rate was facilitated by the prior existence of a floating rate in 1989. Secondly, if the government is unable to sustain a fixed rate for a reasonable period of time, public confidence in economic policy and in the monetary system will be damaged, which will reduce credibility in subsequent stabilisation measures. This may tempt the government to introduce a fixed rate at a depreciated level, which it feels it can sustain over the medium term but which will limit the exposure of domestic enterprises to foreign competition and the counterinflationary effect of convertibility.

Both Poland and Czechoslovakia have been criticised for selecting an excessively devalued exchange rate which weakened the impact of the introduction of convertibility and led to the re-emergence of inflationary pressures after the initial stabilisation period. Poland achieved an immediate and substantial growth in hard currency exports and a reduction in imports which brought the hard currency balances of trade and payments into surplus, allowing a build up of hard currency reserves. However, raw materials and relatively unprocessed goods continued to predominate in Polish exports, while Polish exports to the West (especially those that increased in volume) suffered from major price falls, indicating the possibility of distress selling (Blazyca 1992: 191–2). Critics of the Polish programme claimed that too sharp a devaluation had made exports excessively profitable in relation to the domestic market, which contributed to an overlarge outflow of resources at a time of severe domestic constraint. Inflation, which had fallen from 80 per cent in January 1990 to a monthly rate of 2 per cent in August 1990, started to rise in the autumn and winter of 1990–91 despite tight monetary and fiscal policies, which Portes (1991: 12) attributes to the delayed effect of undervaluation. Poland did succeed in maintaining a fixed exchange rate until May 1991, by which time domestic inflation had made it overvalued and a 17 per cent devaluation was combined with the introduction of a crawling peg system which allowed the zloty to depreciate by 1.8 per cent a month. This has been followed by other 'one-off' devaluations which have attempted to preserve export competitiveness.

## The Russian proposals for convertibility

Although the Soviet government had announced plans to introduce residents' convertibility on 1 January 1992, which would have enabled Soviet residents to buy and sell foreign currency and required enterprises to sell all their hard currency to the state bank, the Soviet authorities appeared unwilling or unable to implement the domestic economic changes that were required to support it (Fedorov 1992: 108; Sutela 1991: 90). The stated policy of the Russian government (Memorandum 1992) was to 'introduce as quickly as possible a single, unified, exchange rate, with a fixed rate for the rouble in order to create a nominal anchor which will play an essential role in our attempts at stabilisation'. The memorandum argues that this goal cannot be achieved without external financial support and proposes a series of stages towards its implementation, starting with the introduction of a two-tier exchange rate, incorporating a single floating rate for all current account operations (including the payment of interest and dividends) and a higher (more appreciated) fixed rate for capital movements. Enterprises would sell a gradually rising proportion of hard currency receipts to the central bank at the market or current account rate. All enterprises would eventually have free access to foreign exchange but would be required to surrender all hard currency earnings to the central bank, subject to an export tax of 20 per cent payable in either hard currency or roubles. The exchange rates for capital and current account transactions were to be harmonised after a fixed rate had been established, but it would require external financing to build up hard currency reserves to defend the rate.

The move towards convertibility and exchange rate unification was to be implemented in the following stages: firstly, specified banks would be authorised to hold currency auctions and to conduct inter-bank currency deals, while currency exchanges would be opened throughout Russia. Finally, non-residents would be permitted to buy and sell currency in the inter-bank market. All export quotas and licences were to be abolished by July 1992 except for fuels, which would be retained until the end of 1993 when domestic prices should have been harmonised with world market prices, and for items whose export will remain restricted on security grounds.

A more detailed timetable for the transition to current account convertibility was announced on 5 May 1992, following negotiations in Washington with the IMF and the group of 10 industrial nations, for the creation of a $6 billion stabilisation fund which would enable the Russian authorities to increase the supply of hard currency onto the market in order to defend a more appreciated rate for the rouble than prevailing market rates. Existing multi-tier exchange rates were to be unified into a single floating rate for current account purposes on 1 July 1992. It was initially proposed that a fixed rate (which was to be maintained within a band of plus or minus 7.5 per cent) would be established on 1 August. Export quotas and licences for all goods except energy, arms and goods subject to quotas imposed by trade partners were to be abolished on 1 July, while the abolition of multiple rates would free exporters from the need to surrender 40 per cent of their hard currency earnings to the state at the overvalued commercial rate.

Within a week it was announced that the fixed rate would not be introduced on 1 August but would be delayed until the autumn of 1992. This was not surprising as the details of the stabilisation fund (including the sources of the funding) had not been fully agreed and it would have been virtually impossible to establish properly equipped and staffed exchange bureaus throughout Russia by that date, while a currency float of only one month would have given little time to establish an underlying rate of exchange that could be defended by the central authorities.

The problem of determining the level of the exchange rate was compounded by the multiplicity of exchange rates and the volatility of the interbank rates and market rates, which were in part determined by imperfections in the embryonic money markets and extreme reactions to inflationary expectations in the first quarter of 1992. On 2 January the Russian Central Bank established a 'market rate' for cash transactions at which households could obtain foreign exchange. This rate appreciated from 140 roubles to the dollar at the end of January to 70 roubles in February (Granville 1992: 11). Enterprises were obliged to surrender 50 per cent of hard currency earnings to the central bank at a special commercial rate which was half the market rate, which enabled the bank to build up a hard currency fund. An interbank currency market was also established, incorporating weekly auctions for non-cash operations conducted by banks on behalf of enterprises (Granville 1992: 41). The interbank auction rate appreciated from 230 roubles at the end of January to around 112 roubles to the dollar in June but with more violent short-term fluctuations.

Supporters of 'shock-therapy' reforms argue that the appreciation of the rouble indicates the successful implementation of a tight monetary policy, which forced enterprises to sell hard currency for roubles and which could lead to the establishment of a single rate in the region of 80 roubles to the dollar, while the possibility of a longer-term rate in the region of 50–60 roubles has been discussed. Critics of the reform (Yavlinsky 1992) argue that currency markets are highly imperfect and have been manipulated by the Central Bank, which increased the supply of hard currency to the market sharply, and that the rate could plummet at any moment. The discussion may seem academic but the question of a sustainable rate has major implications for inflationary pressures and living standards. As domestic energy prices are aligned with world market prices the exchange rate will have a direct effect on a significant proportion of industrial costs and will be a major determinant of the rate of inflation. An undervalued rate which pushes up energy prices and industrial costs will bring demands for compensating wage and pension increases which, if not met, could result in more widespread poverty.

## The need for a stabilisation fund

The establishment of a stabilisation fund which can be used to defend the established rate is crucial to the success of the transformation programme. The introduction of internal convertibility in Poland was assisted by a $1 billion stabilisation fund, while Czechoslovakia received loans worth $1.8 billion from the IMF, in addition to assistance from the EC ($0.7 billion) and the World Bank ($0.5 billion) at the time of the introduction of internal convertibility (Hrncir and Klacek 1991). In theory, the mere existence of a stabilisation fund, which provides enterprises and the public with a guarantee that hard currency will be available when required, could be sufficient to encourage the holding of rouble accounts which would receive favourable interest rates and to repatriate or to exchange hard currency receipts with the Central Bank. Similarly, it would provide potential western investors with a guarantee that rouble earnings could be converted into hard currency. A stabilisation fund would need to be backed by tight monetary policies to prevent excess demand leading to a run on hard currency, while a tight monetary policy would also force exporters to surrender hard currency earnings for roubles to pay suppliers and labour, instead of depending on easy credit. Doubts about the ability of the Russian government to implement a tight monetary policy has been one of the major obstacles for western governments and international financial institutions in their deliberations on establishing a fund. The fear is that, without strict guarantees, those with rouble holdings (however obtained) will exchange these for hard currency to finance imports of consumer goods while enterprise behaviour remains unaltered. The problem is further complicated in Russian circumstances by the inability of the Russian Central Bank to control the supply of rouble credits in non-Russian republics, which is discussed in Chapters 11 and 12.

## OPPOSITION TO THE GAIDAR PROGRAMME

The impact of price liberalisation on output and living standards led to severe criticisms of the reform programme, not just from former party members opposed to the basic idea of reforms, but also from prominent supporters of radical economic reforms in the Gorbachev era. This reflects a fundamental division of opinion between supporters of market reforms (who could be described as social democrats), who support a greater role for the government in the transition process, and the 'Gaidar school' in the government, who derive their inspiration from the radical free market traditions of the Chicago school and who favour a greater use of market forces and a balanced budget. The criticisms of the first school were summarised in a set of proposals that were distributed to the Russian Supreme Soviet on 2 April 1992 by Ruslan Khasbulatov, the speaker for the Russian parliament and a leading opponent of the government programme. Khasbulatov said that the proposals had been drawn up by the Supreme Economic Council with the advice of economists including Petrakov, Shatalin and Yavlinsky, indicating that it could be regarded as a serious alternative reform programme.

Khasbulatov argued that there was 'no alternative to a profound transformation' of the economy, but that existing policies were based on over-optimistic assessments of their impact on the level of output and the standard of living and of the people's tolerance to these measures and underestimated the possibility of a major political reversal if the reforms did not command greater popular support. He contended that the decline in agricultural and industrial output had been estimated by independent research centres to be as high as 23–28 per cent in the first quarter of 1992 compared with official estimates of 15–18 per cent, leading to the real danger of complete economic collapse, and that prices had in practice risen by 8–12 fold in the first quarter, compared with initial predictions of increases in the order of 3.5 times, indicating that hyperinflation had already arrived and that the economic forecasts on which parliamentary support for the programme had been based had not been realised. He blamed this situation on the liberalisation of prices before the creation of proper competitive market conditions. Consequently, enterprises had used their monopoly powers to increase prices while either reducing output or withdrawing produce from the market. Furthermore, he argued that a balanced budget could not be achieved under current circumstances without causing multiplied damage to output, as the slump in budget revenues would enforce cuts in expenditure and finance, which would lead to further cuts in output, which in turn would lead to further cuts in revenue (BBC Summary of World Broadcasts, 4 April 1992).

Khasbulatov proposed that it was necessary, firstly, to halt the slump in output (but did not clearly specify how); secondly, to introduce price and wage controls including 'recommended' prices for most important goods; thirdly, to abandon the target of a balanced or no-deficit budget; fourthly, to strengthen the regulatory controls of the state bank over the commercial banks; fifthly, to establish state priorities for industrial restructuring, and, finally, to improve social security. These proposals imply both a change in the pace and in the sequencing of reform measures and involve slowing the pace of reform in consumer markets until more constructive measures to change enterprise behaviour have taken effect.

## GRADUALIST OR RAPID REFORMS

The arguments in favour of a rapid transition to a market economy are both economic and political. Economic theory contends that all economic actions are interrelated and that economic policies should be assessed in terms of their impact on the economy as a whole. The gradualist implementation of reforms in the Gorbachev era supports the argument that measures designed to deal with specific problems (e.g. decentralisation of trade rights without reform to domestic prices) created even greater distortions elsewhere in the economy which ultimately led to calls for recentralisation. This indicates that reforms should be implemented consistently with a minimum of ad hoc adjustments, or at the very least, that the sequencing of reforms must be very clearly thought out before they are implemented. A strong economic argument in favour of rapid reforms is that the economic distortions arising from the coexistence of inconsistent elements in a common economic system will be minimised, if the period in which they coexist is minimised. This may also be backed up by the argument that, however, well thought out the sequencing is, the formulation and implementation of policy will be subject to human error, which will lead to economic distortions and pressure for backtracking.

Secondly, there is the issue of the credibility and consistency of implementation of the transformation. A key element in the transition to a market economy is to change people's assumptions (as workers and managers as well as consumers) about how the economic system works, while the power of the bureaucracy and the nomenklatura to resist reforms should be broken as quickly as possible. It is important, therefore, to reach a stage as quickly as possible where the reforms are seen to be irreversible. This is also related to the issue of public tolerance for the reforms, which may be strongest in the early stages of reform when the resulting hardship is more closely associated with the inheritance from the past, while public support for essential but unpleasant measures may evaporate if reforms are dragged out over a period of years. Finally, a pressing argument for the rapid introduction of a macroeconomic stabilisation programme involving price liberalisation under Russian conditions was the very real danger of hyperinflation at the end of 1991. Yeltsin argued to the Congress of People's Deputies on 7 April, that 45 per cent of goods were already being sold at free prices by the middle of 1991 and subsidies on the remaining 55 per cent were a major factor contributing to the loss of control over the money supply, which threatened hyperinflation.

Supporters of a rapid transition accept that it is impossible to implement all the transition measures simultaneously and that there is a need for sequencing. Critically it is recognised that the privatisation of large-scale state industry cannot be implemented quickly and consequently other measures, including macroeconomic stabilisation and price liberalisation, will have to precede large-scale privatisation (Sachs 1991). This is unfortunate in a macroeconomic sense as it means that sales of shares cannot play a major role in absorbing excess savings in the initial stages of the stabilisation programme. More critically, it also raises a key microeconomic question of whether the distortion of a highly protected and monopolised industrial sector will be so important that it vitiates all other reform measures.

## CONCLUSION

The main microeconomic weakness of the initial stage of the government programme was that the major vehicle for altering enterprise behaviour was to force enterprises to operate in a restricted retail market, while the government did not have the instruments to impose hard budget constraints on enterprises or to expose them to greater competition. As tight monetary and fiscal policies squeezed the retail sector and exposed consumers to tightening budget constraints, enterprises still enjoyed easy access to credit. Under these circumstances enterprise managers continued to restrict output and increase prices. Furthermore, as the change in consumer markets led to a different structure of demand (towards relatively cheaper goods and away from higher priced goods), the slow response of enterprises to changing demand resulted in either the production of the wrong goods (greater waste) or a fall in output and employment.

This suggests that alternative measures to improve enterprise performance, to harden budget constraints and to expose enterprises to competition should be considered before privatisation can take effect. This could be achieved by opening the economy to foreign competition, either by encouraging direct sales on the retail market or through foreign investment for the domestic market, which supports the case for the early introduction of internal convertibility. Foreign competition has practical limitations in the Russian case, as the sheer size of the Russian market makes the level of imports needed to submit domestic enterprises to competition far greater in relation to the existing volume of exports than is the case in any individual country in Eastern Europe, indicating the need for balance of payments support in the early stages of the transition.

Some of the criticisms in the Khasbulatov programme carry some merit. Firstly, it appears to be as important to restrict credit to enterprises and to exercise strict control over the commercial banking system as to squeeze the household sector. Secondly, price ceilings for the products of monopolised industries could be established (which would be similar to the process for regulating prices for public, or privatised, utilities in the West) at levels just above world market prices, which would both attract foreign competition and limit the worst excesses of monopoly behaviour. This would again require the early introduction of internal convertibility at a fixed or pegged exchange rate to provide a direct link between domestic and world market prices. The highest exchange rate that can be defended will bring the greatest reduction in domestic inflationary pressures.

Bank personnel (both central and local) who gathered their experience under communism lack experience in evaluating the actual or potential profitability of enterprises; there are few grounds to suppose that their decisions about investment or enterprise closures would be better than those taken by a more centralised system attempting to channel investment and encourage inward investment towards areas of the greatest importance (including energy and agriculture). Russian industry is heavily localised with a preponderance of large factories employing several thousands of workers and with a very poorly developed labour and housing markets. It is therefore to be expected that closures of large enterprises will result in large-scale, highly localised and enduring unemployment. A study by the International Labour Organisation estimated that the level of unemployment in Russia could rise to between 10 and 11 million by the end of 1992, a far higher figure than the 6 million anticipated by the government (*Financial Times*, 28 April 1992). This is particularly true in the case of the powerful defence industries, who would then become a focal point for opposition to market reforms.

# Chapter 11

# Russian external trade and economic relations

## THE BREAKDOWN OF INTERREPUBLICAN TRADE

The breakdown of economic relations between the republics of the Soviet Union was a major factor contributing to the decline in industrial production from the end of 1989 onwards and the virtual collapse of the fiscal and monetary system in 1990–91 as republican governments (following the lead of the Russian government) withheld local turnover tax revenues from the central budget from the autumn of 1990 onwards. Russian pressure for greater economic sovereignty within the Union, including control of tax revenues, money supply and prices, accelerated after the election of Yeltsin as Russian president in 1990, while the emergence of a new voice capable of arguing for republican sovereignty in economic affairs in Moscow itself, gave a further lead to national governments to reflect growing domestic centrifugal and nationalist tendencies.

Gorbachev's attempts to formulate new policies to sustain the Union involved the creation of a looser federation, which gave greater autonomy to the republics, but did not adequately reflect the greater economic and political weight of the Russian republic in the 'common economic space'. At the same time fundamental and mutually incompatible differences of opinion over the pace and nature of economic reform widened between republican governments, with the Russian government adopting a more radical approach to questions of price reform and monetary stability than the other republics, which professed a willingness to remain within a form of economic union. In the four months between the failed coup and the collapse of the Soviet Union itself, the Russian government increasingly attempted to control Soviet economic institutions on Russian territory (including Vnesh-ekonombank) and to convert them into Russian institutions. This in part reflected the need to defend Russian interests as far as possible from the effects of the collapse of the monetary system, which could have resulted in an uncontrollable influx of roubles from non-Russian republics, as the latter established separate and independent currencies, and which could have initiated pressures for the breakup of the Russian republic itself.

## RUSSIAN TRADE DEPENDENCE AND INTERREPUBLICAN TRADE

The State Committee for Statistics (Goskomstat) has estimated the value of imports and exports of the individual republics of the Soviet Union in internal prices, subdivided into interrepublican trade and foreign trade (trade outside the borders of the Soviet Union), together with a breakdown of this trade by industrial branches for 1988 (Vestnik 1990, no. 3: 36–53). These data form the basis of Tables 11.1 and 11.2. Total imports of the Russian Republic came to 135.9 billion roubles, of which interrepublican imports accounted for 69 billion roubles and imports from outside the Soviet Union 66.9 billion roubles. Total Russian imports were equivalent to 35.5 per cent of Russian NMP at internal prices while Russia received 68.5 per cent of the value of all imports into the Soviet Union. Total exports of the Russian Republic came to 102.5 billion roubles (26.6 per cent of Russian NMP), of which interrepublican exports came to 69.2 billion roubles and exports outside the Soviet Union to 33.3 billion roubles (contributing to 76.2 per cent of Soviet exports). Russian trade with the other republics of the Soviet Union resulted in a small outflow of resources (surplus) measured in internal prices, while Russian trade with the world beyond the Soviet borders contributed to a net gain in internal prices (deficit) of 33.6 billion roubles, equivalent to 8.8 per cent of Russian NMP. The deficit in foreign trade reflects the fact that the Soviet authorities deliberately imported goods with high internal prices and exported goods with low domestic prices to pay for them. However, the net contribution of trade to the Russian economy is overestimated as a result of the artificially low price of energy exports.

A precise commodity composition of trade cannot be derived from Tables 11.1 and 11.2, as the data refer to industrial branches,

*Table 11.1*  External trade of the RSFSR in domestic prices in 1988
(million roubles)

| | Total trade: All partners | | | Interrepublican trade | | |
|---|---|---|---|---|---|---|
| | Exports | Imports | Balance | Exports | Imports | Balance |
| **Total** | **102,538** | **135,865** | **−33,327** | **69,224** | **68,964** | **+260** |
| **Industry** | **100,574** | **124,796** | **−24,222** | **68,499** | **64,666** | **+3,833** |
| of which: | | | | | | |
| Electroenergy | 592 | 527 | +64 | 491 | 527 | −36 |
| Oil and gas | 16,929 | 2,396 | +14,533 | 7,475 | 1,606 | +5,868 |
| Coal | 1,163 | 462 | +701 | 462 | 183 | +279 |
| Other fuel | 3 | 25 | −23 | 2 | 25 | −23 |
| Metallurgy: | | | | | | |
| Ferrous | 6,872 | 8,874 | −2,002 | 5,372 | 6,368 | −996 |
| Non-ferrous | 4,640 | 2,837 | +1,803 | 3,047 | 1,588 | +1,459 |
| Chemicals (a) | 11,088 | 11,673 | −585 | 8,253 | 6,189 | +2,064 |
| MBMW (b) | 36,711 | 45,427 | −8,716 | 27,115 | 20,849 | +6,266 |
| Wood, paper, | | | | | | |
| cellulose | 7,235 | 2,141 | +5,094 | 4,177 | 796 | +3,382 |
| Building | | | | | | |
| materials | 1,319 | 1,328 | −9 | 1,152 | 752 | +400 |
| Light industry | 7,852 | 25,442 | −17,590 | 6,392 | 11,561 | −5,168 |
| Food industry | 3,744 | 21,698 | −17,955 | 2,598 | 13,135 | −10,537 |
| Other industry | 2,428 | 1,966 | +462 | 1,964 | 1,087 | +877 |
| **Agriculture** | **637** | **9,545** | **−8,908** | **333** | **3,950** | **−3,617** |
| **Other goods** | **1,326** | **1,524** | **−198** | **393** | **348** | **+45** |
| | | | | | | |
| **Total at world** | | | | | | |
| **market** | | | | | | |
| **prices** | **132,700** | **101,900** | **+30,800** | | | |

*Sources:* Inter-industry flows in domestic prices from Vestnik Statistik 1990, no.
3: 39. World market prices from Narkhoz 1989: 639.
*Notes:* a) Includes petrochemicals.
b) Machine building and metal working.
Rounding may affect totals.

not products, which means that imports of machinery and
equipment were recorded by the receiving industry (e.g. the food
industry, the energy industry, etc.). The effects of this should be
most pronounced on the import data where imported machinery
and components will be entirely different from the finished
product. The RSFSR was a net recipient of resources in internal
prices from all sources (Table 11.1, column 3) for the food
industry (18 billion roubles), light industry (17.6 billion roubles),
agriculture (8.9 billion roubles) and machine tools and metal
working (8.7 billion roubles). The principal net exporting

Table 11.2 Trade of the RSFSR outside the Soviet Union in domestic prices in 1988 (million roubles)

|  | Exports | Imports | Balance | RSFSR as % Soviet | |
|  | (million internal roubles) | | | Exports | Imports |
| --- | --- | --- | --- | --- | --- |
| Total | 33,314 | 66,901 | −33,588 | 76.2% | 68.4% |
| Industry | 32,076 | 60,130 | −28,054 | 71.4% | 68.8% |
| of which: | | | | | |
| Electroenergy | 101 | 0 | +101 | 11.1% | − |
| Oil and gas | 9,454 | 789 | +8,665 | 91.3% | 100.0% |
| Coal | 702 | 279 | +423 | 50.0% | 75.0% |
| Ferrous metallurgy | 1,501 | 2,506 | −1,005 | 39.5% | 75.8% |
| Non-ferrous metallurgy | 1,593 | 1,249 | +344 | 84.2% | 80.0% |
| Chemicals and petro | 2,835 | 5,484 | −2,649 | 73.6% | 71.0% |
| MBMW | 9,596 | 24,578 | −14,981 | 77.4% | 78.3% |
| Wood, paper etc. | 3,058 | 1,345 | +1,712 | 100.0% | 61.9% |
| Building materials | 166 | 576 | −410 | 50.0% | 85.7% |
| Light industry | 1,460 | 13,882 | −12,422 | 41.0% | 60.1% |
| Food industry | 1,146 | 8,563 | −7,418 | 57.8% | 59.3% |
| Other industry | 465 | 879 | −415 | 83.3% | 80.0% |
| Agriculture | 304 | 5,595 | −5,291 | 75.0% | 63.6% |
| Other goods | 934 | 1,177 | −243 | 81.8% | 85.7% |

Source: Vestnik Statistik 1990, no. 3.
Note: Percentages estimated by aggregating trade from trade of all republics.
Components and/or balances do not sum to totals because of rounding.

industries were oil and gas (14.5 billion roubles) and timber, wood, paper and cellulose (5.1 billion roubles). In the majority of industries Russia was a net recipient or net exporter in both inter-republican trade and foreign trade. The Russian food industry was a net recipient of resources of 7.4 billion roubles from foreign trade (Table 11.2, column 3) and 10.5 billion roubles from interrepublican trade, light industry by 12.4 billion and 5.2 billion roubles and agriculture 5.3 billion and 3.6 billion roubles respectively. The oil and gas industry was a net exporter of 8.7 billion roubles in foreign trade, 5.9 billion roubles in inter-republican trade. The major exception was that the Russian machine building and metal working industry (MBMW) was net recipient of resources from foreign (including CMEA) suppliers to the value of 15 billion roubles, but a net exporter to the value of 6.2 billion roubles in interrepublican trade. In addition, the chemical industry was a net recipient of resources from the foreign sector of 2.6 billion roubles and a net exporter in interrepublican trade by 2.1 billion roubles, reflecting the imports of machinery and equipment for the chemical industry from the West which exported chemical products to other republics within the Soviet Union.

The figures for trade in internal prices are distorted by a number of problems relating to the accounting methodology used to estimate internal prices. As turnover taxes are levied on finished goods and not intermediate goods (which would be the case in a value-added tax system), internal prices underestimate the relative cost of production of less-processed goods in relation to processed goods. Similarly, consumer subsidies on the wholesale price of food and other basic staple goods mean that real production costs of these items are underestimated. As Russia was a major net importer of these goods from other Soviet republics the calculations underestimate Russian static gains from trade. Goskomstat has made allowances for these (Vestnik 1990, no. 3: 38), which add 3.4 billion roubles and 5.1 billion roubles respectively to the total Russian trade deficit (net resource inflow), which (as the totals for the Union as a whole cancel out) can be attributed to interrepublican trade. This converts the Russian inflow of resources from all sources to 41.7 billion roubles (equivalent to 10.9 per cent of Russian NMP in 1988). A further correction is also made to incorporate the effects of the price reform for heavy industrial goods in June 1988, which reduces Russian trade gains by 16.6 billion roubles, half of which can be attributed to imports from outside the Union.

These estimates, however, are still based on administered prices, not genuine market or scarcity prices (McAuley 1991), and the effect of the reform of heavy industry prices indicates how sensitive the estimates are both to price changes and to the evaluation of Soviet heavy industrial priorities. Goskomstat re-estimated trade flows for each republic in world market prices (Narkhoz 1989: 638–9), which provides an approximation to scarcity prices and an estimate of Russian trade potential following the introduction of world market prices into the domestic trading system, but does not subdivide the results into interrepublican and foreign trade (see Table 11.1, final row).

The principal effect of the estimates is that oil, gas, ferrous and non-ferrous metals and many types of equipment which Russia exports are more highly priced on world markets, while food and light industry products which Russia imports are cheaper (Narkhoz 1989: 639). Consequently, the value of Russian exports 'rises' to 132.7 billion external roubles, while the value of imports 'falls' to 101.9 billion external roubles, resulting in a large trade surplus of 30.8 billion roubles. Goskomstat has also provided estimates of Republican trade balances in domestic and world market prices, subdivided into interrepublican trade and foreign trade for 1987 (IMF *et al.* 1991, vol. 1: 227). These indicate that while Russia made a 'surplus' in interrepublican trade of 3.6 billion roubles in 1987 in domestic prices, this grew to 28.5 billion roubles in world market prices, while a net inflow of resources from foreign trade of 32.4 billion roubles in domestic prices was converted into a surplus of 12.8 billion roubles in world market prices, resulting in a total surplus of 41.3 billion roubles. All the other republics incurred trade deficits when trade was evaluated at world market prices.

The figures in both studies should be treated with considerable caution. The studies do not say how detailed (disaggregated) the original data for the estimates were, or what exchange rates were used to convert world market prices into roubles. Although the estimates in world market prices are stated to be in 'valuta' roubles, implying that they are not strictly comparable with estimates in domestic prices and roubles, Goskomstat does in fact make such comparisons. The estimates provide a rough indication of the opportunity cost of interrepublican trade to the Russian economy and of the possible strength of the Russian economy in world markets.

## RUSSIA'S CONTRIBUTION TO SOVIET EXPORTS AND HARD CURRENCY EARNINGS

Columns 3 and 4 in Table 11.2 provide an estimate of the Russian Republic's contribution to Soviet exports and imports in internal prices by broad industrial groups. These figures do not distinguish between trade in hard and soft currencies. Despite the undervaluation of energy exports Russia accounted for 76 per cent of total Soviet exports in domestic prices, while Russian exports were above this average for industries which were predominant in Soviet hard-currency exports (oil and gas 91 per cent; non-ferrous metals 84 per cent; machinery and metal working 77 per cent; wood and lumber 100 per cent). The Russian Republic only accounted for 68.4 per cent of total Soviet imports in internal prices, with above-average imports predominantly in the investment goods industries (machine tools 78 per cent; chemicals 71 per cent; ferrous and non-ferrous metallurgy 76 and 80 per cent respectively) and below average imports for the consumer goods industries (light industry 60 per cent; food industry 59 per cent; agriculture 64 per cent).

The structure of Russian imports from extra-Soviet markets reflects the preponderance of imports for the machine building and metal working industries which came to 24.6 billion roubles, followed by imports for light industry 13.9 billion, food industry 8.6 billion, agriculture 5.6 billion and chemicals 5.5 billion. Surprisingly, the MBMW sector (which includes the armaments industry) made the largest contribution to Russian exports on foreign markets in internal prices (9.6 billion roubles) while the oil and gas industry contributed 9.5 billion roubles, although in external prices total Soviet exports of oil and gas came to 25.5 billion roubles and were more than double the level of machinery and equipment exports which were only 10.8 billion roubles in 1988. This discrepancy cannot be explained by differences between the structure of exports of the RSFSR and the Soviet Union as a whole, as all exports from the oil and gas industry were recorded as originating from Russia, whereas only 78.3 per cent of total Soviet exports from the machine building and metal working industry originated from Russia. The principal explanation for these discrepancies is the undervaluation of oil and gas products and the overvaluation of heavy industrial goods in Soviet internal prices. In addition, over 20 per cent of Soviet oil exports in 1988 were re-exports and presumably are not included in any of these figures. Finally, however, it also reflects the fact that some exports of armaments that were included in unspecified residuals and were not included in Soviet export statistics for machinery and equipment have been included in the exports of the Russian MBMW industry and give an indication of the importance of this sector for the Russian economy.

## RUSSIAN ENERGY EXPORTS

The major factor contributing to the increased size of Russian exports in world market prices is the re-evaluation of Russian energy exports, energy which is also the major item that Russia would be capable of selling on world markets as an independent state. Russian oil production in 1988 came to 569 million tonnes and production of natural gas to 590 billion cubic metres, while coal production came to 425 million tonnes. According to Russian official statistics Russian exports (outside the Soviet Union) of crude oil came to 125 million tonnes, refined oil products to 30 million tonnes (see Table 11.3). These figure show that total Soviet exports of crude oil (144 million tonnes) were comprised of Russian exports plus re-exports (19 million tonnes) while Russia contributed to only half of total Soviet exports of refined oil products. However, as non-oil producing republics (notably Lithuania) were recorded as oil exporters, Russian exports of crude oil to other Soviet republics also contributed to Soviet exports of refined oil products, that were not recorded as direct Russian exports. Even if we assume that the Russian Republic accounted for 70 per cent of total Soviet oil consumption (441 million tonnes) Russia would have consumed 309 million tonnes, leaving 260 million tonnes available for export. On the basis of a world market price of $20 a barrel, Russian oil exports alone would have been worth $36 billion at world market prices. An approximate estimate indicates that, at best, only 70 million tonnes were actually exported for hard currency (less than $10 billion) while 105 million tonnes went to interrepublican trade and 85 million tonnes went to clearing markets (including CMEA and Finland).

Russian natural gas production in 1988 came to 590 billion cubic metres (out of a total Soviet production of 770 billion). Total Soviet exports were 88 billion cubic metres, all of which came from Russian fields. Assuming that Russia consumed 70 per cent of Soviet gas consumption or 480 billion cubic metres (a high estimate), total Russian exports would have been 110 billion cubic metres, 41 billion of which were for hard currency, 47 billion for clearing and 22 billion (a low estimate) for interrepublican trade. At 1988 Soviet gas prices these would have been worth $6.8 billion, whereas total hard currency receipts were only $2.5 billion.

*Table 11.3* Estimated exports of oil and gas from RSFSR in 1988

|  | Oil (million tonnes) | Gas (billion cubic metres) |
|---|---|---|
| Production | 569 | 590 |
| Consumption | 309 | 480 |
| Availability for exports | 260 | 110 |
| Extra Soviet exports | 155 | 88 |
| Hard currency | 70 | 41 |
| Soft currency | 85 | 47 |
| Interrepublican | 105 | 22 |
| Value of availability | $36 billion | $6.8 billion |

*Sources:* Production and exports: Narkhoz RSFSR 1989: 365, 644.
All other figures are estimates (see text for explanation).

These approximate estimates indicate that Russia could have increased its hard currency earnings from sales of oil and gas alone by approximately $30 billion in 1988 (which is equivalent to $200 per head) if it had been able to sell them all for hard currency at prevailing world market prices, without taking any steps to reduce Russian consumption. This would not have been a net gain as Russia received imports of food, machinery and equipment in exchange for oil and gas exports in interrepublican trade and in clearing arrangements. Furthermore, it is unlikely that western markets could have absorbed the additional volumes without some impact on prices, not to mention physical constraints on delivery systems, particularly in the case of natural gas, which would have to be delivered by pipeline and would require the negotiation of long-term contracts.

Russian oil production fell by 108 million tonnes between 1988 and 1991 to 461 million tonnes (and fell by a further 13 per cent in the first half of 1992), while consumption was not significantly affected by falling industrial production. The fall in Soviet exports of crude oil from 144 million tonnes to 52 million tonnes and of refined oil products from 61 million tonnes to 41 million tonnes in 1991 can be entirely attributed to falling Russian production. The impact of declining Russian oil production on Soviet hard currency earnings was limited by the move to settlements in hard currency in trade with former CMEA countries, but only at the cost of the virtual collapse in imports from former CMEA partners which created additional bottlenecks in the domestic economy. The increase in Russian natural gas production to 643 billion cubic metres was one of the few positive areas in the Russian energy scene which facilitated the continuation of exports.

The basic difference between the external payments position confronting the Soviet Union as a whole and the separate Russian Federation was well known to Russian economists. The Sarafanov study (1992) also estimated the Russian balance of pay- ments for extra-Soviet trade (in actual external prices) in 1990 and 1991. The estimates were based on relatively simple assumptions that have a decisive effect on the results. It was assumed that Russia contributed 78 per cent of Soviet exports, and this figure was applied uniformly to Soviet exports to each trade zone (hard currency, clearing and CMEA) to arrive at the value of Russian exports. This figure made an explicit allowance for the higher share of the Russian Republic in arms production, which was then equally distributed between the three trading regions. The Russian share of total Soviet imports was assumed to be 68 per cent in 1990 and 67 per cent in 1991. These figures are broadly consistent with the Russian share of total Soviet imports and exports in internal prices in the Goskomstat study. Of Soviet gold exports, 67 per cent were allocated to Russia, reflecting the Russian share in Soviet gold production.

The estimates are summarised in Table 11.4. Comparison of the data for 1990 with 1991 is complicated by the inclusion of trade with the former GDR in trade with Germany in 1991, and by the redesignation of trade with Finland from clearing to hard currency in 1991. The estimates indicate that Russia made a deficit in extra-Soviet trade in 1990 of $2.0 billion, which was turned into a surplus of $9.1 billion in 1991 by a 45 per cent cut in imports. The deficit in trade with former CMEA countries was reduced by a major cut in imports. Surpluses in trade with non-CMEA countries based on clearing ($1.6 billion in 1990 and $4.8 billion in 1991) partly reflect arms sales for non-convertible currencies based on credit. Russia made a surplus in its trade in convertible currencies of $2 billion in 1990 and $4.8 billion in 1991, but deficits on invisibles of $3.7 billion and $3.9 billion, largely attributed to the Russian share of interest on Soviet debt, turned these into a deficit of $1.7 billion in 1990 and a surplus of only $0.9 billion in 1991. However, gold sales of $1.8 billion in 1990 and $2.5 billion in 1991 restored an overall surplus in the hard currency operations' current account of $0.1 billion in 1990 and $3.4 billion in 1991. The study concludes that these figures

*Table 11.4* Russian balance of trade and payments in 1990 and 1991
($ billion)

|  | 1990 | | | | 1991 | | | |
|---|---|---|---|---|---|---|---|---|
|  | Hard | CMEA | Soft | Total | Hard | CMEA | Soft | Total |
| Exports | 26.1 | 40.7 | 14.1 | 80.9 | 24.8 | 17.0 | 12.9 | 54.7 |
| Imports | 24.1 | 46.3 | 12.5 | 82.9 | 20.0 | 17.5 | 8.1 | 45.6 |
| **Balances** | | | | | | | | |
| **Trade** | +2.0 | −5.6 | +1.6 | −2.0 | +4.8 | −0.5 | +4.8 | +9.1 |
| **Services** | −3.7 | −0.4 | 0.0 | −4.1 | −3.9 | −0.6 | 0.0 | −4.5 |
| Gold sales | 1.8 | – | – | 1.8 | 2.5 | – | – | 2.5 |
| **Current account** | | | | | | | | |
| a) | −1.7 | −6.0 | +1.6 | −6.1 | +0.9 | −1.1 | +4.8 | +4.6 |
| b) | +0.1 | −6.0 | +1.6 | −4.3 | +3.4 | −1.1 | +4.8 | +7.1 |

*Sources:* Ekonomika i Zhizn 1992, no. 6 (Sarafanov *et al.* 1992)
Notes a) excluding gold sales; b) including gold sales.
Hard, CMEA, Soft = Russian trade conducted with partners in hard currency,
CMEA and other clearing arrangements respectively.
Data for 1991 include Finland and the former GDR in hard currency trade.

indicate that 'until very recently, Russia financed the imports of
the other republics, without compensation', which, it claims, com-
plicates the problem of allocating the Soviet debt burden between
the republics.

The Russian government can be expected to give greater
weight to specifically Russian economic interests in its relations
with former Soviet republics than formerly (and will continue to
view the resource-bearing regions of Siberia as remaining under
Russian control). The evidence outlined above suggests that,
although Russia's trade relations with other republics in domestic
prices was broadly balanced, Russia experienced a substantial net
outflow of resources when trade flows were re-evaluated at world
market prices which was not reflected in the accumulation of
capital claims against recipient republics. The available data is too
aggregated (and possibly too selective) to assess the scale of these
resource transfers, but the potential size of Russian energy exports
suggests that Russian forgone gains in intrarepublican trade were
significant. This was not the result of specific aid policies designed
and pursued by the Russian government but arose from the
nature of the Soviet planning system. Furthermore, the Sarafanov
study also indicates that although Russia may have run surpluses
in hard currency trade which effectively financed the imports of

non-Russian republics of the former Soviet Union, it now finds itself in the position of having to bear the chief responsibility for the collective debt of the former Soviet Union.

## THE ORGANISATION OF MONETARY AND TRADE RELATIONS WITH FORMER SOVIET REPUBLICS

### The costs and benefits of a common rouble zone

What will be the optimal form for organising economic relations between the former Soviet Republics? Aleksashenko (1992: 118) distinguishes between a confederation of republics embodying a single currency, with a banking and monetary system based on the 'common action of the member banks' and a far looser economic community which would embody separate national currencies and banking systems with the possibility of flexible exchange rates between them. In both systems, the central budget would be funded by taxes levied by the individual republics, but central expenditure (common defence, interrepublican infrastructure) would be expected to play a greater role in a confederation. Soviet theory tended to address the problem from the initial perspective of finding the optimal conditions for generating efficiency in production on a union-wide basis before considering the problems of interrepublican distribution. These arguments supported the maintenance of a single currency area, which was embodied in the Shatalin plan and which envisaged a single banking system modelled on the US Federal Reserve (see Brown 1992: 133–4).

The principle of a single currency area, which would involve Republics that wanted to join the rouble zone maintaining accounts with the Central Bank of Russia and coordinating their monetary policy, was maintained in the Russian Memorandum on Economic Policy. The memorandum also states that the Russian government will 'adopt all possible measures for preserving the common economic space', will facilitate direct trade links between enterprises in different republics with a limited role for the state and will limit quantitative restrictions in interrepublican trade to those that apply in trade relations with third parties.

The critical danger of a common rouble area is that attempts by the Russian government to implement a tight monetary policy could be nullified by excess credit emission by other republics over which the Russian government has no de facto or de jure control. Without strict controls over the supply of money, a common currency area provides member governments with an incentive to run budget deficits in the expectation that they will be financed by other republics, which is inherently inflationary. Russian economists contend that Russian attempts to impose strict credit controls over its own enterprises in the first half of 1992 were largely nullified by loose credit expansion in other republics (notably the Ukraine). The only way out of the problem appears to be that the Russian monetary authorities (which in the absence of a CIS central bank have effectively taken over responsibility for monetary policy and rouble stabilisation) will have to impose strict rules on the monetary authorities in other republics who wish to stay in the rouble zone, concerning credit ceilings, reserve requirements and rediscounting debt to prevent the emergence of inflationary pressures. Republican governments that do not wish to submit to these controls would be required to leave the rouble zone and establish their own separate currencies. This has the danger of an unregulated withdrawal which could lead to an influx of roubles into republics that stay in the rouble zone, although the potential impact of this has been reduced by the erosion of rouble balances by price liberalisation. The memorandum envisages that special agreements will be reached on the 'regulated withdrawal of the rouble' with those republics that wish to introduce their own currencies. This will entail detailed negotiations between the Russian Central Bank and the central banks of republics that wish to withdraw from the rouble area, concerning such matters as how to collect cash and the methods of financing interrepublican trade. A successful agreement was reached with Estonia, which introduced a separate currency (the kroon) on 20 June 1992 and agreed to return the stock of roubles to the Russian Central Bank.

The economic wisdom of establishing a common monetary system embracing republics with vastly different resource endowments and economic structures is questionable. Under central planning, movements of physical capital were chiefly determined by administrative fiat while flows of resources between republics were largely determined by input–output criteria resulting from centralised investment decisions. Relative cost advantages and disadvantages between republics were nullified by administered prices and subsidies. As the market starts to play a greater role, relative prices, wage levels and exchange rates will start to determine interrepublican trade and investment to a far greater extent. Republics that have historically been highly dependent on trade flows with Russia (which would be difficult to redirect) would be the worst affected by withdrawal from the rouble zone, and trade flows could suffer badly in the short term from fluctuations in exchange rates between the new domestic currency and the rouble. In 1989 interrepublican trade accounted for more than 30 per cent of GNP, in internal prices, for all republics except Russia, the Ukraine and Kazakhstan, while interrepublican trade accounted for 86–89 per cent of total trade for all republics except Russia and the Ukraine (*European Economy* 1990, no. 45; Granville 1992: 22). This might suggest a strong impetus to preserving a common rouble area. However, these trade flows reflect irrational patterns of production and specialisation and the preference for interrepublican (as opposed to foreign) trade imposed by central planners on the republics. The Baltic republics, the Ukraine and Kazakhstan (which has substantial energy and mineral wealth) and Moldova (which could link into a Black Sea trading zone) all have potential for developing and expanding their trade links outside the former Soviet Union and reducing dependency on trade with Russia. For all the republics (with the exception of Kazakhstan) this is also a political objective and they have announced their intention to establish their own currencies. Georgia is not a member of the CIS and Armenia and Azerbaidzhan, torn apart by the question of Nagorno-Karabakh, are unlikely to be able to fulfil strict monetary requirements, even if they wished to. Granville (1992: 22–3) also suggests that the central Asian republics could strengthen their trade links with India, Pakistan, Iran, the Gulf States and Turkey.

The main economic incentive for the non-Russian republics to stay within the rouble zone would be to effect a transfer of resources from Russia, either by importing energy on more favourable terms than could be obtained in trade outside the CIS and/or by effectively forcing the Russian government to finance non-Russian budget deficits. It is increasingly unlikely that Russia will wish to do this unless it receives external assistance: there are few trade reasons for the non-Russian republics to preserve a common currency and subject their economies to a common exchange rate. As Russia will continue to be a substantial net exporter of oil, gas, raw materials and precious metals in the long term it will be able to defend a higher exchange rate than the equilibrium rate required by republics that are more dependent on exports of manufactured and agricultural goods in foreign markets. Furthermore, the Russian government may wish to adopt as high an exchange rate as possible in the transition stage to reduce inflationary pressures. The adoption of a single exchange rate with Russia would reduce the competitiveness of manufactured exports from non-Russian republics in world markets and the demand for labour in those regions.

The problem of the optimal exchange rate is equally acute for trade relations with Russia itself. The central Asian republics have relatively plentiful supplies of labour (and higher levels of unemployment) but lower living costs, which were not reflected in interrepublican wage differentials, while the past structure of investment has left the central Asian republics with highly specialised output and export structures concentrated in the consumer goods and food industries. These could prove to be highly susceptible to both changing demand patterns in Russia over the long term and even to western aid policies. If Russia redirected energy and raw material exports to the West to boost hard currency earnings, the traditional exports of the central Asian republics would be exposed to increasing competition from western consumer products in the Russian market. Unless labour is both willing and able to move from central Asia to areas of higher labour demand (which appears even less probable as the republics become more distinct political and national entities), demand for labour will have to be stimulated by reducing wage costs relative to Russia and other European republics. Given the difficulty in reducing wage levels, this can be best achieved by devaluation, which would be impossible within a single currency area.

It appears unlikely that the non-Russian republics (and the central Asian republics in particular) will be able to protect their economies fully from a structural tendency towards deficits in their trade with the Russian republic as energy prices in interrepublican trade approach world market prices, which will involve them in a major deterioration in their terms of trade. This problem will be intensified by the collapse in Russian oil production, which will place even greater pressure on the Russian government to favour hard currency exports over interrepublican trade, a trend that will be accelerated if energy production is privatised and/or falls into foreign ownership and the new owners are concerned with profit maximisation. Under these circumstances the optimal trading arrangements may well be to introduce separate national currencies, which would initially be allowed to float against the rouble but which would subsequently be linked to the rouble at a fixed or pegged exchange rate and as such would be convertible into hard currency through the convertibility of the rouble itself.

## THE IMPLICATIONS OF A BREAK UP OF INTERREPUBLICAN TRADE

The arguments outlined above indicated that Russia benefited from a net inflow of resources in trade with the West (measured as the difference between the domestic value of imports and the domestic cost of the exports required to pay for them) but suffered from a net outflow of resources in its trade with the Third World (caused by non-payment of credits). Russia also experienced a net outflow of resources in trade with other Soviet republics and Eastern Europe when trade flows were measured in world market prices (which reflected the opportunity cost to the Russian economy of diverting energy exports away from more advantageous western markets). Consequently, the creation of an open economy, in which domestic enterprises (including producers of energy and raw materials) were exposed to world market prices and international competition and were subject to the threat of take-over (including the possibility of foreign ownership) if they failed to maximise their potential profits, will result in a very different pattern of trade from the one that existed under Soviet circumstances. If Russian producers are required to choose imports and exports on the basis of world market prices according to the principles of comparative advantage they will be forced to demand substantial improvements in their terms of trade with other former Soviet republics and to re-direct trade away from loss-making areas. Although this would offer significant long-term benefits to Russia it would also involve a major redistribution of income away from the majority of the non-Russian republics towards the Russian republic and would involve a major dislocation of trade and production in the short term.

The effects of the redirection of Russian trade can be analysed by the following categories:

1 Trade flows which involved a 'negative sum game' whereby Russian resources were transferred to recipients who were required to use them in uneconomic activities, particularly in heavy engineering. The elimination of trade that created 'value-subtracting' activities will result in a net economic gain in the long term, although this may not be equally distributed and could cause substantial economic and social dislocations in the short term. The long-term benefits to Russia's trade partners of the cessation of uneconomic activities may not be very great if the initial trade flows involved a large element of subsidy and would depend on the speed of response of the affected republic to new trade conditions.

2 Trade which was a zero sum game, involving the transfer of Russian resources on terms that were less favourable to Russia, but more favourable to the trade partner than those that could be obtained in world markets. The move to trade in world market prices will eliminate the 'subsidy' element of trade and redistribute resources towards the Russian republic, provided that the recipient can overcome the resulting income effects and maintain imports. If not, trade flows will be reduced with a dislocation of trade. In either case the trade partner will be worse off as a result of the change.

3 Trade that was a positive sum game, in that there are net gains from trade, but these are distributed in favour of the trade partner to such a degree that the Russian republic actually loses from the trade. The long-term outcome will again depend on whether the trade partner can withstand the long-term income effects of a redistribution of the benefits to Russia. In both cases the trade partner will be worse off.

**The short-run economic effects of trade dislocation**

Although the analysis of Russian trade patterns with other republics indicates that the redirection of Russian trade away from former Soviet republics would bring significant economic benefits to the Russian Federation in the long term, it is also apparent that this process will impose significant costs on the former Soviet republics in the short term and possibly on Russia itself. A significant part of the gains to the Russian Federation will involve uncompensated transfers of income from the poorer non-Russian republics, either directly through changes in the terms of trade or indirectly through trade diversion. The experience of the collapse of intra-CMEA trade and the resulting fall in industrial output in Eastern Europe, following the move to trade in hard currency at world market prices, indicates that the process of transition will also involve a major short-term dislocation of trade flows, which will have a multiplied effect on production in both the non-Russian republics and Russia itself.

The analysis in Chapter 5 indicated that the former Soviet republics are suffering from a systemic inability to produce and export the commodities that are demanded in world markets, which suggests that many non-Russian republics would be unable to respond quickly to changing trade relations with Russia and either produce goods which would be in demand in Russian markets, or divert their trade to alternative markets in order to buy imports from Russia. This problem is aggravated by the reluctance of many republics to implement reforms which would enable them to respond to changing circumstances in Russia itself. This suggests that several non-Russian republics will respond far more slowly to changing trade conditions than Eastern Europe and, given their greater dependence on interrepublican trade and geographical isolation from alternative foreign markets, that the depth and length of the ensuing recession will be substantially longer than that facing Eastern Europe.

It is unlikely that the Russian economy will be able to protect itself fully from the impact of supply problems that would result from a further breakdown in interrepublican trade in the short term. The situation that would result can be compared with the collapse in intra-CMEA trade in 1991. The dislocation of production in the Soviet Union following the breakdown in intra-CMEA trade was largely caused by the fall in Russian oil output, which meant that the Soviet authorities could not divert oil exports to Eastern Europe to alternative markets to compensate for the fall in imports from Eastern Europe. This process will be repeated in the case of interrepublican trade if Russian oil production cannot at least be stabilised at 1990 levels, let alone recover to those of the late 1980s. Many Russian enterprises will find it difficult, if not impossible, to restore (or even preserve) trade relations with partners in former Soviet republics as well as Eastern Europe and will require new markets for their products as well as suppliers if they are to survive under these new circumstances.

# CONCLUSION

The problem of the collapse of interrepublican trade will be greatest for the machine tool and metal working industries, which accounted for 40 per cent of Russian exports to other republics in 1988 and 7 per cent of Russian NMP in internal prices. This sector also includes defence-sector enterprises that were dependent on Soviet defence contracts and bilateral trade agreements operated by the former Soviet government with third world countries and were funded by the All-Union budget who are now faced by loss of markets and the break up of the sophisticated Union-wide supply networks that insulated them from the supply constraints that plagued civilian industry and are being forced to seek alternative markets for their products. An open defence industry lobby, led by directors of defence industry enterprises, alarmed at the proposal for military conversion and for the decentralisation of Union authority to the republics expressed in the Shatalin plan, emerged during 1989 and was widely believed to have played a critical role in dissuading Gorbachev from adopting Shatalin's proposals (Cooper 1991: chapters 5, 6). Not only is the defence industry largely located in Russia, but senior personnel in defence plants in non-Russian republics are predominantly Russian and have traditionally been administered directly from Soviet authorities based in Moscow, not in the republics (Cooper 1991: chapters 5, 6). Not surprisingly this sector, which was capable of exercising major economic and political influence in the Soviet Union and which is now faced with the collapse of both its internal and external markets for its products, is seen by radical reformers as one of the greatest sources of resistance to economic reform in Russia and a defender of the interests of Russians in non-Russian republics. Although the defence industry is not universally hostile to economic reforms, the military-industrial complex remains essentially conservative and has been associated with Russian nationalism. An alliance between supporters of the interests of heavy industry (especially the defence industry), who could articulate the genuine concerns of industrial workers faced with widespread unemployment, and Russian nationalists, who are opposed to the concept of foreign investment and ownership in Russia and fear that market reforms will destroy a significant proportion of Russia's industrial strength, present a major threat to the reform process. More seriously, the accelerated collapse of interrepublican trade and the resulting economic dislocation could exacerbate ethnic tensions.

# Chapter 12

# Russia and the world economy: problems of integration and the role of the West

## THE PROSPECTS FOR THE TRANSITION

### The optimistic scenario

Two extreme scenarios can be presented for the process of transition to a market economy in Russia. The optimistic scenario attributes a major proportion of the blame for the poor perform- ance and the relative backwardness of the Russian economy to the failure of the economic system created by Stalin to provide a functional system of incentives to management, labour and owners of capital, which would provide them with an incentive to innovate and diffuse technology and new working practices rapidly through the economy without the use of wide-scale coercion and terror. As the use of terror and coercion as a means of economic mobilisation has become less effective (as the successful application of modern technology increasingly requires a well motivated and better educated and trained labour force), economic growth has decelerated and the capital stock has become increasingly obsolete. The logical outcome of this argument is that, if the former Soviet republics can replace an outmoded economic system and modernise their capital stock, they have the potential to reverse the decline in output and then to grow faster than economies at equivalent or higher levels of development and narrow the gap in production and living standards between themselves and the industrialised economies.

Even those who take an optimistic view accept that this process will not be easy and will take several decades to achieve. The scale of the problem can be indicated by some 'ball park' figures. Collins and Rodrik (1991: 76–80) attempted to estimate how much investment would be required for a 'full catch-up' which would involve a complete modernisation of the capital stock of the former Soviet Union to enable all of the republics to close the gap between their levels of labour productivity and the average of the industrialised West. This necessarily involved making heroic assumptions which may even have underestimated the scale of the problem. They estimated the level of the existing capital stock in the former Soviet Union to be $1.7 trillion and that it would need to grow sevenfold to reach western levels of capital per head over a decade which would require investment of $1.2 trillion per annum. Collins and Rodrik also estimated the level of investment that would be required to generate a rate of growth of 7 per cent per annum in the former Soviet Union, which would be comparable to that achieved by the newly industrialising countries (NICs) of South-East Asia as an alternative to the 'full catch-up scenario'. A rate of growth of this magnitude (from the 1989 output base) could be expected to provide a majority of the population with an expectation of long-term income growth and economic stability which would permit reasonable labour incentives and reduce social tensions. Collins and Rodrik estimate that it would require investment of $571 billion per year to achieve this objective throughout the Soviet Union.

These estimates refer to the level of investment required to modernise the capital stock, not to the level of direct assistance or to the level of net capital inflows (including investment, asset sales, etc.) that would be required. However, it is apparent that the former Soviet republics do not have either the physical or financial capacity to generate investment on anything approaching this scale and that a significant proportion of the resources would have to come from outside the domestic economy in the form of financial support and imported equipment. Even the smaller sum of $571 billion, however, would be equivalent to 4 per cent of OECD GNP, and 20 per cent of their annual level of investment, and would exceeds current levels of western defence expenditure directed towards the Warsaw Pact. Furthermore, these estimates do not include any provision for the preliminary costs of environmental clean up, additional investment in transportation related to the geographical problems associated with developing Siberia, or attempts to boost or even maintain living standards during the transformation period. Capital transfers on this scale are beyond the capacity of the West to deliver or the ability of the former Soviet republics to absorb investment and would have major repercussions on the world economy. The estimates provide a telling insight into the scale of the problem and give some indication of the length of the transition process that might be expected.

**The pessimistic scenario**

These estimates indicate that any appreciable narrowing of the gap between living standards in Russia and the industrialised economies of western Europe cannot be expected for a decade, while in the interim the process of transition to a market economy will inflict major economic and social costs on large sections of the population in both Russia and the non-Russian republics in the form of large-scale unemployment, falling consumption and open inflationary and hyperinflationary pressures. The pessimistic scenario indicates that there is a real danger that the cost of the transition will be so severe that it will aggravate social and ethnic tensions that were largely suppressed under Soviet control, with the result that, at best, economic recovery is substantially delayed or, at worst, large areas of the former Soviet Union become engulfed by instability and ethnic violence.

A more specific danger is that the Russian government may feel itself compelled by domestic economic pressures to pursue an overtly 'Russia-first' policy, which involves the redirection of energy supplies from non-Russian republics to hard currency markets, or to demand major changes in Russian terms of trade with other republics (including energy price increases) which provoke anti-Russian feelings. This could extend to attacks on the Russian population domiciled in non-Russian republics, many of whom have not become integrated with the native population, do not speak the native language and enjoy living standards that are significantly higher than those of the non-Russian population. This could lead to increased popular support within Russia itself for Russian military intervention in support of Russian nationals in other republics, which would increase the possibility of a return of a more nationalist-authoritarian government with the support of the military and the defence industry.

## THE COSTS OF THE TRANSITION

The potential difficulties associated with the transition can be illustrated by some of the specific institutional factors that were inherited from the Soviet economy. The need for a radical structural transformation of industry will result in major shifts in the demand for labour and the prospect of widespread unemployment in an economy in which industrial workers have traditionally enjoyed a high degree of job security and have very limited experience of the need to search for alternative employment. Industry is, in the main, highly concentrated into large plants, with entire regions heavily dependent on a single industry and large towns dependent on a single enterprise which was the chief source of social, cultural and welfare facilities as well as employment. These factors, together with the virtual absence of a housing market, suggest that labour could be slow to respond to changing demands in the labour market and that unemployment resulting from factory closures, or even reductions in demand for labour, resulting from greater internal efficiency or reduced demand, will be of long duration. Furthermore, high concentrations of localised unemployment make it unlikely that there will be sufficient demand for the development of a local service sector to absorb displaced labour. This indicates that the level of unemployment that would be consistent with a low or stable level of inflation will be far higher and of far longer duration in Russia than in a mature market economy.

Consequently, the Russian authorities are faced with a major problem in steering economic policy between the threat of hyperinflation on the one hand and unacceptable levels of unemployment on the other. The transition to a market economy entails the move from a shortage economy in the retail market, in which a large proportion of the population had excess money balances but experienced difficulties in actually obtaining goods, to a demand or budget-constrained economy in which retail goods are rationed by price, while subsidies on basic staple goods are being rapidly removed. While this should lead to improved consumer supplies in the aggregate in the long term, many poorer individuals and families (plus those who become unemployed), who depended more heavily on the state retail network and who do not have high levels of savings and whose incomes do not keep up with inflation, will be permanently disadvantaged.

Furthermore, stabilisation policies have to be implemented following a fall in production in the former Soviet Union, the depth and length of which is unprecedented in an industrial economy in peacetime this century, which reduces the availability of consumer goods to satisfy demand and reduces the government's room for manoeuvre. All the East European economies experienced a significant fall in output following the collapse of communism at the end of 1989 and it is probable that the fall in production in many of the former Soviet republics will be sharper and of longer duration. The severity of the fall in output in Eastern Europe was in part caused by the collapse of the CMEA trading system and cuts in Soviet energy supplies in particular. However, the majority of the former Soviet republics are more dependent on trade with Russia both for supplies of energy and raw materials and markets for their products than the East European nations were in the late 1980s, and, if only as a result of geography, will face greater difficulties in finding alternative suppliers and customers. The Soviet Union, however, was incapable of protecting its own economy from the effect of the disintegration of trade with Eastern Europe, and the immediate impact of the collapse of interrepublican trade can be expected to be equally severe.

Fortunately, the impact on living standards of structural transformation should not be as severe as the fall in output alone suggests, provided that reductions in output are concentrated on industrial activities that make a marginal contribution to added-value in the economy (or even value-subtracting activities) and goods that are largely dedicated to the overdeveloped defence sector. However, it seems inevitable that industries that are viable in the longer term will also be affected by the disruption and uncertainty involved in the transition.

Consequently, any Russian government that is seriously attempting to introduce a market economy will be forced to make very difficult choices between policies that may generate apparently unacceptable levels of inflation (or hyperinflation) and unacceptable levels of unemployment. The need to maintain tight fiscal and monetary policies to prevent the re-emergence of hyperinflationary pressures during the period when structural changes start to take effect and open unemployment takes effect will slow down the process of economic recovery, as the economy will depend to a greater degree on private demand and market forces, which will place greater pressure on the government to identify and preserve industries that have long-term potential but are suffering from short-term financial problems. At the same time the pursuit of tight fiscal and monetary policy will be complicated by the potential erosion of budget revenues following the establishment of a legally defined, ex ante tax system based on value-added and income taxes, which will depend on economic recovery for revenues in place of ex post expropriations of enterprise profits and increased pressure for expenditure on social-welfare programmes.

## TRADE LIBERALISATION: INTERNATIONAL EXPERIENCE

There are no exact precedents for the circumstances inherited by the Russian government, given that the experience of Eastern Europe is of limited duration and still of uncertain outcome. Given that the high proportion of national income devoted to military expenditure (in a vain attempt to maintain strategic parity with stronger economies) was a major factor which turned relative economic decline into absolute decline, it may be appropriate to compare Russia with a defeated military power. Japan and Germany both provide positive examples of defeated military powers who were required to reduce defence expenditure and relinquish their former military dominance and developed highly successful peacetime economies. Other successful examples of trade liberalisation as a means to economic development are to be found in South East Asia.

The post-war experience of Japan, which recovered from substantially lower pre-war levels of income than the West European economies (but had shown the fastest growth of GNP and exports in the inter-war period), has parallels with the problems facing Russia. Japan was faced with the destruction of much of its capital stock as a result of the Second World War, while that which survived consisted largely of military capacity and heavy industry, which was of little use in generating a successful peacetime economy. Japan also suffered from the destruction of its historic markets and major restrictions on its exports to western Europe. Under occupation, Japan was required to undertake a rather arbitrary land reform (which created a large class of owner farmers), deconcentrate industry (which was subsequently reversed), institute democracy and abolish its armed forces (Maddison 1969: 44–5) Following initial inflationary pressures, which averaged 85 per cent a year from 1945–51, a fixed (but relatively undervalued) exchange rate was established in 1949. The shortage of hard currency allied to a fixed exchange rate required Japan to pursue restrictive fiscal and monetary policies when demand for imports outstripped export growth and was the major constraint on what was nevertheless explosive growth until the mid-1960s when trade started to move into regular surpluses. During this period Japan operated a number of restrictive import policies, including import quotas, strict rationing of foreign exchange (which was allocated to targeted industries) and tight controls over foreign investment (Yoshitomi 1991).

Thus for nearly 20 years after the war, Japan pursued a policy of 'protected export promotion' during which period infant industries were heavily protected from foreign competition and received priority allocation of foreign currency. This period coincided with a rapid expansion of output of labour-intensive goods, including small manufactures and textiles. Yoshitomi (1991: 135–7) shows that protectionist policies involved 'positive adjustment' – the encouragement of export industries, not support for declining industries, in order to build up an export sector to overcome the shortage of foreign exchange. In the 1960s Japan progressively liberalised import quotas and controls on foreign exchange and reduced tariffs but did not remove all controls over foreign investment until 1973. During this period imports of electric consumer goods and electronics, which were to become Japan's staple exports, were progressively liberalised.

Japan's export structure gradually shifted from labour-intensive products through capital-intensive products to R&D intensive products. This process was neither entirely spontaneous or government-led as small independent export industries also emerged during this period. Yoshitomi (1991: 139) attributes the dynamism and high degree of innovation of Japanese industry to fierce domestic competition (most industries supported 10 or more firms) in a protected market, combined with a long-term approach by companies, incorporating job security which required them to look for an expanding markets to secure employment, rather than short-run profit maximisation. The search for an increased market share stimulated product innovation, falling unit costs, and provided a stimulus to exports. Until the

1970s the government also financed large-scale investment in infrastructure out of taxation.

Yoshitomi (1991: 145) draws four conclusions from this experience, which can be adapted to the analysis of the conditions facing Russia today. Firstly, domestic industries were only innovative because they were exposed to domestic competition. In the absence of domestic competition import controls would have slowed down development. Secondly, the government selected and supported potential 'winners', progressively liberalising import controls according to an announced timetable. Thirdly, the government stimulated high rates of saving within a 'disciplined fiscal and monetary policy framework' and, fourthly, success also depended on the special nature of Japanese business relations.

Japan's experience is not unique. David Gordon, a former Director of the World Bank (UNCTAD 1990: 3) argues that 'the world leaders in economic growth... have generally been those countries that, following a brief period of protective import substitution have fought vigorously and effectively to promote exports'. This requires not just that import protection (tariffs and quotas) should be removed as soon as possible, preferably according to a pre-announced schedule, but also that the state should provide special incentives to encourage the export of new products. Studies of the trade strategies of the more successful newly industrialising economies of South-East Asia support the argument in favour of export-oriented strategies over import-substituting strategies, after an initial period of import protection intended as a short-run stimulus to the development of an export sector. Balassa (1991) shows that in the initial import-protecting stage, NICs produced simple labour-intensive consumer goods. Once the domestic market for these products had been saturated, the country had to either shift production to a new range of (protected) import substitutes or export consumer goods in which the country has developed an initial comparative advantage. At this stage import liberalisation was important in exposing producers to international competition, to ensure that their products met international standards of price and quality. Balassa (1991: 80) also shows that Far-Eastern NICs, which pursued an export-oriented strategy, achieved higher rates of per capita growth incorporating 'high levels of investment efficiency ... with high and rising ratios of exports to GDP'.

Several developing and industrialised countries which once

combined an essentially market economy with a protectionist
foreign trade system based on quotas have liberalised their foreign
trade regimes, replacing quantitative restrictions by price indicators, while other centrally planned economies have attempted
to liberalise foreign trade both as part of reforms to a centrally
planned economy and as part of the transition to a market
economy. The experience of these countries supports the argument that the transition should be conducted as rapidly as is
consistent with social cohesion. A World Bank study (Choksi *et al.*
1991), which analysed the experience of 36 successful and
unsuccessful attempts at trade liberalisation in market economies
in 19 different countries (the majority of which were developing
countries), concluded that trade liberalisation was more likely to
be successful if the following criteria were met:

1 Bold policies should be pursued and should 'start with a bang'
  (p. 55).
2 Quantitative import controls should be dismantled rapidly;
  there was a 'powerful link between a bold relaxation of [quantitat-
  ive restrictions] and the long-term success of the liberalisation
  effort' (p. 44).
3 The programme should begin with a substantial depreciation
  of the currency, which provides price protection for domestic
  producers, which stimulates exports, which in turn stimulates
  employment and growth and reduced pressure on the balance
  of payments, and reduces subsequent pressure for the
  restoration of quantitative restrictions on competitive imports.
4 'A stable macroeconomic environment is an absolute essential.'
  Restrictive monetary and fiscal policies were required to
  prevent the erosion of competitive price gains resulting from
  currency depreciation. This is also essential to prevent the
  emergence of hyperinflationary pressures following major
  depreciation. The study concluded that 'expansionary fiscal
  and monetary pressures are the single most important factor in
  causing a reversal of trade reforms' (p.47).

### The relevance of the experience of NICs for the Russian economy

Although the economic circumstances confronting the central
Asian republics (and some of the autonomous republics within the
Russian Federation) can be compared with initial conditions

facing the NICs, the Russian economy differs from many NICs in five crucial respects. Firstly, Russia is a substantial net exporter of energy and raw materials, which under market circumstances will tend to drive up the long-term equilibrium exchange rate and reduce the competitiveness of exports of other goods. Secondly, it has a relatively well educated (but demoralised) labour force with skills in engineering but which is used to job security and has little or no experience of responding to market stimuli. Thirdly, Russia has an existing, although poorly functioning, industrial structure with a largely obsolete capital stock excessively geared towards heavy industry and armaments, much of which will have to be destroyed before it can be replaced. This will involve major economic as well as social costs, and could create a psychological barrier to economic recovery. Fourthly, there is the problem of major environmental pollution that will require initial clean-up cost before investment can be attracted. Finally, there is the sheer size of the country, which increases the need for investment in transport, communications and infrastructure and which implies that the optimum trade to GNP ratio for Russia will be lower than for many NICs.

The last point also suggests that the republics of the former Soviet Union will have to be far more dependent on the generation of domestic capital (particularly in the non-energy sector) and the development of internal markets for economic recovery than either the NICs or the economies of central-eastern Europe, which are also undergoing the transformation from central planning to a market economy.

## THE CASE FOR WESTERN ASSISTANCE IN THE PROCESS OF TRANSITION

The case for western governmental support in the process of transition to a market economy rests as much on self-interest as on humanitarian or moral factors. The successful transition to a democratic system of government based on a demilitarised market economy in Russia and the former Soviet republics offers major strategic and security advantages to the western powers. It also offers significant long-term economic advantages in the form of a potentially large reduction in defence expenditure (the 'peace dividend'), as well as commercial advantages for western producers and consumers arising from the potential opening up and expansion of undeveloped markets and alternative sources of supply. Without substantial external assistance the Russian government will be unable to generate sufficient hard currency earnings to finance the desired level of imports of investment goods and technical knowledge to modernise Russian industry, infrastructure, agriculture and food processing, and to service their own share of Soviet debt, as well as meeting the energy demands of the non-Russian republics without imposing an intolerable strain on domestic consumption. This would increase popular opposition to market reforms and potentially strengthen the coalition of Russian nationalists and conservatives. The potential economic and political gains of the end of cold war could be lost if a nationalist authoritarian government came to power with military support, or if the region, which contains an estimated 30,000 nuclear warheads, became increasingly unstable and degenerated into ethnic warfare.

Major questions remain about the size of external assistance: what form it should take from the standpoint of the recipient (technical advice, education and training, investment in infrastructure and productive capital, etc.) and from the donor (grants, credits, investment); how assistance should be funded and administered and by whom; the impact of such assistance on other international economic and political concerns (e.g. the environment, assistance to the Third World) and what economic and political conditions should be attached to such assistance.

## PRIORITIES FOR INVESTMENT AND ASSISTANCE

The study by Collins and Rodrik (1991) indicated that the level of investment required to generate a single percentage growth rate across the former Soviet Union as a whole is in the order of $80 billion (equivalent to 0.5 per cent of OECD GNP). These figures refer to a permanent increase in output generated by a growth of the capital stock and it appears probable that specific investment and assistance directed towards alleviating the most critical problem areas and bottlenecks would have a far greater short-term impact. A successful policy in the long term will involve significant foreign direct investment in the Russian economy in the form of multinational investment either in the acquisition of existing plants or the construction of new plants or in the form of capital shares in newly privatised industries, which will require the investor to bear the risk of bad decisions and consequently to ensure that investments are appropriate to the circumstances and to ensure the subsequent efficient operation of the plant. Although several western firms are actively investigating the prospects for investment in the former Soviet Union they have been deterred from undertaking major investment by both political and economic uncertainty and by specific problems, including the neglect of infrastructure, problems of environmental pollution that will have to be overcome before investment can commence, and the lack of financial skills and practical experience in the operation of a market economy of local management.

The most urgent priorities for western governmental or multilateral assistance are therefore to stimulate measures that will encourage trade liberalisation, domestic competition and the development of a market economy. These should include specific measures to facilitate inward investment, including measures to improve transportation and communications and environmental clean up; expenditure on education and training in the skills required to make a market function; measures to underwrite the political risks involved in investing in the former Soviet Union; and measures to alleviate the costs of the transition process on the domestic population, including assistance in the development of a welfare programme, humanitarian aid (including food and medicine) and balance of payments support to help maintain living standards during the initial transition period. Ideally this form of 'start-up' assistance should be reduced gradually as private capital flows take over. Finally, the reduction and removal of existing impediments to trade, including CoCom restrictions on the transfer of civilian technology with military uses, and EC and US constraints on potential (not just actual) imports of manufactured goods (including textiles), will help to stimulate Russian hard currency earnings and western investment in export-oriented industries in the former Soviet Union.

### Western assistance to stimulate trade liberalisation and economic efficiency

The Russian government inherited a trading system that was virtually the opposite of that developed by Japan and the successful NICS, including a highly monopolistic domestic industrial structure together with an inward-looking, import-substituting, protectionist system of organising and administering foreign trade which was reflected in the commodity structure of trade, based on exports of raw materials and imports of capital goods.

The most important target for western assistance is to provide support for the introduction of residents' convertibility (and in the longer term full capital convertibility) which will expose enterprises to foreign competition in the domestic market by liberalising imports, and will provide a basic currency anchor to restore a minimum value to the rouble in the domestic economy. This will involve critical judgements concerning the level of the exchange rate. An excessively low rate will stimulate further inflationary pressures, while an excessively high rate will expose viable enterprises to excess competitive pressures in both domestic and foreign markets. The volume of trade in manufactured goods in relation to the domestic market, however, suggests that inflationary pressures are the greater danger during the transition process and that the provision of a stabilisation fund which would enable the authorities to support the highest rate that can be sustained without a major run down of reserves and/or damage to viable industries should be a major priority. The low level of Russian gold and foreign exchange reserves indicates that the Russian contribution to the fund will be lower than was once anticipated and that a significant proportion of the stabilisation fund (in the region of $6 billion) will have to be provided externally.

A stabilisation fund must be supported by Russian guarantees on the supply of money and credit to both ensure that enterprises are genuinely forced to improve efficiency and to prevent a run down of reserves. The Russian authorities will be unable to exercise realistic control over the money supply unless they can control credit expansion by the central banks of the individual republics. This will either require the creation of a new central banking system (on the lines of the US Federal Reserve) or measures to ensure that the central banks of republics that remain within the rouble zone submit to rules on credit and monetary control established by the Russian central bank. The discussion in Chapter 11 indicates that, instead of attempting to sustain a single currency zone, the majority of the non-Russian republics should be encouraged to establish separate currencies, which would involve an initial devaluation against the rouble to increase the competitiveness of exports in the Russian market and would then have to bear responsibility for their own money supply. This would require the provision of external assistance to create an asset base for the newly independent central banks and to provide education and training for banking personnel.

The discussion in Chapter 11 also suggests that the preservation of trade levels with Russia after the introduction of trade in world market prices (assuming that demand for Russian oil is price inelastic) would result in substantial deficits for the non-Russian republics and that this is a potential area of interrepublican tension. The provision of transitional relief (or short-term balance of payments support) to the republics would enable them to maintain imports from Russia (if they wished) and indirectly would assist Russia (who would be able to sell energy to the non-Russian republics on similar terms to those prevailing in world markets). Assistance would be gradually phased out over a period of five years to stimulate domestic adjustment. Western companies might also be encouraged to establish ventures in the non-Russian republics by the prospect of lower wage costs, with the intention of marketing to Russia, which would also expose Russian enterprises to competition. These measures would help to prevent a major collapse of the former Soviet market and would also help to reduce potential economic disputes between those non-Russian republics that wish to preserve economic links within the former Soviet Union and Russia itself.

## THE SIZE AND COSTS OF WESTERN ASSISTANCE

Several writers have compared the provision of financial assistance to the former Soviet republics and Eastern Europe to the financial support provided by the USA to western Europe under the Marshall Plan after the war. These comparisons attempt to quantify the size of equivalent assistance from the perspective of the donor or the recipient. The Marshall plan provided $12.4 billion of grant aid and concessionary loans to western Europe between April 1948 and December 1951, which would be equivalent to $65 billion or $17.3 billion per year at today's prices (Collins and Rodrik 1991: 81). In practice, a sum of this size shared between all the former Soviet republics and Eastern Europe would be equivalent to approximately 1 per cent of the recipient countries' GNP and could not be expected to have a very large impact.

Chalmers and Lawson (1991: 23) estimate that Marshall plan aid was equivalent on average to 5–6 per cent of recipient GNP during the late 1940s (but as much as 14 per cent of Austrian GNP). Estimates of Soviet GNP vary substantially according to the methodology chosen, ranging from $1,735 dollars per head to $9,230. These estimates imply that assistance equivalent to 5 per cent of former Soviet GNP would range from $25 billion per annum to $133 billion. If Soviet per capita GNP is estimated at $5,000 per head (equivalent to 25 per cent of US GNP) the equivalent sum would be $75 billion per year, which is approximately equivalent to 0.5 per cent of the combined GNP of the USA, the EC and Japan. This sum (which excludes assistance to Eastern Europe, which could double the amount) is clearly significant and would have a significant impact on world capital markets if it were not accompanied by reductions in expenditure elsewhere. However, it is only equivalent to 15 per cent of the combined defence expenditure of the Group of Seven industrialised countries that was directed against the Warsaw Pact ($500 billion) and may not be considered as quite so large in the context of the potential (but not guaranteed) long-term savings in defence expenditure which could result from a permanent end to the cold war.

An alternative approach is to consider what levels of assistance the western nations might be expected to advance and to estimate its likely impact on the former Soviet economy. An annual sum in the order of $35–40 billion, which would be gradually reduced over a five-year period as both export earnings and private capital flows replace grants and credits would represent 0.25 per cent of OECD national income, is not unreasonable in view of the potential security benefits. It still seems improbable, however, that financial assistance to the former Soviet Union on this scale will be forthcoming, particularly in the form of direct grants, although a combination of humanitarian assistance involving medical and food aid, technical assistance, tied credits, and one-off payments in the form of relief on repayments of debt and interest and standby credit arrangements could push published figures towards this total. The initial figures would also be inflated by 'one-off' stabilisation funds that might not be drawn on. These sums would not represent a net loss of resources to the West. Food aid would largely be provided by running down excess stocks created as a by-product of western agricultural stabilisation programmes; technical assistance programmes generate income for western consultancies and colleges and, at a time when the OECD economies are experiencing a lengthy savings-led recession (which will be further aggravated by cuts in defence expenditure), government assisted or guaranteed investment programmes and balance of payments assistance would provide a Keynesian boost to the capital goods industries. Finally, although debt relief does not involve a flow of new money or resources and the real net cost would be reduced by the possibility that the Russian government would experience major difficulties in meeting scheduled repayments, it could have a critical impact on confidence and on future lending to the country.

## THE ECONOMIC AND POLITICAL CONDITIONS FOR ASSISTANCE

It can be argued that economic assistance that is not granted on purely humanitarian grounds should be linked to conditions to ensure that it is used efficiently and will help to achieve its stated objective. In many cases, however, it is difficult to discern whether aid has been granted on economic, strategic or humanitarian grounds. For example, I have argued above that the primary rationale for granting substantial amounts of aid and credits to Russia and the former Soviet republics was an attempt to guarantee stability within the region, which is in effect an attempt to 'buy' security. This, however, has a basically humanitarian aspect, as instability could result in both loss of life and a large number of homeless people and refugees, and an economic aspect in that it may be cheaper to grant assistance now than to attempt to cope with the aftermath of civil war. Even this involves a considerable degree of speculation as it cannot be guaranteed that such expenditure will prevent the outbreak of nationalist-inspired violence or even major conflict in the region, nor could the outbreak of violence in one or several regions of the former Soviet Union be taken as proof that a policy of assistance had failed. I do not personally believe that economic assistance to the states of the former Yugoslavia on the levels discussed above would have prevented the outbreak of civil war. All that can be said is that economic assistance that reduces the number of potential flashpoints and misunderstandings that could result from economic pressures will reduce the probability of a major and uncontrollable conflagration.

There is a not unreasonable concern that large-scale western assistance could be used to build up a new Russian superpower whose interests would conflict with those financing economic reconstruction in the longer term. The collapse of the Warsaw Treaty Organisation and the scale of investment required to generate even a small reduction in the gap between the national income of the Russian Republic and the NATO countries makes a direct military confrontation improbable. The possibility that Russian foreign policy objectives, which could be supported by force, could conflict with those granting assistance is far less improbable and it is a legitimate security interest to link large-scale assistance to agreements that ensure a sustained and permanent reduction in the military threat of the former Soviet Union and which reduce potential sources of instability in the region. These should include agreements to demilitarise the economy subject to monitoring and verification, as well as an economic objective that will facilitate the transfer of resources to civilian uses, plus agreements not to intervene militarily in the internal affairs of other republics, other than on humanitarian grounds and subject to the approval of the United Nations.

In many cases western political and security interests may directly conflict with either Russian economic interests or the dictates of a pure market economy. It was indicated in Chapter 5 that Russia had developed a comparative advantage in arms production and that pure economic interests might be best served by increasing arms exports to finance imported goods rather than by attempting to convert military plants to civilian production. To some extent this problem could be countered by requiring the Russian authorities to abide by international agreements to limit arms transfers as a condition of economic assistance. It is possible, however, that western governments might wish to see more stringent controls applied to Russian weapons sales than are applied to western companies themselves. This implies that governments that wish to impose greater controls over Russian exporters than over their own companies or nationals should bear at least some, if not all, of the costs to the Russian economy. Under these and other circumstances external assistance could be provided to underwrite the additional costs of measures that are being undertaken on security grounds. This could include underwriting the costs of providing housing for Russian troops withdrawn from former Soviet republics. Security interests may also indicate that investment to provide secure employment and maintain living standards should be directed to areas of above-average political risk, while private investors (both inside and outside the former Soviet Union) will be deterred from investing in the region for that very reason. External assistance could therefore be geared towards insuring or underwriting the additional costs incurred on security grounds.

In practice western governments and international financial agencies appear to have been more concerned with the economic conditions linked to western assistance programmes than with the political conditions. These have come under the purview of the IMF, which has developed considerable expertise in the formulation, approval and supervision of economic programmes that must be implemented by governments seeking multilateral assistance before credits are advanced. Governments are required to submit a letter of intent which contains commitments to the introduction of current account convertibility, price liberalisation, a broadly balanced budget and the development of an extensive private sector. The economic policy of the Russian government was based on the Economic Memorandum which formed its letter of intent to the IMF, while western governments are unwilling to advance bilateral credits and loans to Russia until the IMF gives approval to the Russian government stabilisation programme.

Negotiations between the Russian Government and the IMF, which will ultimately release an estimated $24 billion of multilateral and bilateral trade credits (comprised of an initial $1 billion credit tranche with fewer conditions attached; second, a more conditional $4 billion standby agreement, thirdly, a $6 billion stabilisation fund, $2 billion of debt rescheduling which would then pave the way for the release of $11 billion bilateral governmental trade credits and multilateral credits agreed with the World Bank and the European Bank for Reconstruction and Development), were stalled in the summer of 1992 over the severity of the Russian budget deficit and monetary control. The IMF wants the deficit to be reduced to below 5 per cent of GNP (excluding foreign borrowing) and inflation to be brought below 10 per cent before it will advance even the first $1 billion tranche of the standby agreement.

The Russian government will have difficulty in complying with these demands, given that it cannot control credit emission in the other Republics and that the level of the budget deficit in Russia itself is both a subject of controversy and cannot be calculated with any accuracy. (At the same time some western governments have discovered that their own budget deficits have been substantially underestimated at a time of recession.) This raises fundamental questions about the suitability of IMF conditions, which were largely intended to manage and supervise the stabilisation programmes of Latin American countries which were experiencing the dual problems of hyperinflationary pressures and external indebtedness (and which have been criticised for aggravating poverty), in the case of the transition to a market economy in Russia which has security and strategic as much as purely economic implications. It can be argued that the problems of indebtedness and hyperinflationary pressures in Russia are very similar to those experienced in Latin America and that economic recovery will be impossible without stringent monetary and fiscal policies, which are also necessary to prevent the misuse of funds. The principal counter-argument is that economic reform will be impossible without major western assistance and that the scale of the international problems which could result from the failure of Russian reforms is of an altogether different magnitude from projects that the IMF has overseen on a economic basis in the past.

Slavophiles contend that the Russian (and Slav) people differ from any other people and that the policies that have generated economic modernisation (with varying degrees of success) in other parts of the world will not necessarily work in Russia. The counter-argument is that the Russian economy is inherently similar to other economies, and subject to the same economic 'laws' as other economies and that Russia should pursue policies that are broadly similar to those pursued by successful newly industrialising economies that have embraced a free market philosophy and accepted substantial foreign direct investment. The truth probably lies somewhere between these two extremes. The clearest example of a long-term 'successful' industrialising economy in the post-war era is Japan, which has combined national traditions (particularly in labour relations) with the acceptance of some foreign ideas and capital. Japan also adopted a far more interventionist policy than the IMF seems willing to countenance in Russia. Stabilisation was achieved over a period of six years in Japan and overt protection for industry was maintained for 20 years.

## CONCLUSION

One of the major paradoxes of Russian and Soviet economic development has been that the continual quests for centralised modernisation (which involved forcing economic sacrifices on the population to generate the capital to overcome economic backwardness), from Ivan the Terrible, through Peter the Great, Catherine the Great, Witte, Stalin and most recently Gorbachev, all failed to establish a lasting modernised economic structure. The failure of attempted modernisation has determined Russian and Soviet trade patterns which continued to reflect the pro-duction structure of a relatively backward economy, dominated by imports of machinery, equipment and industrial components and exports of goods with a relatively low degree of industrial processing (agrarian products until the 1950s and energy and raw materials more recently). In this context it is possible to view the attempted rapid transition to a market economy as the con-tinuation of a historical sequence of attempts to inculcate western values to overcome inherited backwardness and halt the process of relative decline. Even if rapid systemic change can be achieved, the process of economic recovery will take several decades. A sudden reduction in the gap between Russian living standards and those of western Europe cannot be expected and success should be measured in terms of a gradual improvement in the standard of living. Even this limited goal may not be achieved without substantial western assistance, while the failure to provide such assistance could have incalculable consequences for global peace and stability. The response of the western powers and international institutions to the problems confronting the Russian government in the first eight months following the collapse of communist power in the Soviet Union has displayed a lack of vision and awareness of the problems confronting the Russian government and of the long-term advantages to the West if they are to be overcome. The economic conditions attached to IMF-backed assistance (the satisfacton of which western powers have accepted as prerequisites to additional bilateral aid) have been virtually impossible to achieve under Russian conditions and have raised the genuine question for many Russian citizens of whether the cure is worse than the illness and have badly undermined the reform process.

Although the major justification for large-scale assistance in both the short and long run is humanitarian (to alleviate the most immediate economic suffering and to reduce the prospect of widespread ethnic unrest which could result in civil wars and/or the prospect of the creation of a an unprecedented number of refugees), humanitarian assistance may be justified on the economic grounds that limited assistance now may be cheaper than the cost that will result from attempting to limit intractable problems after they have arisen. In the long term, the West needs to develop new instruments to 'buy' security in a volatile region. Assistance in the region of a single percentage point of the GNP of the OECD countries may appear relatively small when compared with western defence budgets in the cold war period.

# Bibliography

Aganbegyan, A. (1988) *The Challenge: Economics of Perestroika*, London: Hutchinson Education.

Aleksashenko, S. (1992) 'The economic union of republics: federation, confederation, community', in A. Aslund (ed.) *The Post Soviet Economy*, London: Pinter.

Aslund, A. (1990) 'How small is Soviet national income?', in H.S Rowen and C. Wolf (eds) *The Impoverished Superpower*, San Francisco: ICS Press.

—— (ed.) (1992) *The Post Soviet Economy: Soviet and Western Perspectives*, London: Pinter.

Balassa, B. (1991) 'Policy choices in the newly industrialising countries', in A. Koves and P. Marer (eds) *Foreign Economic Liberalisation*, Oxford: Westview Press.

Bash, Yu., Belous, N. and Kretov, I. (1986) 'Ekonomicheskii Eksperiment v Promyshlennosti i Razvitie Eksporta', *Vneshnyaya Torgovlya* 7.

Baykov, A. (1946) *Soviet Foreign Trade*, Princeton, New Jersey: Princeton University Press.

Bergson, A. (1989) *Planning and Performance in Socialist Economies*, London: Unwin Hyman.

Bertsch, G. and Elliot-Gower, S. (1991a) 'US Cocom policy: from paranoia to perestroika?', in G. Bertsch, H. Vogel and J. Zielonka (eds) *After the Revolutions*, Boulder, Colorado: Westview.

Bertsch, G. and Elliot-Gower, S. (eds) (1991b) *The Impact of Governments on East–West Economic Relations*, Basingstoke and London: Macmillan.

Birman, I. (1978) 'From the achieved level', *Soviet Studies* 30, 2: 153–72.

Blazyca, G. (1992) 'Poland', in I. Jeffries (ed.) *Industrial Reform in Socialist Countries*, Aldershot: Gower.

Bofinger, P. (1991) 'Options for the payments and exchange rate system in Eastern Europe', in *European Economy* 1991, 2: 243–61, Brussels: Commission of the European Communities.

Bogomolov, O. (1990) 'The Soviet economy on the eve of the 1990s: prospects for international cooperation', in NATO *The Central and East European Economies in the 1990s*, Brussels: NATO Economics Directorate.

Bradshaw, M. (1992) 'Foreign trade', in *Eastern Europe and the Commonwealth of Independent States*, London, Europa Publications.

Brown, S. (1992) 'Federalism and marketization in the Soviet Union in A. Aslund (ed.) *The Post Soviet Economy*, London, Pinter.

Bukharin, N. and Preobrazhensky, E. (1970) *The ABC of Communism*, Harmondsworth: Penguin.

Bykov, A. N. (1991) 'Institutional framework of foreign trade relations of the Soviet Union', in M. Kaser and A.M. Vacic (eds) *Reforms in Foreign Economic Relations of Eastern Europe and the Soviet Union*, New York: UN Economic Commission for Europe.

Chadwick, M., Long, D. and Nissanke, M. (1987) *Soviet Oil Exports: Trade Adjustments, Refining Constraints and Market Behaviour*, Oxford: Oxford University Press.

Chalmers, M. and Lawson, C. (1991) *Western Security and Soviet Reform*, Bristol: Saferworld Foundation.

Choksi, A., Michaely, M. and Papageorgiu, D. (1991) 'The design of succesful trade liberalisation policies', in A. Koves and P. Marer (eds) *Foreign Economic Liberalisation*, Oxford: Westview Press.

CIA (1980) *Communist Aid Activities in Non-Communist Less Developed Countries, 1979 and 1954–79*, Washington DC: Central Intelligence Agency, National Foreign Assessment Center.

CIA (1984) *Handbook of Economic Statistics, 1984*, Washington DC: Central Intelligence Agency.

Collins, S. and Rodrik, D. (1991) *Eastern Europe and the Soviet Union in the World Economy*, Washington DC: Institute for International Economics.

Cook, L.J. (1992) 'Brezhnev's "social contract" and Gorbachev's reforms', *Soviet Studies*, 44, 1: 37–56.

Cooper, J. (1991) *The Soviet Defence Industry: Conversion and Reform*, London: Pinter, for Royal Institute of International Affairs.

Crisp, O. (1976) *Studies in the Russian Economy before 1914*, London: Macmillan.

Deger, S. (1985) 'Soviet arms sales to developing countries: the economic forces', in R. Cassen (ed.) *Soviet Interests in the Third World*, London: Sage.

Dyker, D. (1992) *After the Soviet Union: the International Trading Environment*, London: Royal Institute of International Affairs.

Efrat, M. (1985) 'The economics of Soviet arms transfers to the Third World', in P. Wiles and M. Efrat (1985) *The Economics of Soviet Arms*, STICERD Occasional paper 7. London: London School of Economics.

Ekonomika i Zhizn: see Note on Soviet statistical sources (ii), below.

Ellman, M.J. (1975) 'Did the agricultural surplus provide the resources for the increase in investment in the USSR in the First Five Year Plan?' *Economic Journal* 85.

—— (1982) 'Did Soviet economic growth end in 1978?', in J. Drewnowski (ed.) *Crisis in the East European Economy*, London: Croom Helm.

Ericson, P. and Miller, R. (1979) Soviet economic behavior in a balance of payments perspective', in *The Soviet Economy in a Time of Change*, Washington DC: Joint Economic Committee of the US Congress.

*European Economy* (1990) *Stabilization, Liberalization and Devolution. Assessment of the Economic Situation and Reform Process in the Soviet Union*, Brussels: Commission of the European Communities. Directorate-General for Economic and Financial Affairs. No. 45.

*European Economy* (1991) *The Path of Reform in Central and Eastern Europe.* Commission of the European Communities, Brussels: Commission of the European Communities. Directorate-General for Economic and Financial Affairs. Special edition no. 2.

Falkus, M. (1972) *Industrialisation of Russia, 1700–1914*, London: Macmillan.

Fedorov, B. (1992) 'Monetary, financial and foreign exchange policy', in A. Aslund (ed.) *The Post Soviet Economy*, London: Pinter.

Foot, M.D. (1992) *Currency Issues in Eastern Europe: A Western Perspective*, London: Royal Institute for International Affairs. Briefing Paper.

Gaidar, Y. and Yarushenko, V. (1988) Nulevoi Tsikl. *Kommunist* 8: 74–86.

Gardner, H.S. (1983) *Soviet Foreign Trade. The Decision Process*, Boston: Kluwer-Nijhoff.

Garvy, G. (1977) *Money, Financial Flows and Credit in the Soviet Union*, Cambridge, Mass: Ballinger.

Gaworzewska, A. (1985) 'Soviet and East European hard currency debt and trade with the West', *EIU Regional Review: Eastern Europe and the USSR 1985*, London: Economist Intelligence Unit.

Geron, L. (1990) *Soviet Foreign Economic Policy under Perestroika*, London: Pinter, for Royal Institute of International Affairs.

Goldman, M. (1980) *The Enigma of Soviet Petroleum*, London: Allen and Unwin.

Gomulka, S. (1971) *Inventive Activity, Diffusion and the Stages of Economic Growth*, Aarhus: Institute of Economics.

—— (1986) *Growth, Innovation and Reform in Eastern Europe*, Brighton: Harvester Wheatsheaf.

Gomulka, S. and Nove, A. (1984) 'Contribution to Eastern growth; an econometric evaluation', in *East–West Technology Transfer*, Paris: OECD.

Granville, B. (1992) *Price and Currency Reform in Russia and the CIS*, London: Royal Institute of International Affairs.

Gruzinov, V.P. (1970) *The USSR's Management of Foreign Trade*, London and Basingstoke: Macmillan.

Gustafson, T. (1989) *Crisis amid Plenty. The Politics of Soviet Energy under Brezhnev and Gorbachev*, Princeton, New Jersey: Princeton University Press.

Hanson, P. (1981) *Trade and Technology in Soviet–Western Relations*, London and Basingstoke: Macmillan.

—— (1988) *Western Economic Statecraft in East–West Relations*, Chatham House Paper no 40. London: Routledge and Kegan Paul.

—— (1992) 'The Russian budget crisis', in *RFE/RL Research Report* 14: 39–43.

Hardt, J. (1990) 'Soviet economy in crisis and transformation', in NATO (1990) *The Central and East European Economies in the 1990s*. Brussels: NATO Economic Directorate.

Hewett, E. (1988) *Reforming the Soviet Economy*, Washington DC: The Brookings Institution.

Hill, M.R. (1983) *East-West Trade, Industrial Co-operation and Technology Transfer*, Aldershot: Gower.

Holzman, F.D. (1974) *Foreign Trade Under Central Planning*, Cambridge, Mass: Harvard University Press.

—— (1979) 'Some systemic factors contributing to the convertible currency shortages of CPEs', *American Economic Review*, 69.

Hough, J. (1991) 'The Soviet attitude toward integration in the world economy', in G. Bertsch and S. Elliot-Gower (eds) *The Impact of Governments on East-West Economic Relations*, London: Macmillan.

Hrncir, M. and Klacek, J. (1991) 'Stabilization policies and currency convertibility in Czechoslovakia', in *European Economy 1991, The Path of Reform in Central and Eastern Europe*, Brussels: Commission of the European Communities.

IMF, The World Bank, OECD, EBRD (1991) *A Study of the Soviet Economy*, 3 vols. Paris: OECD.

Jeffries, I. (ed.) (1992) *Industrial Reform in Socialist Countries*, Aldershot: Gower.

Kaplan, N.M. and Moorsteen, R. (1960) 'An index of Soviet industrial output', *American Economic Review*, 50.

Kaser, M. (1984) 'External relations of Comecon countries: gold sales and prospects', in *External Economic Relations of the Comecon Countries*, Brussels: NATO, Economics Directorate.

Kaser, M. and Vacic, A.M. (1991) *Reforms in Foreign Economic Relations of Eastern Europe and the Soviet Union*, New York: United Nations Economic Commission for Europe.

Kaufman, R.F. (1991) US–Soviet trade policy in the 1980s, in G. Bertsch and S. Elliot-Gower (eds) *The Impact of Governments on East-West Economic Relations*, London: Macmillan.

Kennedy, P. (1989) *The Rise and Fall of the Great Powers*, London: Fontana.

Khanin, G. (1991) Ekonomicheskii rost v SSSR v 80 gody. *EKO*, 5: 25–34.

—— (1992) 'The Soviet economy – from crisis to catastrophe', in A. Aslund (ed.) *The Post Soviet Economy*, London: Pinter.

Kostinsky, B. (1973) *Description and Analysis of Soviet Foreign Trade Statistics*, Washington DC: US Department of Commerce.

Koves, A. (1985) *The CMEA Countries in the World Economy: Turning Inwards or Turning Outwards*, Budapest: Akademiai Kiado.

Khrushchev, N. (1962) *Razvitie Ekonomikii SSSR i Partiinoe Rukovodstvo Narodniim Khozyaistvom*, Moscow: Gospolitizdat.

Lavigne, M. (1985) *Economie Internationale des Pays Socialistes*, Paris: Armand Colin.

—— (1991a) *International Political Economy and Socialism*, Cambridge: Cambridge University Press.

—— (1991b) *Financing the Transition in the USSR: The Shatalin Plan and the Soviet Economy*, New York: Institute for East-West Security Studies.

McAuley, A. (1991) 'The economic consequences of Soviet disintegration', *Soviet Economy* 7, 3: 189–214.

Maddison, A. (1970) *Economic Growth in Japan and the USSR*, London: Allen and Unwin.

Malle, S. (1987) 'Soviet labour-saving policy in the eighties' in *The Soviet Economy: A New Course?*, Brussels: NATO Economics Directorate.

Marrese, M. and Vanous, J. (1983) *Soviet Subsidisation of Trade with Eastern Europe: A Soviet Perspective*, Berkeley, Calif.: University of California Press.

Memorandum (1992) Memorandum ob Ekonomicheskoi Politike Rossiiskoi Federatsii, *Ekonomika i Zhizn*, no. 10.

Milanovic, B. (1992) 'Poland's quest for economic stabilisation 1988–91: Interaction of political economy and economics', *Soviet Studies* 44, 3: 511–31.

Moorsteen, R.H. and Powell, R.P. (1966) *The Soviet Capital Stock 1928–62*, Homewood, Illinois: Irwin.

Morrison, J. (1991) *Boris Yeltsin*, Harmondsworth: Penguin.

Munting, R. (1982) *The Economic Development of the USSR*, London: Croom Helm.

Narkhoz: see Note on Soviet statistical sources (ii), below.

NATO (1990) *The Central and East European Economies in the 1990s*, Brussels: NATO Economics Directorate.

Nechaev, A.A. (1991) 'The industrial depression in the USSR: a mechanism of development', *Communist Economies and Economic Transformation*, 3, 4: 455–66.

Nello, S. S (1991) *The New Europe*, London: Harvester Wheatsheaf.

Nissanke, M. (1987) 'Oil exports and balance-of-payments adjustments: a historical examination', in M. Chadwick, D. Long and M. Nissanke, *Soviet Oil Exports: Trade Adjustments, Refining Constraints and Market Behaviour*, Oxford: Oxford University Press.

Nove, A. (1969) *An Economic History of the USSR*, Harmondsworth: Penguin.

—— (1986) *The Soviet Economic System*, London: Allen and Unwin.

Parrott, B. (1983) *Politics and Technology in the Soviet Union*, Cambridge, Mass: MIT Press.

Pierre, A.J. (1982) *The Global Politics of Arms Sales*, Princeton, New Jersey: Princeton University Press.

Pinder, J. (1991) *The European Community and Eastern Europe*, London: Pinter for Royal Institute of International Affairs.

Portes, R (1983) 'Deficits and detente', *Report of an International Conference on the Balance of Trade in the Comecon Countries*, New York: The Twentieth Century Fund.

—— (1991) 'Introduction', in *European Economy* Special edition no. 2, Brussels: Commission of the European Communities.

Pozdnyakov, V.S. and Sadikov, O.N. (1985) *Pravovoe Regulirovanie Otnoshenii po Vneshnie Torgovle SSSR*, Moscow: Mezhdunarodnye Otnosheniya.

Poznanski, K. (1988) 'Opportunity costs in Soviet trade with Eastern Europe', *Soviet Studies* 40, 2: 290–307.

Quigley, J. (1974) *The Soviet Foreign Trade Monopoly*, Columbus, Ohio: Ohio State University Press.

Roxburgh, A. (1992) 'The August revolution and its consequences', in *Eastern Europe and the Commonwealth of Independent States 1992*, London: Europa Publications.

Rowen, H.S. and Wolf, C., Jr (1990) *The Impoverished Superpower: Perestroika and the Military Burden*, San Francisco: ICS Press.

Sachs, J. (1991) 'Poland and Eastern Europe: what is to be done?', in A. Koves and P. Marer (eds) *Foreign Economic Liberalisation*, Oxford: Westview Press..

—— (1992) 'The grand bargain', in A. Aslund (ed.) *The Post Soviet Economy*, London: Pinter.

Sarafanov, M., Takhtamanov, F., Daniltsev, A. and Ivashura, S. (1992) 'Platyezhnii balans SSSR i Rossii' *Ekonomika i Zhizn* 6: 11.

Seliunin, V. and Khanin, G. (1987) 'Lukavaia Tsifra', *Novy Mir*, 63.

Shatalin, S. (1990) *Perekhod k Rynku* (cyclostyled copy of programme circulated to the Russian and Soviet Parliaments).

Smirnov, G., Zotov, B. and Shagalov, G. (1964) 'Evaluating the effectiveness of foreign trade', *The American Review of Soviet and East European Foreign Trade* 1, 1: 3–15.

Smith, A.H. (1982)'The influence of trade on Soviet relations with the Middle East', in A. Dawisha and K. Dawisha (eds) *The Soviet Union in the Middle East*, London: Heinemann, for the Royal Institute of International Affairs.

—— (1985a) 'Soviet trade relations with the Third World', in R. Cassen (ed.) *Soviet Interests in the Third World*, London: Sage.

—— (1985b) 'International trade and resources', in C. Keeble (ed.) *The Soviet State*, Aldershot: Gower.

—— (1987) 'Foreign trade', in M. McCauley (ed.) *The Soviet Union under Gorbachev*, London: Macmillan.

—— (1989) Can Comecon Survive? WEFA Group, Newsletter, December 1989, Washington DC and London: Wharton Econometric Forecasting Agency.

—— (1992) 'Soviet Economic Relations with Eastern Europe under Gorbachev', in A. Pravda (ed.) *The End of the Outer Empire*, London: Sage.

Sokoloff, G. (1987) *The Economy of Detente*, Leamington Spa: Berg.

Spandaryan, V. and Shmelev, N. (1990) ' "Otkritaya ekonomika" na slovakh i na dele', *Kommunist* 6: 46–57.

Steele, J. (1992a) *Guardian*, 19 February 1992.

Steele, J. (1992b) *Guardian*, 21 February 1992.

Stent, A. (1981) *From Embargo to Ostpolitik. The Political Economy of West German–Soviet Relations 1955–1980*, Cambridge: Cambridge University Press.

Stern, J. (1982) *East European Energy and East–West Trade in Energy*, London: Policy Studies Institute and Royal Institute of International Affairs.

—— (1987) *Soviet Oil and Gas Exports to the West*, Aldershot: Gower.

Sutela, P. (1991) *Economic Thought and Economic Reform in the Soviet Union*, Cambridge: Cambridge University Press.

—— (1992) 'The role of the external sector during the transition', in A. Aslund (ed.) *The Post Soviet Economy*, London: Pinter.

Sutton, A. (1968) *Western Technology and Soviet Economic Development*, Vol. 1, Stanford, Calif.: Stanford University Press.

Treml, V. (1980) 'Foreign trade and the Soviet economy: changing parameters', in E. Neuberger and L. Tyson (eds) *The Impact of International Disturbances on the Soviet Union and Eastern Europe*, Oxford: Pergamon.

—— (1983) 'Soviet dependence on foreign trade', *External Economic Relations of the CMEA Countries*, Brussels: NATO Economics Directorate.

Treml, V. and Kostinsky, B. (1982) *Domestic Value of Soviet Foreign Trade: Exports and Imports in the 1972 Input–Output Table*, Foreign Economic Report no 20. Washington DC: US Department of Commerce.

UNCTAD (1990) *Financing of Exports from Developing Countries*, Geneva: International Trade Centre, UNCTAD/GATT.

Valkenier, E.K. (1983) *The Soviet Union and the Third World: An Economic Bind*, New York: Praeger.

Vestnik (1990) Ekonomicheskie Vzaimosvyazi Respublik v Narodno-khozyaistvennom Komplekce, *Vestnik Statistik* 3: 36–53.

White, S. (1992) 'Nationalism in the USSR', in *Eastern Europe and the Commonwealth of Independent States*, London: Europa Publications.

Wiles, P.J.D. (1982) 'The worsening of Soviet economic performance', in J. Drewnowski (ed.) *Crisis in the East European Economy*, London: Croom Helm.

Williamson, J. (1991) *The Economic Opening of Eastern Europe*, Washington DC: Institute for International Economics.

Yavlinsky, G. (1992) 'Spring '92 Reforms in Russia', *Moscow News*, nos 21–2.

Yoshitomi, M. (1991) 'Micro and macro foundations of Japan's economic success', in A. Koves and P. Marer (eds) *Foreign Economic Liberalisation*, Oxford: Westview Press.

Zoeter, J.P. (1983) 'USSR: hard currency trade and payments', in *The Soviet Economy in the 1980s*, Washington DC: Joint Economic Committee of the US Congress.

## Note on Soviet statistical sources

### i) Trade data

The Ministry of Foreign Trade published an statistical yearbook under the title Vneshnyaya Torgovlya SSSR (Foreign Trade of the USSR) from 1956 until 1988. This was renamed Vneshniye Ekonomicheskiye Svyazi SSSR (Foreign Economic Relations of the USSR) from 1988–90, following the replacement of the Ministry of Foreign Trade by the Ministry of Foreign Economic Relations. For simplicity, both series of handbooks are referred to as Vneshtorg in the text and tables. The Ministry of Foreign Trade also published commemorative issues of Vneshnyaya Torgovlya in 1967, with partial data covering the period from 1918–66, and in 1982, with partial data covering the period from 1922–81. These were used extensively to obtain data on trade before 1956 and for data that was not published in the relevant yearbook.

## ii) Domestic data

The Central Statistical Administration of the USSR (since 1988 the State Committee of Statistics or Goskomstat) produced a statistical yearbook and occasional commemorative editions under the title Narodnoye Khozyaistvo SSSR (National Economy of the USSR). There is a similar publication by the republican statistical authorities for the Russian Republic. These are referred to in the text and tables as Narkhoz and Narkhoz RSFSR respectively. Other official statistical data (monthly, quarterly and annual data for the period after 1990) have been taken from the weekly economic journal Ekonomika i Zhizn (Economics and Life), which was formerly called Ekonomicheskaya Gazeta (Economic Gazette). These are referred to as Ekonomika i Zhizn in the text.

# Index

Abalkin, Leonid 111, 114, 115;
plan 111–12, 113–14, 115–16,
117, 118
Adygai 10
Aganbegyan, A. 103, 108, 115,
125, 130; plan 115
agriculture: Bolshevism 22;
collectivisation 64; fertiliser
industry 62, 66; Russia 8;
Russian Empire,
pre-revolution 15, 16, 19
Aleksashenko, S. 210
Algeria 89, 149–50
Alma Ata declaration (1991) 1–2,
7
anti-alcohol campaign 102–3
Arbatov, G. 113–14
Armenia 1, 2–3, 6, 212
arms and military equipment,
exports 74–5, 79, 88–96, 139,
143, 147–51, 234
Aslund, A. 34, 35
Azerbaidzhan 1, 3, 10, 86, 122,
212

Baku 122
balance of payments, USSR
156–76; collapse of trade
172–5; and domestic economy
164–72; Gorbachev 156–62;
imports 162–4; repressed
deficit 41
Balassa, B. 225
Balcerowicz, L. 189
Baltic Republics 1, 3, 6, 212

banking 20, 40; reforms 109–10;
and transition to market
economy 198 see also Russian
Central Bank;
Vneshekonombank;
Vneshtorgbank
Bash, Yu. 50
Bashkiria 9, 10
Baykov, A. 18, 19, 25, 26, 28
Belous, N. 50
Bergson, A. 26–7, 34
Bertsch, G. 123
Bielarus 10
Birman, I. 38
Black Sea fleet 10
Blazyca, G. 190
Bocharov, Mikhail 115
Bogomolov, O. 112
Bolshevik government: economic
strategy 20–3; foreign
economic relations 23–6
Bradshaw, M. 9, 147
Brezhnev, L.I. 32, 61, 66, 78,
102, 123, 124
Brown, S. 210
budget deficit: Poland 180;
Russia 180; USSR 110–11,
118, 119
Bukharin, N. 21–2, 23, 24
Buryatia 10
Byelorussia 1, 2, see also Bielarus
Bykov, A.N. 131, 132, 136

Cameroon 148–50
Carter, Jimmy 123

Central Intelligence Agency (CIA): arms exports studies 88–95; gold production estimates 96–8; oil study 83
central planning 36–41
Chadwick, M. 80, 82, 84
Chalmers, M. 232
Chechen people 9, 10
chemicals industry 30, 57, 61–3; exports 74–5, 78, 143, 151–3
Chernenko, K. 102, 142, 167
Chernobyl accident 138
Choksi, A. 226
Chuvashia 10
coal industry 84, 144, 146
CoCom (Coordinating Committee for Multilateral Export Controls) 60, 123
Collins, S. 218–19, 228, 231
common rouble zone 210–14
Commonwealth of Independent States (CIS) 1–7, 212; energy production 145–6; stability of 10–12
communal ownership 185–6
consumer goods 39, 171–2
Cook, L.J. 103, 108
Cooper, J. 217
Council for Mutual Economic Assistance (CMEA) 53–5, 123, 145, 162, 172–4, 175
coup (August 1991) 1, 6–7
Crimean War 16
Crisp, O. 16
currency convertibility 187–8, 190, 193; Poland 188–90; Russia 190–4
Czechoslovakia 172, 184, 186

Dagestan 10
De Beers 147
Deger, S. 90, 98
demand: consumer 40–1, 68–70, 113, 166; for labour 65–7
developing countries: debt to USSR 161–2; Soviet exports to 74, 78–9, 88–96, 147–51
diamonds 8; exports 74, 76–8, 143, 146–7

differentiated valuation coefficients (DVKs) 133–5

Eastern Europe: collapse of communism 101, 173; economic planning 53–4; energy 54–5, 84, 87–8, 144–6; trade with USSR 53–5, 123, 162, 172–4, 175; transition to market economy 101, 113, 177
Efrat, M. 89, 92
Egypt 148–50
electricity 8
Elliot-Gower, S. 123
Ellman, M.J. 26, 33–4
energy 8, 84–5; exports to Eastern Europe 54–5, 84, 87–8, 172–5; exports to the West 74–5, 80–8, 124, 138–46; production 138, 141, 144–6; Russian exports 206–10
Ericson, P. 93, 94
Estonia 1, 3, 6, 212
exchange rate: Russia 187–8, 190–4, 230; USSR 45–6, 135, 187
exports 73–9; arms and military equipment 74–5, 79, 88–96, 143, 147–51, 155; Bolshevism 25; Brezhnev era 74, 80–8; and central planning 43–50; diamonds 74, 76–8, 143, 146–7; energy 54–5, 74–5, 80–8, 124, 138–46; gold 74, 76–7, 96–8, 153–4; Gorbachev 138–55; processed goods 74–5, 143, 151–4; Russia 11–13, 199–216; to the West 74–5, 80–8, 124, 138–46, 174–5

Fedorov, B. 191
fertiliser industry 62, 66
financial planning 39–41
food 183; demand for 68–9; imports 170–1; price liberalisation 178–9
Foreign Trade Organisations (FTOs) 42–3, 44, 49, 129, 131
free economic zones 137

Gaidar, Yegor 61, 62, 177, 194
Gardner, H.S. 48, 49
Garvy, G. 67
gas, natural: exports 81, 84–8, 124, 143, 144; exports to Eastern Europe 54–5; production 8, 141, 144–6; Russian exports 206–7
General Agreement on Tariffs and Trade (GATT), Soviet membership 127
Georgia 1, 2–3, 6, 212
Geron, L. 131, 134
GKES (State Committee for Foreign Economic Relations) 42–3, 131
gold 8, 153; exports 74, 76–7, 96–8, 153–4
Goldman, M. 83, 85, 86
Gomulka, S. 27, 33, 59, 64
Gorbachev, Mikhail: and balance of payments 167, 175; democratic reforms 3, 199; economic reform 99–105, 107, 113, 115, 117–18; foreign economic relations reform 124–5, 127, 187; and imports 63, 142, 175; and privatisation 185; resignation 1–2; and Russia 4; and Yeltsin 5–7
Gordon, David 225
Gorno-Altai 10
Gosbank (State Bank) 40, 109–10
Gosplan (State Planning Committee) 30–1, 37–8, 42–3
Gospriemka (State Quality Control Board) 103
Gossnab (State Committee for Material Supply) 37, 40, 42, 130
grain imports and exports 55, 68–9, 124, 171
Granville, B. 192, 212
growth: Bolshevism 25; and labour demand 65–7; post-war 30–5; Russian Empire, pre-revolution 15–19; Stalinist model 26–30, 59–60; wages, and consumer demand 68–70; Western estimates of 33–4

Gruzinov, V.P. 42, 44, 49
Gustafson, T. 9, 61, 83, 84, 122

Hanson, P. 31, 58, 62–3, 66, 122, 180
Hardt, J. 104
Hewett, E. 37
Hill, M.R. 60, 63, 66
Holzman, F.D. 28, 29
Hough, J. 24
Hrncir, M. 193
Hungary 128, 172

imports: Bolshevism 25–6; Brezhnev period 55–6; and central planning 43–50, 52–3; Chernenko period 142; Gorbachev 143, 162–4, 167–9; grain 55, 68–9; machinery and equipment 31, 56–64, 125, 168–9, 205; Stalinism 28; technology 26–35
incomes 110, 118, 119–20, 182–3
India 148–50
industrialisation 26–7, 34, 64
industry: Bolshevik nationalisation 20–1; and central planning 37–9; chemicals 30, 57, 61–3; energy demands 84; and labour demand 65–7; Russia 8; Russian Empire, pre-revolution 16, 18–19
inflation 41, 109, 116
Ingush people 9, 10
integration of Russia with world economy 218–38; costs of 221–3; transition scenarios 218–20; and western assistance 227–36
International Labour Organisation (ILO), employment study 198
International Monetary Fund (IMF): conditions for aid to Russia 235–6, 237; estimates of Soviet trade 156–9, 163–4; Soviet membership 127
investment, foreign 73, 218–20,

228–31; Russian Empire, pre-revolution 17–18
Iran 86
Iraq 89

Japan 86–7, 223–5, 236
Jeffries, I. 112, 116
joint ventures 128–30, 136–7

Kabardino-Balkaria 10
Kalmykia 10
Kaplan, N.M. 29
Karachai-Circassia 10
Karelia 10
Kaser, M. 96, 153
Katushev, Konstantin 131
Kaufman, R.F. 123
Kazakhstan 1–2, 3, 84, 212
Kennedy, John F. 124
Kennedy, P. 15, 16
Khakassia 10
Khanin, G. 34–5, 119
Khasbulatov, Ruslan 194–5, 197–8
Khrushchev, N. 30–1, 32, 57, 67, 97
Kiselev, V.P. 108
Klacek, J. 193
Komi 10
Korean War 53
Kostinsky, B. 48, 49, 58, 76, 163–4
Kosygin, A.N. 31
Koves, A. 28–9
Kretov, I. 50
kulaks 22
Kyrgyzstan 1–2, 3

labour market 65–7, 198
Latvia 1, 3, 6, 212
Lavigne, M. 46, 78, 97, 116, 134, 164
Lawson, C. 232
Lenin, V.I. 20–1, 23–4, 42
Libya 89, 148–50
liquefied natural gas (LNG) 86–7
Lithuania 1, 3, 6, 212
living standards 107, 182–3, 222, 237

McAuley, A. 203

machinery and equipment: exports 74–5, 143, 151–3; imports 31, 56–64, 125, 168–9, 205
Maddison, A. 15, 17–18, 224
Malle, S. 65, 66
management: and central planning 38–9; and reforms 105–6
Mari 10
market economy, transition to see transition
Marrese, M. 55
Marshall Plan 231–2
Marx, Karl 20, 29
Milanovic, B. 189
Miller, R. 93, 94
minerals 8; exports 74–5, 143, 146–7
Ministry for Foreign Economic Relations (MVES) 131–2
Ministry of Foreign Trade 42–4, 128, 131
modernisation, investment required 218–20, 228–31
Moldova 1, 3, 6, 10, 11, 212
monetary policy: Russia 179, 181–2, 192–3; USSR 20, 39–41
Moorsteen, R. 29
Mordovia 10
Morrison, J. 4, 6, 115
Munting, R. 15, 16, 18–19

Nemchinov, V. 105
nepmen 22
New Economic Policy (NEP) 21–4, 36, 42, 105
newly industrialisaing countries (NICs) 219, 225–7
Nissanke, M. 80, 82, 97
Nove, A. 16, 64
nuclear power 138

oil 8, 121–2, 138–9; exports to Eastern Europe 54–5, 172–5; exports to the West 80–4, 138–46; investment in 122; production 138, 141, 144–6; Russian exports 206–7

Ossetia 10

Parrott, B. 31–2
Pavlov, Valentin 118
Petrakov, N. 113–14, 194
Pierre, A.J. 89
planning, economic 20, 36–51;
    CMEA countries 53–4;
    domestic 36–9; financial and
    monetary 39–41; and
    Gorbachev reforms 103–4;
    Lenin 20; state monopoly of
    foreign trade 41–51
Poland 128, 172; budget deficit
    180; currency convertibility
    188–90; privatisation 184, 186;
    transition to market economy
    113, 177
Politburo 37
Portes, R. 94, 190
Pozdnyakov, V.S. 43
Poznanski, K. 55
precious metals 8; exports 74,
    76–8, 96–8, 146–7, 153–4
*preisausgleich* 46, 48
Preobrazhensky, E. 21–2, 23
prices: domestic and world 46;
    fixed 40–1, 45, 48; inflation
    109, 182; liberalisation and
    stabilisation, Russia 178–82;
    reform, under Gorbachev
    107–9, 114, 118–19
privatisation: Russia 183–6, 196;
    Soviet reform plans 112,
    116–17, 118
production: falling (1991) 118–19;
    post-war 30, 32–5

Quigley, J. 24

railways 17, 19
Rapallo, Treaty of 25
Reagan, Ronald 122, 123–4
reform, under Gorbachev 99–120;
    Abalkin plan (1989–90)
    111–14; compromise attempt
    117–18; deterioration (1991)
    118–20; failure of gradualist
    approach 106–8; first phase

(1985–87) 102–3; foreign
    economic relations 127–37;
    growing inflation (1988–90)
    109–11; joint ventures 136–7;
    radicalisation of reforms
    99–102; Shatalin plan (1990)
    114–17; streamlining
    (1988–90) 103–6
reform, Russia 177–98; currency
    convertibility 187–8, 190–4;
    gradual *vs* rapid 195–7;
    macroeconomic stabilisation
    and living standards 182–3;
    opposition to 194–5; price
    liberalisation and stabilisation
    178–82; privatisation 183–6,
    196
Rodrik, D. 218–19, 228, 231
Romania 128
rouble: common rouble zone
    210–14; convertibility 45–6,
    135, 187, 190–4
Roxburgh, A. 7
Russia 2–3
Russian Central Bank: and
    common rouble zone 210–12;
    and rouble supply 182, 193,
    194
Russian Empire, pre-revolution
    4, 15–20
Russian Federation: and the CIS
    1; economic importance of
    7–10; integration with world
    economy 218–38; trade and
    economic relations 11–13,
    199–217; trade with other ex-
    Soviet republics 210–16;
    transition to market economy
    177–98; and Ukraine 10–11
Russian Soviet Federal Socialist
    Republic (RSFSR) 2–4; energy
    exports 206–10; and Shatalin
    plan 114–17; and Soviet
    exports 204–5, 208–9; trade
    199–210; trade with other
    Soviet republics 199–204
Ryzhkov, Nikolai 112, 114–15,
    125–6, 158–9, 172–3; plan
    112, 113

Sachs, Jeffrey 177, 196
Sadikov, O.N. 43
Sarafanov, M. 150, 156–7, 161, 172–4, 208–10
savings 70, 110, 119–20, 179
self-management 105–6
Seliunin, V. 34–5
Shagalov, G. 31
Shatalin, S. 113, 194; plan 6, 115–17, 210, 217
Shmelev, Nikolai 171–2
Siberia 8–9, 84, 85, 144, 209
Slavophile school 4–5, 13, 236
Smirnov, G. 31
Smith, A.H. 31, 55, 78, 83, 84, 86, 93, 94, 173
Sokoloff, G. 31, 58, 60
South Africa 147
Soviet Union see Union of Soviet Socialist Republics (USSR)
Spandaryan, V. 171–2
stabilisation 182–3, 222; fund 191–2, 193–4, 230–1
Stalin, J.V. 22, 24, 29, 42, 53, 97
State Bank (Gosbank) 40, 109–10
State Bank for Foreign Economic Relations (Vneshekonombank) 129, 131, 133
'State Capitalism' 20
State Certificate of Quality 49
State Committee for Foreign Economic Relations (GKES) 42–3, 131
State Committee for Material Supply (Gossnab) 37, 40, 42, 130
State Enterprise Law 105–6
State Foreign Economic Commission 128, 131–2
State Foreign Trade Bank (Vneshtorgbank) 42, 131
State Monopoly of Foreign Trade 41–51; Lenin 23–4; optimal operation of 46–8; in practice 48–50
State Planning Committee (Gosplan) 30–1, 37–8, 42–3
State Quality Control Board (Gospriemka) 103

steel production 8
Steele, Jonathan 4, 11
Stent, A. 124
Stern, J. 55, 82, 85, 88, 124
Stockholm International Peace Research Institute (SIPRI) 89
Stolypin agriculture reforms 16
Sutela, P. 4, 103, 104, 112, 131, 191
Sutton, A. 29
Syria 89, 149–50

Tadzhikistan 1–2, 3
Tatarstan 9, 10
technology, imported, Stalinist growth model 26–35
trade, foreign: Bolshevism 23–6; with CMEA countries 53–5, 123, 162, 172–4, 175; and domestic economy 164–72; export problems under Gorbachev 138–55; Gorbachev's initial strategy 124–6; Gorbachev's reforms 127–35; liberalisation of 223–7; post-war 30–5; Russian contribution to 201–10; Russian Empire, pre-revolution 16–20; Stalinism 26–30; USSR and USA 122–4; with the West 31, 55–64, 80–8, 122–35, 138–46, 174–5 see also balance of payments
trade, interrepublic 199–204, 210–16
Transcaucasian republics 2–3, 86
transition to market economy, Russia 177–98; costs of 221–3; currency convertibility 187–94; gradual vs rapid reform 195–7; and NIC development 225–7; opposition to Gaidar programme 194–5; price liberalisation 178–82; privatisation 183–6; prospects for 218–20; stabilisation 182–3; western assistance 227–36

Treml, V. 48, 49, 58, 70, 163–4
Trotsky, Leon 21, 24
Turkmenistan 1–2, 3

Udmurtia 10
Ukraine 1, 2, 10–11, 144, 212
unemployment 198, 221
Union of Sovereign Republics,
    plan for 6–7
Union of Soviet Socialist
    Republics (USSR): balance of
    payment problems 156–76;
    Bolshevik government 20–6;
    borrowings 121, 160; CMEA
    trade 53–5; dissolution of 1–2;
    economic planning 20, 36–51;
    export problems 138–55;
    formation of 2–3; imports,
    demand for 52–71; integration
    with world economy 125–6;
    interrepublic trade 199–204;
    post-war 30–5; reforms, under
    Gorbachev 99–120, 121–37;
    Russian contribution to trade
    201–10; Stalinist growth
    model 26–30; -USA relations
    122–4
United States of America (USA):
    CIA studies 83, 88–95, 96–8;
    Marshall Plan 231–2; and
    Soviet natural gas 86–7, 88;
    -USSR relations 122–4
Uzbekistan 1–2, 3

Valkenier, E.K. 31, 89
Vanous, J. 55
Vlasov, Alexander 114–15
Vneshekonombank (State Bank
    for Foreign Economic

Relations) 129, 131, 133
Vneshtorgbank (Foreign Trade
    Bank) 42, 131
Vyshnegradsky, I.A. 18

wages 67, 182–3
'War Communism' 21
West: assistance with transition to
    market economy 227–36;
    conditions for assistance
    233–6; size and costs of
    assistance 231–3; Soviet
    exports to 74–5, 80–8, 124,
    138–46, 174–5; Soviet imports
    from 31, 55–64; Soviet trade
    reform, Gorbachev 122–35;
    and stabilisation fund 193–4,
    230–1
westernisation school 4–5, 12–13
White, S. 6
Wiles, P.J.D. 34
Witte, Sergei 17, 19
wood and paper products,
    exports 74–5, 143, 151–3

Yakutia 10, 86–7
Yarushenko, V. 61, 62
Yavlinsky, Grigory 96, 98,
    115–16, 153–4, 180, 183–4,
    193–4
Yeltsin, Boris 5–7, 114–15, 177,
    196
Yoshitomi, M. 224, 225
Yugoslavia 185, 233

Zhirinovsky, Vladimir 4
Zoeter, J.P. 93, 94, 95
Zotov, B. 31